PROMOTING DEMOCRACY

Democracy in the World

A project of
The Robert Maynard Hutchins
Center for the Study of
Democratic Institutions
Robert Wesson, General Editor

Other volumes
Share: **The Making of Spanish Democracy, 1986**

PROMOTING DEMOCRACY
Opportunities and Issues

Edited by
Ralph M. Goldman
William A. Douglas

PRAEGER

New York
Westport, Connecticut
London

Library of Congress Cataloging-in-Publication Data

Promoting democracy: opportunities and issues / edited by Ralph M.
  Goldman, William A. Douglas.
        p.   cm. — (Democracy in the world)
    Bibliography: p.
    Includes index.
    ISBN 0-275-92814-4 (alk. paper)
      1. Democracy.   2. United States—Foreign relations.
    3. Propaganda, America.   I. Goldman, Ralph Morris, 1920–
    II. Douglas, William A.   III. Series.
    JC421.P77   1988
    321.8—dc19   87-21482

Library of Congress Catalog Card Number: 87-21482

ISBN: 0-275-92814-4

First published in 1988

Praeger Publishers, One Madison Avenue, New York, NY 10010
A division of Greenwood Press, Inc.

Printed in the United States of America

♾

The paper used in this book complies with the
Permanent Paper Standard issued by the National
Information Standards Organization (Z39.48-1984).

10 9 8 7 6 5 4 3 2 1

CONTENTS

v

A NOTE ON THE SERIES

This is the second book of a series entitled "Democracy in the World," sponsored by the Center for the Study of Democratic Institutions. The Center's mission is to help clarify basic issues confronting a democratic society, particularly issues involving justice and freedom in the interplay of twentieth-century institutions. The Center has worked mostly through interdisciplinary dialogues. However, the publication of books and monographs has been one of its oldest traditions, going back to a series of volumes on "Communism in American Life" under the editorship of Clinton Rossiter in the 1950s, and including works of many distinguished scholars.

This new series will treat a range of subjects, such as the failures and successes of democracy, studies of particular democratic institutions in one or various countries, relations of democracy to economic and social conditions, problems such as human rights that are closely related to democracy, questions of democracy and foreign policy, proposals for the improvement of democratic institutions, and interpretations and theories of democracy. It is hoped that the series will make information and ideas about democratic systems more widely available and also encourage study of their problems.

The general editor of the present series is Robert Wesson, Senior Research Fellow at the Hoover Institution in Stanford, California. Associate editor is Jeffrey D. Wallin, Program Director at the Center. The views and judgments expressed in these works are those of the authors only. The Center is responsible only for determining that their writing meets the highest standards of American scholarship.

Donald McDonald
Acting Director of the Center

FOREWORD

The opposite of democracy is simply self-imposed or irresponsible rulership, whereby a few who have gained possession of the state use its resources and means of coercion to keep themselves in power and dominate the community without answering to it. Only democratic government can really be considered legitimate in the modern world, and dictatorial governments call themselves democratic, often holding elections without real choice, in order to claim legitimacy.

This may be considered a matter of internal affairs of the state. However, it is very important to other states. A democratic country finds other democracies more reliable partners with whom trade and other exchanges prosper and understanding comes more easily. Democratic countries probably have better promise of economic development. They do not promote terrorism or undertake aggressive wars. They are better neighbors.

It is consequently natural that, as the world becomes increasingly integrated by trade, travel, and communications, the feeling has grown that it is proper to concern ourselves with the political development of other, especially less affluent countries. We would like to help them, in a friendly and pacific fashion with due respect for sovereignty, toward more democratic institutions.

The promotion of democracy has thus become an important ingredient of foreign policy of the United States and to some extent of Western European countries. It has, however, been subject of little systematic analysis. This book is hence an important contribution, as it considers what has been done, problems encountered, and recommended ways to proceed. It merits careful consideration by makers of foreign policy.

Ralph Goldman and William Douglas and their contributors are much less observers than experienced practitioners of the promotion of democracy. The Center for the Study of Democratic Institutions is happy to present their work in hopes that it will contribute to the cause we share.

Robert Wesson

PREFACE

The United States is one of several evangelistic nations in the contemporary world. Our objectives are secular, although U.S. rationales are often formulated in the language of Judeo-Christian religious themes and symbols. The global millennium for Americans will presumably be a world in which all nations are democratic and functioning within the framework of democratic world institutions. This goal has been pursued in many ways since the founding of this unique republic. Recently, the grand political dream has been subordinated to policies more pertinent to military security and international economic competition, usually pursued in the name of democracy, however.

The emergence of the totalitarian state earlier in this century and the prevalence of authoritarian regimes throughout the world in the post–World War II era have impressed upon leaders in the United States and other Western democracies the need to do more than make the world militarily safe for democracies, as important as safety may be. It has not been sufficient to give the democratic concept philosophical and propagandistic expression. The democracies need to give the nondemocracies information, skills, and practical institution-building help, that is, political aid.

It has also become clear that government-sponsored political education is not easily carried on by pluralistic, open societies in which many ideologies compete freely. In this regard. U.S. promotion of democracy abroad, in its recent forms, has varied in circumstance, approach, and theory. Issues of political implementation and effectiveness are many. In the United States, for example, modest steps to promote democracy were taken under the Kennedy administration's Alliance for Progress. Collateral efforts resulted from the Carter administration's human rights policy. More recently, the Reagan administration has embarked upon the Democracy Initiative. At the instigation of the private sector, Congress has established the National Endowment for Democracy, already the subject of substantial controversy. The desire to pursue the democratic mission has persisted regardless of which party is in office. This book is offered as a contribution to this difficult effort.

The authors endeavor to describe and analyze some aspects of the U.S. experience in promoting democracy abroad. They also assess the difficulties of and prospects for this policy. Goldman's historical chapter on the United States' democratic mission describes the long-term background of contemporary efforts; promoting democracy is not new for Americans. Gastil places the mission into a contemporary context, suggesting where and what work may be required. Schott demonstrates why and how it is possible to nurture democratic institution building even in authoritarian systems, particularly if we focus attention on essentially political factors. Goldman notes that foreign assistance may interfere too much or too little in the affairs of recipient nations or groups. Hence, a donor's aid, no matter how well meaning, may result in dependency when the objective really is independence for the aid recipient.

There are many channels through which various types of aid, mainly economic, have flowed or could flow: private businesses, free trade unions, cooperatives, peasant organizations, international nongovernmental organizations, and, prospectively, transnational political parties. Chapters by Sullivan, Godson, Weihe, Hough, and Goldman report on these developments, citing policy-making dilemmas, tactical problems, and issues for further public consideration.

Straus tells of emerging movements to bring the democracies together formally for a better integrated collaboration to preserve and promote democracy. The volume concludes with Douglas's argument that private sector activities may afford foreign policy flexibilities not now enjoyed by the government. Goldman's last word is that programs to promote democracy need better theoretical models, better empirical knowledge, more demanding evaluation of results, and more public support. The time is right. Democracies are beginning to help one another. Political aid programs are beginning to acquire sophistication. The campaign for a democratic world is gathering force and effectiveness.

What gives the surveys and analyses of this book a particularly sharp edge is the existence of other evangelistic nations whose concepts of a global millennium are quite different from the democratic. So also is their readiness to forgo human rights and employ violence in the pursuit of their particular millennia. The Soviet Union is the principal of these other nations: totalitarian in political organization, rigidly ideological in its analysis of world politics and the pursuit of its global mission, disdainful of human rights and individual dignity, and unhesitant in the use of force and terror as tactical measures. Comparable cases, less potent and less organized, are Khomeini's Iran and Qaddafi's Libya. These are significant competing approaches to Truth and Political Valhalla, undergirded by substantial military and economic resources. If the United States has a competitive advantage over these other systems, it may simply be because Americans, experienced in the ways of democracy, are more accustomed to and skilled in political competition itself, that is, if and when Americans realize that a competition is in progress.

To appreciate the problem of American awareness, we need only recall Pogo's famous observation: "We have met the enemy and they are us." Americans have a number of traditional attitudes and policies that are self-created hurdles for a foreign policy promoting democracy abroad. Americans, for example, tend to be pragmatists and reformers, hence skeptical of the absolutist goals and other certainties of ideologues. This tends to make Americans uncomfortable with apparently ideological campaigns on behalf of democracy, particularly since our own version, by our own standards, is constantly subject to our own critiques as less than perfect.

The second hurdle is our respect for the independence and right of self-determination of other peoples. This is the basis for U.S. nonintervention policies promulgated in an earlier and less interdependent time. A third hurdle arises from the tendency of Americans to view with suspicion the practice of politics generally. This is often most clearly observed in negative attitudes toward our own political parties, despite the widely held belief that the parties have been among the principal proponents and practitioners of democracy within the United States, the democratic nations of the Western world, and, more recently, transnationally.

Despite these mixed attitudes and policies, the United States has enthusiastically fought costly wars on grounds that they were necessary to make countries, continents, and the world safe for democracy. It has invested heavily in foreign aid programs to bolster the security and the economy of allies that are either democratic or likely to become so. United States foreign policymakers regularly recite the concepts, goals, and principles of democracy as justifications for military, economic, and diplomatic actions.

Implied in these words and actions, intended or not, is the assumption—first articulated by Thomas Jefferson—that the United States has a special responsibility as a prime model of democracy in the world. Today, many question the relevance of the model by arguing that the United States is unique in its history, geography, and national development generally. The consequences of this apparent "exceptionalism" have been mixed. Many nations have copied the language of the U.S. Constitution but have been unwilling or unable to produce imitations that work. In contrast, the postwar Japanese constitution, recognizing indigenous traditions and conditions, has made its "copy" of the U.S. Constitution work. Whether as a model or not, how best may the United States carry on its part in the promotion of democracy? The purpose of this book is to report on important aspects of the U.S. experience, not to engage in chauvinism. There are now 40 or 50 democracies with a variety of institutional structures. It is to be hoped that the information, perspectives, and suggestions provided here will be generally relevant for democratic development everywhere.

ACKNOWLEDGMENTS

As editor of the Center for the Study of Democratic Institutions' series of books on democracy in the world, Robert Wesson first identified the need for a collection of essays such as this. The concept was endorsed by Jeffrey W. Wallin, the center's program director, and by Allen Weinstein during his tenure as the center's president. Wesson has kept this project moving along and has served as a most helpful source of friendly criticism. We wish to express our appreciation to all three.

The contributors, without exception, are busy workers in the vineyard of democratic development. In contributing their essays, they devoted substantial amounts of their scarce time to set down their experiences, perceptions, and theories for the edification of a concerned public. We think the reader will join us in applauding the results.

The book may seem too American a product; all its authors are Americans. It should be said, therefore, that no one of us believes that the American Way is the only, or even the best way to have or promote democratic institutions. We respect the experiences and wisdom of the West Germans, the British, the French, and others. Promoting democracy is a task to be shared with them. What is particularly American about this book is the earnestness of its authors, each of whom is eager to have his country get on quickly and thoughtfully with the very difficult task of lending a helping hand and mind to other peoples in their indigenous efforts to acquire for themselves the precious benefits of democracy.

Pluralists of the world, unite! You have nothing to lose but your dictators.

Ralph M. Goldman
William A. Douglas

Washington, D.C.

PROMOTING DEMOCRACY

1 THE DEMOCRATIC MISSION: A BRIEF HISTORY
Ralph M. Goldman

From the founding of the Republic to the present day, many Americans have viewed the democratic political system of the United States—the first modern republic—as a model for other peoples. For some leaders, the sharing of this model with others has become an explicit and ardent mission. That the Founding Fathers, as leaders of some 3.5 million people widely scattered along the east coast of a continent distant from the center of world politics in Europe, should design a republic and then declare for themselves this democratic mission could well evoke ridicule or awe, and it did both. Two centuries later, the United States is recognizedly the most powerful, affluent, and vital democracy in the world, and the sense of democratic mission persists. What is the content and origin of such missionary zeal?

THE VISION OF THE FOUNDING FATHERS

The answer begins with the Declaration of Independence, which was hardly an humble document. It spoke of the right of revolution not only for the British colonies in America but also for all peoples and all political systems.

[G]overnments are instituted among men, deriving their just powers from the consent of the governed; that whenever any form of government becomes destructive of these ends [inalienable rights], it is the right of the people to alter or to abolish it, and to institute new government, laying its foundation on such principles, and organizing its powers in such form, as to them shall seem most likely to effect their safety and happiness.

Here was a declaration about all governments and all peoples, a generalization for which the complaints and actions of the colonies constituted a particular case. Although revolutions and civil wars were familiar events by the eighteenth century, the philosophical rationale and the particulars of the colonial case against the British king expressed in the Declaration of Independence have served as a model and an inspiration for many subsequent revolutionary movements.

The principal author, Thomas Jefferson, most assuredly had in mind that the United States should be a model for nations suffering tyranny or yet unborn. This ambition was shared by most of the Founding Fathers, including the often reticent George Washington.

Jefferson reiterated his expectations many times over. In 1788 he wrote to John Rutledge: "We can surely boast of having set the world a beautiful example of a government reformed by reason alone, without bloodshed. But the world is too far oppressed, to profit by the example." Two years later, in correspondence with William Hunter, he wrote proudly, "It is indeed an animating thought, that while we are securing the rights of ourselves and our posterity, we are pointing out the way to struggling nations, who wish like us to emerge from their tyrannies also." As president in 1802 he was effusive in a letter to Delaware's Governor Hall.

We have the same object, the success of respresentative government. Nor are we acting for ourselves alone, but for the whole human race. The event of our experiment is to show whether man can be trusted with self-government. The eyes of suffering humanity are fixed on us with anxiety as their only hope.

In 1820, after the new nation had survived three tumultuous decades, Jefferson wrote from retirement to Benjamin Rush as follows:

We exist, and are quoted, as standing proofs that a government, so modelled as to rest continually on the will of the whole society, is a practicable government. Were we to break to pieces, it would damp the hopes and efforts of the good, and give triumph to those of the bad through the whole enslaved world. As members, therefore, of the universal society of mankind, and standing in high and responsible relation with them, it is our sacred duty to suppress passions among ourselves, and not to blast the confidence we have inspired of proof that a government of reason is better than one of force.

Jefferson's sense of mission for the U.S. political model and his devotion to popular self-government were shared by others, most notably President Washington. In his farewell address, Washington advised his countrymen on several matters, but chiefly on the relations of the United States with other nations. "Observe good faith and justice toward all nations. Cultivate peace and harmony with all. Religion and morality ·enjoin this conduct. And can it be that good policy does not equally enjoin it? It will be worthy of a free, enlightened, and at no distant period a great nation to give to mankind the magnanimous and too novel example of a people always guided by an exalted justice and benevolence."

Jefferson's and Washington's eloquent phrases express themes that continue to move U.S. leaders and policy to this day. They also moved the leaders of the French Revolution. The Declaration of the Rights of Man, proclaimed by the revolutionary Estates General in 1789, was based on the American Declaration of Independence. A written constitution, two years in the making, was adopted in 1791 and established the First French Republic. Cordial relations with the United States, particularly with the Jeffersonian Democratic-Republicans, were established and prevailed for the decade prior to the Napoleonic empire, at which time France regressed into autocracy.

THE MISSION ACQUIRES A TERRITORIAL DIMENSION

As Napoleon's armies and influence spread across Europe, Spain agreed to cede the Province of Louisiana, west of the United States, to France. This placed the important port city of New Orleans under the jurisdiction of Napoleon, whose dictatorship and imperial ambitions caused consternation among Americans, particularly those dependent upon trade through this port. President Jefferson tried to arrange for the purchase of New Orleans, only to have Napoleon respond with an offer to sell all of Louisiana. The offer gave rise to a lively constitutional and financial debate regarding presidential capacity to arrange such a purchase and the treasury's capacity to pay for it. It was no surprise that the extension of democracy to the Province of Louisiana should be one of the principal arguments in favor of the purchase.

During the debate in Congress, the argument for the extension of democracy was made by Senator John Breckenridge on November 3, 1803.

Why not then acquire territory on the west, as well as on the east side [a reference to efforts to purchase Florida] of the Mississippi? Is the Goddess of Liberty restrained by water courses? Is she governed by geographical limits? Is her dominion on this continent confined to the east side of the Mississippi? So far from believing in the doctrine that a Republic ought to be confined within narrow limits, I believe, on the contrary, that the more extensive its dominion the more safe and more durable it will be. In proportion to the number of hands you intrust the precious blessings of a free government to, in the same proportion do you multiply the chances for their preservation.

The Louisiana Purchase doubled the geographical area of the United States and, according to the cession treaty, assured its inhabitants "all the rights, advantages and immunities of citizens of the United States." Here was a literal application of the democratic mission, achieved without force of arms. The acquisition and the westward movement that followed gave the young nation its first taste of its "Manifest Destiny," a phrase that was coined in 1845 to describe other territorial aspirations related to the impending war with Mexico.

The rationale for a concept of Manifest Destiny was already in the making by 1819 when the purchase of Florida from Spain was added to that of Louisiana. In Latin America, Spanish provinces were rebelling and declaring their independence from the mother country. John Quincy Adams, President Monroe's secretary of state, put the case candidly in his diary notes about a cabinet discussion on November 16, 1819. Geographical inevitability became meshed with concern for the advancement of democracy abroad. The subject under discussion was the impression in Europe that the United States was "an ambitious and encroaching people." What should be done to remove this impression? Wrote Adams:

Nothing that we could say or do would remove this impression until the world shall be familiarized with the idea of considering our proper dominion to be the continent of North America. From the time when we became an independent people it was as much a law of nature that this should become our pretension as that the Mississippi should flow to the sea. Spain had possessions upon our southern and Great Britain upon our northern border. It was impossible that centuries should elapse without finding them annexed to the United States; not that any spirit of encroachment or ambition on our part renders it necessary, but because it is a physical, moral, and political absurdity that such fragments of territory . . . should exist permanently contiguous to a great, powerful, enterprising, and rapidly growing nation. Most of the Spanish territory which had been in our neighborhood had already become our own by the most unexceptionable of all acquisitions—fair purchase for a valuable consideration.

THE MONROE DOCTRINE: A FIRST DEFENSE
OF DEMOCRACIES

This was the thinking that paved the way for the Monroe Doctrine, articulated by the president in his message to Congress on December 2, 1823. The background for the message was the defeat of Napoleon in 1815, the creation of the Holy Alliance among the monarchies of Europe, and, by 1820, the possibility that the alliance would endeavor to reestablish European colonial jurisdiction over the new republics of Latin America.

The immediate occasion was the signing of a treaty with Russia clarifying the manner in which the fur trade and other Russian commerce would be conducted in the Northwest. In reporting on the treaty, President Monroe asserted "as a principle in which the rights and interests of the United States are involved, that the American continents [*sic*], by the free and independent condition which they have assumed and maintain, are henceforth not to be considered as subjects for future colonization by any European powers." He continued:

With the movements in this hemisphere we are of necessity more immediately connected, and by causes which must be obvious to all enlightened and impartial observers. The political system of the allied powers [the Holy Alliance] is essentially different in this respect from that of America. This difference proceeds from that which exists in their respective Governments; and to the defense of our own, which has been achieved by the loss of so much blood and treasure, and matured by the wisdom of their most enlightened citizens, and under which we have enjoyed unexampled felicity, this whole nation is devoted. We . . . declare that we should consider any attempt on their part to extend their system to any portion of this hemisphere as dangerous to our peace and safety.

If nothing else, the Monroe Doctrine was an audacious statement by a militarily weak and isolated nation, addressed to a victorious alliance that had just vanquished no less an adversary than Napoleon. In a single policy statement, Monroe placed the United States at the head of the nations of the New World to serve as the protector of their newborn democracies, rationalizing it all as a U.S. national security measure. It was a formulation that is relevant and reiterated to this day.

Monroe's distinction between the New World and the political system of the Old World was the clear distinction between democratic and autocratic governments. The Monroe Doctrine reflected the national commitment to the advancement of democratic institutions wherever possible and the protection of the democratic way of life in the United States as the example for others. The haste with which the new Latin American republics adopted large components of the U.S. Constitution, regardless how inappropriate for indigenous political conditions, is testimony that the Monroe Doctrine was a democracy-promoting as well as a national security policy.

These themes of democratic mission, national security, and geographical predestination were already present at the end of the American Revolution in treaty negotiations with Great Britain. At that time the Americans successfully argued that the Mississippi River rather than the Appalachian Mountains was the natural defensible western boundary for the new nation. This mission-security-predestination mix was later present in the purchase of Louisiana and Florida, in the treaty with the Russians, and, as just noted, in the Monroe Doctrine. The themes became the slogan *Manifest Destiny* in the 1840s.

THE MISSION BECOMES MANIFEST DESTINY

The 1840s were an expansionist period in which Mexico was incapable of serious self-defense. U.S. settlers in Texas declared themselves a free state. Negative European reaction to annexation of Texas led President Polk to restate the Monroe Doctrine.

The people of the United States can not . . . view with indifference attempts of European powers to interfere with the independent action of the nations of this continent. The American system of government is entirely different from that of Europe. . . . We must ever maintain the principle that the people of this continent alone have the right to decide their own destiny. Should any portion of them, constituting an independent state [Texas, in this case], propose to unite themselves with our Confederacy, this will be a question for them and us to determine without any foreign interposition. (Message to Congress, December 2, 1845).

During this period, Manifest Destiny was the popular rationalization for the so-called "God-given right" of the United States to take lands from Indians, from English fur traders in Oregon (1846), and from Mexico (1848). The God-given right was also rationalized by the unfounded charge that Indians, Mexicans, and others failed to cultivate the soil or pursue democratic ways of life. Manifest Destiny was a populist and expansionist aberration of the democratic mission, hardly the mission that Jefferson, Adams, and Monroe had in mind. The result, nonetheless, was to make the Pacific Ocean the western boundary of the United States.

One unanticipated consequence of Manifest Destiny was the series of events it triggered, leading to removal of the U.S. model's major undemocratic blemish: slavery. The acquisition of western territories sparked a race between free-state Northern farmers and slave-state southern planters for possession of the new lands and for new state constitutions that either prohibited or permitted slavery. The contest produced an abolitionist president, Abraham Lincoln, and the Civil War. This was a tragic way to remove the blemish and further legitimize the mission. Unfortunately, vindictive postwar Reconstruction policies delayed democracy's return to much of the South for the next 100 years. The racist tarnish on the democratic mission continues to be evident in many places and under many circumstances in the United States to this day.

MISSIONARIES: THE CHURCHES JOIN UP

The Industrial Revolution arrived in the United States during the Civil War, particularly in the arms and related war production industries. The pace of economic transformation was stepped up during the postwar period as investment capital and new technologies created an industrial base and a merchant fleet that, even prior to 1900, was second only to the British. Westward migration, the discovery of vast deposits of gold, silver, and other minerals, and the intensification of internal trade between east and west coasts gave Americans an exalted sense of their basic democratic and religious values: rugged individualism; free enterprise; a work ethic; and the godliness of economic and social success, that is, as evidence of being God's "Chosen." It was but a small step from exaltation to missionary zeal in preaching these values to others.

Protestant and Catholic missionaries were not novel features of U.S. physical expansion. They had arrived in Hawaii by 1820; the Dole family, for example, were missionaries before they became pineapple growers and businessmen. Methodist and Presbyterian missionaries were active in the Pacific Northwest as early as the 1830s. More than 80 missions were established in China between 1830 and 1860, making a substantial impact upon the Chinese upper class and often serving as translators for merchants and diplomats. By the end of the nineteenth century, overseas missionary work had become a highly organized endeavor of many U.S. churches.

In general, the missionaries followed trade, particularly in the Pacific and Far East, teaching U.S. and Christian values. Their role as representatives of "American ways" during the latter half of the nineteenth century did much to establish the social and political trust so essential for long-term growth of U.S. trade and political relations with Asia and Latin America. These were precisely the regions where trade and political relations were on the rise. Some men of the cloth, such as the Reverend Josiah Strong of the Social Gospel movement, went a bit overboard in their excessive commitment to a "white man's burden" that presumably justified carrying on an "imperialism of righteousness" for the purpose of "Christianizing the world."

REACHING BEYOND NORTH AMERICA

Internal developments in the United States affected external affairs in significant ways during and after the Reconstruction period. Trade with Europe prospered as U.S. cotton, whose production was recovering from the devastation of the Civil War, was exchanged for British and French manufactures. The longstanding U.S. commerce in the Caribbean was revived and extended to Central America. Transportation across the Isthmus of Panama became increasingly important for traffic between California and the east coast. The Americans on the west coast and in Hawaii became more and more preoccupied with trade with China and Japan. The growing "export" of U.S. citizens, goods, and values was drawing the one-hundred-year-old Republic toward a major role in world affairs.

This outward thrust began to concern a great many historians, businessmen, and others who pondered its relationship to the closing of the frontier in 1890. In the analysis of the historian Fredrick Jackson Turner, U.S. democracy and prosperity had been strongly linked to the frontier and the westward movement. With the end of the frontier, could U.S. institutions, democracy, freedom, and prosperity survive? Turner left the question unanswered, but implicit was an argument for expansion overseas. Brooks Adams was more explicit and pessimistic. He saw elements of decay in U.S. society and argued that only overseas expansion could save democracy at home. Imperialism became a major issue in the presidential election of 1900 as a consequence of the territorial acquisitions of the Spanish-American War. The Republican incumbent William McKinley, having just approved the annexation of the Philippines, won; the Democrat, William Jennings Bryan, who opposed imperialism and expansion overseas, lost.

The Spanish-American War was in the making for nearly four decades. Cuban uprisings against Spanish rule were recurrent from the 1860s on, evoking strong U.S. sympathy for the revolutionaries seeking freedom from autocratic Spain. At the beginning of their Ten Years' War (1868-78), President Ulysses Grant expressed his willingness to risk war to aid the Cubans, but he lacked public support for such an undertaking. That support materialized during the Cuban uprising of 1895, which was in large measure directed and financed by groups in the United States supportive of independence and a democratic Cuba.

By 1898 the Spaniards in Cuba had suffered 100,000 military casualties. Public opinion in the United States, aroused by chauvinistic elements in the press, was virtually panting to get into the fight. The sinking of the U.S. battleship *Maine* in Havana harbor, with a loss of 260 lives, provided the justification for bringing the United States into war with Spain. The outcome was another confluence of democratic mission and territorial aggrandizement. The Treaty of Paris ending the war provided for Cuban independence and the cession of the Philippines, Guam, and Puerto Rico to the United States.

Although committed to the sovereign independence of Cuba, the United States insisted on a "special relationship" with that island. This was arranged in the Platt Amendment to the army appropriation bill for 1901 and later incorporated in the Cuban constitution. It provided that Cuba would never allow a foreign power to gain a foothold in its affairs and gave the United States the right to intervene, if necessary, "for the preservation of Cuban independence, the maintenance of a government adequate for protection of life, property, and individual liberty." The Platt Amendment was abrogated in 1934, ending the protectorate relationship but not the problems of democracy in Cuba, which has since endured one dictatorship after the other.

Great Britain was the principal industrial nation and world power throughout the nineteenth century, giving impetus to the movements for laissez-faire, free trade, and open seas. By 1900, however, the United States took first place as the world's leading manufacturing country. Domestic industrial, transportation, and financial monopolies had produced huge accumulations of liquid capital and a financial elite ready and willing to take risks in overseas enterprises. By the turn of the century, Manifest Destiny was looking less like a democratic mission and increasingly like outright economic imperialism. Expansionist policies, emphasizing free enterprise and free trade, seemed only coincidentally to carry the democratic cause along.

In foreign affairs, Theodore Roosevelt believed in speaking softly but carrying a big stick, particularly in the implementation of U.S. policies in the Caribbean and South America where U.S. companies were actively exploiting agricultural economies. The term *Dollar Diplomacy* was coined during the administration of William Howard Taft, a firm endorser of U.S. corporate investment overseas.

It was Woodrow Wilson who revived the political aspects of the mission of the United States by assuming the awesome task of "making the world safe for democracy."

MAKING THE ENTIRE WORLD SAFE FOR DEMOCRACY

When the Central Powers and the Allies went to war in 1914, popular attitudes and official policy in the United States were as one in support of neutrality. Wishing to be a peacemaker, President Wilson sent numerous special emissaries to try to arrange a termination of hostilities. By 1916, however, British propaganda and German unrestricted submarine warfare against neutral shipping, mainly U.S., combined to draw Americans to the Allied side. The British successfully portrayed Kaiser Wilhelm II as an evil tyrant and his armies as "Huns." The submarine was a new military technology, and the Germans used it intensively, taking many American lives and ships in the process.

Also tilting the Americans in favor of the Allies were the Anglo-Saxon origins of U.S. institutions and sympathies for an English-speaking democracy. Public opinion and the president slowly but surely moved to the conclusion that freedom and democracy would be better off if the Allies won the war. This became quite explicit in President Wilson's war message to Congress on April 2, 1917.

Our object now . . . is to vindicate the principles of peace and justice in the life of the world as against selfish and autocratic power and to set up amongst the really free and self-governed peoples of the world such a concert of purposes and of action as will henceforth insure the observance of those principles. Neutrality is no longer feasible or desirable where the peace of the world is involved and the freedom of its peoples, and the menace of that peace and freedom lies in the existence of autocratic governments backed by organized force which is controlled wholly by their will, not by the will of their people. . . .

[W]e shall fight for the things which we have always carried nearest our hearts—for democracy, for the right of those who submit to authority to have a voice in their own Governments, for the rights and liberties of small nations, for a universal dominion of right by such a concert of free peoples as shall bring peace and safety to all nations and make the world itself at last free.

Wilson, a political scientist by profession, quickly sought to institutionalize this "concert of free peoples." In an address to Congress on January 8, 1918, Wilson set forth his fourteen-point program of war aims. To make the world "fit and safe to live in," he proposed "a general association of nations" that would guarantee the political independence and territorial integrity of all nations. The Allies agreed with the Fourteen Points as a general statement of war aims, the British and French establishing special committees to plan the new organization. In the United States, Wilson and his confidant, Col. E. M. House, took personal charge of drafting provisions for what became the Covenant of the League of Nations.

When completed, the covenant had the structural appearance of a confederation with a bicameral representative assembly and, in Article 23, many of the goals for social and economic cooperation familiar in domestic politics in the United States: fair and humane conditions of labor in all countries; protection of women and children; prevention of drug traffic; control of the arms trade; freedom of communication, transportation, and trade; and prevention of disease. Wilson's view of the democratic mission was clearly evidenced in the covenant. It was an exercise in global institution building that would have to be repeated in 1945 after a second world war.

The U.S. Senate refused to ratify the league covenant without numerous controversial reservations. U.S. participation in the league became the preeiminent issue in the presidential election of 1920. Rejection of the league was followed by a decade of isolationism. The major arguments of isolationists were reminiscent of several earlier foreign policy postures. (1) Stay out of the League of Nations to avoid foreign entanglements. (2) Avoid interventionist policies, particularly those that hold a risk of getting the United States into other peoples' wars. (3) Exercise influence across the world by providing a "good example," that is, building prosperity and freedom under democracy at home. The issue transcended party and ideological lines up to and into the New Deal era.

THE TOTALITARIANS VERSUS THE FOUR FREEDOMS

Without the United States, the League of Nations became a European-centered organization, dominated by Great Britain and France, and incapable of coping with challenges from Japan (in Manchuria), fascist Italy (in Ethiopia), and Nazi Germany (in Austria, Czechoslovakia, and elsewhere). The Bolshevik revolution in Russia, the aggressive activities of the Communist International (Comintern), and Stalin's purges added to the threat and turmoil that dominated the international arena during the 1920s and 1930s. From their safe haven of freedom in the United States, Americans found it difficult to comprehend, let alone believe, the scope, cruelty, and intensity of the new totalitarianisms developed by Hitler, Stalin, and Mussolini. Matters were made even worse by the Great Depression of the early 1930s, a worldwide economic disaster that inhibited early military response to the totalitarian threat to democracies everywhere. The Nazi invasion of Poland in September 1939 finally compelled an Anglo-French response that triggered World War II. The Japanese attack on the U.S. naval base at Pearl Harbor on December 7, 1941, brought the United States into the war.

President Franklin D. Roosevelt began in 1937 to turn his attention from his domestic New Deal efforts to the conduct of a difficult foreign policy, namely, the support of the European democracies against the rising tide of fascism. This meant nothing less than completely reversing U.S. isolationism and neutrality policies. This also meant finding ways to support the Allies against the Axis without getting involved militarily. Roosevelt was reliving many of the dilemmas of his old chief, Woodrow Wilson. As early as October 1937, Roosevelt moved assertively, calling for a "quarantine" of aggressors.

The democratic mission once again found voice in Roosevelt's call upon his countrymen to make U.S. arms production "the arsenal of democracy." In his message to Congress on January 6, 1941, Roosevelt argued that "enduring peace cannot be bought at the cost of other people's freedom." To this he added:

In the future days, which we seek to make secure, we look forward to a world founded upon four essential human freedoms.

The first is freedom of speech and expression—everywhere in the world.

The second is freedom of every person to worship God in his own way—everywhere in the world.

The third is freedom from want—which, translated into world terms, means economic understandings which will secure to every nation a healthy peacetime life for its inhabitants—everywhere in the world.

The fourth is freedom from fear—which, translated into world terms, means a world-wide reduction of armaments to such a point and in such a thorough fashion that no nation will be in a position to commit an act of physical aggression against any neighbor—everywhere in the world.

This is no vision of a distant millennium. It is a definite basis for a kind of world attainable in our own time and generation.

This democratic mission of the United States became Anglo-American with the issuance of the eight-point Atlantic Charter drafted by

Roosevelt and British Prime Minister Winston Churchill at a secret ren-
dezvous off the coast of Newfoundland in August 1941. Among other
things, the document called for the destruction of tyranny and the
restoration of peoples' right to self-government.

DESIGNING DEMOCRACY FOR THE UNITED NATIONS
AND THE DEFEATED AXIS

The next step beyond the successful conduct of war against the Axis
was, as it had been in 1917-18, the creation of a "concert of nations" to
organize and maintain the peace at the end of World War II. The Atlantic
Charter called it a "permanent system of general security," an objective
reiterated in the Joint Four-nation Declaration issued in Moscow in
October 1943. A priori support came from Congress in the form of the
Fulbright Resolution passed in November 1943.

Largely a U.S. initiative and a U.S. draft, the Charter of the United
Nations was composed at Dumbarton Oaks between August and October
1944 by representatives of the United States, Great Britain, the Soviet
Union, and China, and signed in San Francisco on June 26, 1945. All this
occurred prior to public awareness of the atomic bomb and prior to its
use over Hiroshima and Nagasaki.

The preamble of the charter reads like a modern version of the preamble of the U.S. Constitution, opening with the phrase "We the Peoples
of the United Nations." The new world organization would be dedicated
not only to eliminating the "scourge of war" but also to such democratic-
sounding values and objectives as "fundamental human rights," "dignity and worth of the human person," "equal rights of men and women
and of nations large and small," "better standards of living in larger
freedom," and "tolerance." While the term *democracy* was nowhere
used, essential components of democracy were present in many parts of
the charter.

The principle of bicameralism was again applied in the creation of the
Security Council and the General Assembly. The appearance of a system
of separation of powers was provided by adding to these two bodies the
United Nations Secretariat and the International Court of Justice. It
could have been a cross between the U.S. Articles of Confederation and
the Constitution on a global scale. What were not anticipated by the
drafters of the United Nations Charter were the atomic bomb, the Cold
War, and a rancorous Third World, the last having grown out of a
trebling of the number of nations.

A more immediate and pressing task was assisting the defeated Axis
powers design and inaugurate viable democratic institutions. Italy and
Germany had had brief and intense experiences with freedom, democracy, and constitutionalism. Pre-Fascist and pre-Nazi political leaders

were still available to manage a democratic revival. However, Soviet unwillingness to cooperate in the reconstruction of a unified Germany created an impasse. This situation continued until 1948, when the United States, Great Britain, and France reached an agreement in London to authorize those Germans under Western military government to establish a provisional government, democratic and federal in character, based on a constitution prepared by the Germans themselves. The United States and its allies, having diligently sought out and recruited the pre-Nazi leaders, helped them establish pluralist regimes and fend off communist efforts to capture control of unions, political parties, and governmental bodies. Unaccustomed to this type of political warfare and uneasy about intervening in the domestic politics of other nations, U.S. political aid, mainly financial, was channeled covertly to prodemocracy parties and groups through the Central Intelligence Agency (CIA) and nongovernmental organizations such as the American Federation of Labor.

In the case of Japan, an authoritarian monarchy, democracy building had to start almost from scratch. As early as September 6, 1945, the United States declared that its policy toward postwar Japan was to ensure that it would not again become an international menace and to bring about the establishment of a democratic system of government. "The United States desires that this government should conform as closely as may be to principles of democratic self-government but it is not the responsibility of the Allied Powers to impose upon Japan any form of government not supported by the freely expressed will of the people." The Japanese constitution promulgated in 1946 established a constitutional monarchy with ultimate sovereignty residing with the people.

BIPOLARIZATION AND MILITARIZATION OF WORLD POLITICS

The atomic bomb gave future world wars the potential of literally detroying human civilization and the human race, and, as such, became a deterrent to further resort to major warfare as an instrument of national policy. Limited wars, wars of "national liberation," and state-supported terrorism became the contemporary modes of military engagement. Surrogates, in the form of militarized revolutionary movements or transnational political party affiliates, often carried out the maneuvers of competing nations. Given their openness, regard for dissent, and concern for the human individual, many developing nations and emergent democracies became particularly vulnerable to wars of national liberation and state-supported terrorism. As a consequence, the United States found itself serving as policeman for the world, a role that sometimes put its democratic mission into jeopardy or in reverse, for example, by giving aid to Franco and other dictators in exchange for access to strategic military bases.

The Cold War created a bipolar global military and political contest between the Western democracies and the Eastern totalitarians. An ostensibly nonaligned Third World, usually led by authoritarian regimes, divided in its leanings toward one superpower or the other. Cycles of Cold War or detente between the superpowers came to be recognized as tactical measures for reducing the cost of the arms race, controlling allies, impressing domestic constituencies, or stabilizing superpower economies. The bipolarization of the global contest also brought into sharp relief the contrasts between democracy and totalitarianism. The difference appeared clearly in the preparation of the Universal Declaration of Human Rights adopted by the United Nations General Assembly on December 10, 1948.

The U.S. delegation to the Commission on Human Rights was led by Eleanor Roosevelt, whose views and energy did much to shape the document. The General Assembly, with only about 55 members at that time and led by the United States, voted unanimously for the declaration. The Soviet bloc, South Africa, Saudi Arabia, and Yugoslavia abstained. Subsequently, the declaration became the basis for condemning the denial of human rights in several nations, for example, Rhodesia and South Africa.

Security and defense rather than freedom and democracy became the salient concerns of U.S. foreign policy as the Cold War progressed. Soviet troops and local Communist parties were converting the nations of Eastern Europe into a ring of satellite buffer states. A peace treaty with Austria was held up for years because Soviet troops refused to leave. The partition of Berlin was a source of constant difficulty, eventually leading to the Berlin airlift. The Soviet Union was actively supporting Communist parties and Communist factions in trade unions throughout Western Europe in the hope of either gaining control of the devastated democracies or at least neutralizing Europe in global politics. By 1953 the creation of the United States Information Agency (USIA) and the revitalization of the Voice of America and other international communication activities gave the United States a major instrument for the defense of democracy and U.S. foreign policy during the intensifying propaganda warfare of the 1950s and 1960s.

Territorial encroachments, limited wars, civil wars, and terrorism became constant preoccupations for the Western democracies. U.S. responses initially tended toward military options as the country reversed its rapid demobilization at the end of World War II, created a large permanent military force under the new Department of Defense, and established military alliances with former enemies as well as former allies. Economic measures were initiated with the Truman Doctrine and the Marshall Plan in 1947.

Ideological and political organizational measures began to receive attention with the creation of President Kennedy's Alliance for Progress, President Carter's campaign for human rights, and, most recently, President Reagan's Democracy Initiative. The tardy and limited resort to overt ideological and political measures—to be referred to below as political aid—has been ironic, for Americans almost universally have perceived World Wars I and II as battles between democracy and dictatorship and the Cold War as a struggle between democracy and communist totalitarianism.

The Truman Doctrine, responding to Soviet-supported efforts to dismantle constitutional regimes in Greece and Turkey, called attention to the long-term character of the Cold War and launched a U.S. commitment to aid threatened democracies with substantial and continuing economic resources. In his message to Congress on March 12, 1947, Truman reiterated the democratic mission:

The peoples of a number of countries of the world have recently had totalitarian regimes forced upon them against their will. The Government of the United States had made frequent protests against coercion and intimidation, in violation of the Yalta Agreement, in Poland, Rumania and Bulgaria. I must also state that in a number of other countries there have been similar developments.

At the present moment in world history nearly every nation must choose between alternative ways of life. The choice is too often not a free one.

One way of life is based upon the will of the majority, and is distinguished by free institutions, representative government, free elections, guarantees of individual liberty, freedom of speech and religion, and freedom from political oppression.

The second way of life is based upon the will of a minority forcibly imposed upon the majority. It relies upon terror and oppression, a controlled press and radio, fixed elections, and the suppression of personal freedoms.

I believe that we must assist free peoples to work out their own destinies in their own way.

I believe that our help should be primarily through economic and financial aid which is essential to economic stability and orderly political processes.

With this, Truman asked Congress to fund $400 million in economic aid for Greece and Turkey. In June of the same year, at Truman's behest, George C. Marshall, the secretary of state, proposed an unprecedented program of economic aid to the countries of Western Europe: the Marshall Plan. Between 1948 and 1952 alone, over $15 billion was given to Western European countries as loans or grants-in-aid. So great was the success of the Marshall Plan in preventing economic and political chaos among the struggling democracies that economic aid became an enduring instrument of U.S. foreign policy. The Marshall Plan is also credited with providing a major impetus to the development of the European

Communities. A significant factor, of course, was prior European experience with the political and economic institutions that could give maximum economic effect to the funds they received.

The containment of communism, the Korean War, the anticommunist spirit of the McCarthy era, and the escalation of warfare in Vietnam were among the developments that provided a significant rationale for the militarization of U.S. foreign policy in its new role as world policeman. The Eisenhower administration devoted much of its attention to rebuilding the armed forces and condemning international communism.

THE ALLIANCE FOR PROGRESS: A TURN TOWARD POLITICAL AID

Since the 1950s, economic and military aid to friendly, sometimes democratic, regimes have become familiar and substantial instruments of U.S. diplomacy. The taxpayer has willingly carried the multitrillion dollar cost of these foreign aid programs, which U.S. leaders nearly always justify on grounds of national security or the economic interdependence of the United States and its allies. Political aid—usually in the form of assistance to particular political parties, unions, organized interests, politicians, or press—has been quite another matter. Political aid (the term does not represent an explicit established policy) has been encumbered by its apparent breach of a longstanding U.S. diplomatic principle, namely, nonintervention in the politics of other sovereign nations.

What little political aid the United States has attempted in the past 35 years has been more or less covert, largely financial, and most often administered through the CIA. It did not take long for most policymakers to realize that such covert political operations were inappropriate, awkward, and embarrassing—even un-American. Political aid seemed to run counter to the U.S. preferences for open politics, an informed citizenry, nonintervention in the domestic politics of other nations, and ethical use of money in politics. Covert political aid, however defined or justified, simply would not do; such a program had only the narrowest constituency in the United States.

These ambivalences have been confined strictly to the United States. Historically, major European imperial powers have rarely been reluctant to transfer their national ideologies, political institutional forms, political parties, politicians, and policies from their homelands to the territories of their empires. Gandhi, for example, delivered India into nationhood through the application of a kind of political judo; he brought down the British under the weight of their own political values and institutional structures, which they had so conscientiously installed on the Indian subcontinent. Similarly, the Soviet Union has had no qualms about training political cadres, establishing Communist parties, promoting front organizations, engaging political leaders, financing a procommunist press, or otherwise providing political aid to its partners in some 96 nations of the world. The U.S. inhibitions are in part a consequence of a tradition that is skeptical about politics generally, politicians particularly, and political parties usually.

Ambivalence notwithstanding, superpower status since the end of World War II has given the United States, almost against its will and certainly beyond its international political experience, the role of political as well as military and economic leader of the world. With regard to the last two roles, the weaponry of military aid and the dollars of economic aid have been readily understood as tools of world politics—buy-'em-or-bomb-'em policy alternatives. Not until the 1960s did policies resembling a contemporary conception of political aid begin to surface, initially in connection with the Alliance for Progress.

Suggested by President John F. Kennedy, the Alliance for Progress was designed as a ten-year development program for Latin America. The agreement was signed at Punta del Este, Uruguay, in 1961 by all the American republics except Cuba. The United States expected to provide at least $20 billion over the life of the program. The first of the 12 goals stated in the agreement was "to improve and strengthen democratic institutions through application of the principle of self-determination by the people." It was the express national interest of the United States to help Latin America evolve a new set of political institutions that would be capable of coping with and even promoting social and political change.

It very soon became evident that democratic institutions do not arise with the wave of a wand or the expression of a good intention; democracy requires an experienced citizenry, a technically as well as philosophically knowledgeable leadership relatively trusting of one another and of the citizenry, and a civic culture that, at minimum, values the individual, human rights, dissent, and popular sovereignty. But the Alliance for Progress goal was a beginning in that it acknowledged that the development of political institutions could be "aided."

TITLE IX

During 1961 and 1962, at the initiative of Senator Hubert H. Humphrey and Representative Clement J. Zablocki, the Foreign Assistance Act was amended to declare that the policy of the United States is to "encourage the development and use of cooperatives, credit unions, and savings and loan associations" as well as "programs of community development which will promote stable and responsible governmental institutions at the local level." Both men, reared in the populist states of Minnesota and Wisconsin, were keenly aware of the training for democracy that citizens could acquire through these particular financial institutions. For them democracy was a grass-roots-up, not a nation-state-down development. Unfortunately, the administrators of the provisions of the act were not entirely certain how to go about promoting democratic institutions.

In ensuing years the degree to which popular participation in the development programs of aid-receiving countries increased was far too little to satisfy the expectations of Zablocki's Foreign Affairs Committee. It was apparent that the Foreign Assistance Act needed something more. At about the same time a group of twenty-five Republican congressmen launched a six-month study of foreign assistance. This group issued a statement that became influential in the formulation of the "something more," namely, Title IX of the Foreign Assistance Act. The Republican statement (*Congressional Record*, March 15, 1966) included a call to U.S. labor unions to help organize democratically oriented labor unions in developing countries, to private foundations to help promote popular participation in the development programs of countries receiving U.S. assistance, and to the Republican and Democratic parties, acting in concert, to undertake carefully devised programs to promote greater contact among U.S. and Latin American politicians.

In 1966, Title IX, Utilization of Democratic Institutions in Development, was incorporated into the Foreign Assistance Act. It instructed the Agency for International Development (AID) to find new and imaginative ways to strengthen the existing and latent democratic forces of aid-receiving countries and to increase AID's reliance upon nongovernmental organizations with demonstrated competence for enlisting popular participation in the development process. To this day Title IX has been more aspiration than implementation.

Representative Donald M. Fraser (Democrat, Minnesota), an author and interpreter of Title IX, became one of the principal advocates of political aid. Writing in *World Affairs* (vol. 129, no. 4, 1967), Fraser argued that the major shortcomings in developing nations lay in their political and social institutions. He complained that the existing U.S. aid programs tended to reinforce traditional and authoritarian systems rather than promote the pluralism that has facilitated change and progress in the more developed nations. He urged reforms that would direct U.S. programs toward strengthening cooperatives, labor unions, citizen participation, private enterprise, educational institutions, and political parties dedicated to pluralism.

POLITICAL FOUNDATIONS

Meanwhile, in West Germany, a model for a systematic approach to political aid was being inaugurated. Statutes were enacted that established special political foundations (*Stiftungen*) with distinct domestic functions in the field of civic education and a capacity to extend these functions to pluralistically oriented partners in foreign nations, particularly in the Third World (see chap. 5). A separate foundation was created for each of West Germany's major political parties: the Friedrich Ebert Foundation for the Socialists, the Konrad Adenauer Foundation for Christian Democrats, the Friedrich Naumann Foundation for Liberal Democrats, and the Hanns Seidel Foundation for the Bavarian Christian Social Union. Each was to engage in research and training for the advancement of democracy among its partisans at home. Each could—and very soon did—assist labor, civic, and other political groupings of similar partisan persuasion in other countries to strengthen themselves. For numerous Americans the *Stiftungen* and their rich experience became the model for a similar approach by the United States.

Few academicians and political leaders have acknowledged the importance of political aid as a dimension to be added to the military and economic aid techniques of the United States. One of these was George E. Agree, an experienced Washington, D.C. political consultant and organizer, who directed a project—Transnational Interactions of Political Parties—for Freedom House of New York City. Late in 1977, citing the West German experience, Agree proposed the creation of the American Political Foundation as a similar vehicle for promoting communication and understanding between the two major U.S. political parties and democratic parties elsewhere in the world. By early 1980 he had recruited officers for the foundation: William E. Brock, then U.S. special trade representative and former chairman of the Republican National Committee, to serve as the foundation's chairman, and Charles T. Manatt, then chairman of the Democratic National Committee, as vice chairman. Agree became president.

This was the first joint venture of the two major parties that was of their own creation. The first project of the foundation was to host 31 foreign political party leaders as observers at the Republican and Democratic national conventions during the summer of 1980. The project was funded by contributions from the U.S. International Communication Agency and several major corporations.

The American Political Foundation established an office in Washington, D.C., from which it provided briefings, appointments, and other assistance to foreign party, parliamentary, and academic visitors to the United States. It invited groups of foreign party representatives to seminars in Washington and facilitated their observation of important stages in the U.S. party and election process. It received invitations to send Republican and Democratic leaders to various congresses of foreign and transnational political parties. The foundation's funds came from corporations, labor unions, private foundations, individuals, and, for specific projects, the U.S. International Communication Agency. By 1982 the foundation had established its credentials as a serious and potentially significant organization for linking U.S. parties, private interest associations, academic specialists, and others involved in the pluralist politics of this nation with like-minded organizations and individuals in other countries.

The role of the foundation changed dramatically in 1982 when President Ronald Reagan revived, with strong personal endorsement, the languishing concept of political aid. In a carefully drawn speech delivered to the British Parliament during his visit to Europe in June 1982, Reagan called for a "Crusade for Freedom" in which he contrasted life under totalitarian and democratic systems and invited the democracies to assert their cause more vigorously and skillfully throughout the world

The objective I propose is quite simple to state: To foster the infrastructure of democracy—the system of a free press, unions, political parties, universities— which allows a people to choose their own way, to reconcile their own differences through peaceful means. . . .

We in America now intend to take additional steps, as many of our allies have already done, toward realizing this same goal. The chairmen and other leaders of the national Republican and Democratic party organizations are initiating a study with the bipartisan American Political Foundation to determine how the United States can best contribute—as a nation—to the global campaign for democracy now gathering force. They will have the cooperation of congressional leaders of both parties along with representatives of business, labor, and other major institutions in our society.

I look forward to receiving their recommendations and to working with these institutions and the Congress in the common task of strengthening democracy throughout the world. It is time that we committed ourselves as a nation—in both the public and private sectors—to assisting democratic development.

We plan to consult with leaders of other nations as well. There is a proposal before the Council of Europe to invite parliamentarians from democratic countries to a meeting next year in Strasbourg. That prestigious gathering would consider ways to help democratic political movements.

This November in Washington there will take place an international meeting on free elections and next spring there will be a conference of world authorities on constitutionalism and self-government hosted by the Chief Justice of the United States. Authorities from a number of developing and developed countries—judges, philosophers, and politicians with practical experience—have agreed to explore how to turn principle into practice and further the rule of law.

The Reagan administration gave an initial grant of $300,000 to the American Political Foundation for a six-month study to develop proposals for a democracy program. An executive board for the planning project was created. It included the chairmen of the national committees of the Republican and Democratic parties, Richard Richards (later, Frank

Fahrenkopf) and Charles Manatt respectively, Lane Kirkland, president of the AFL-CIO, Michael Samuels, international vice president of the U.S. Chamber of Commerce, Representative Dante B. Fascell, chairman of the House Subcommittee on International Operations, and other distinguished leaders and experts. Professor Allen Weinstein of Georgetown University was selected to be project director.

THE NATIONAL ENDOWMENT FOR DEMOCRACY

Out of the planning project came a report and bills introduced into the House of Representatives (H.R. 2915) and the Senate (S. 1342). (See Woldman for legislative history.) Congress established the National Endowment for Democracy (NED) as an independent nonprofit corporation under the laws of the District of Columbia; the endowment would not be an agency or establishment of the United States Government.

NED would have a 15-member board of directors, a president, and such other offices as were created by the board. Basic support funds would take the form of grants from the USIA, although other contributions from nongovernmental sources were expected to form an important part of the endowment's budget.

Specified sums were to be transmitted by the NED to the Free Trade Union Institute, a nonprofit agency of the AFL-CIO, and to the Center for International Private Enterprise, an organ of the U.S. Chamber of Commerce. These would be the principal private sector avenues for providing political aid to democratic labor and business partners overseas. The legislation also designated funds for newly created institutes of the Republican and Democratic national parties, but this provision has since been controversial and has been modified. The general purposes of the NED were enumerated as follows:

1. To encourage free and democratic institutions throughout the world through private sector initiatives, including activities that promote the individual rights and freedoms, including internationally recognized human rights and fundamental freedoms, which are essential to the functioning of democratic institutions;

2. To facilitate exchanges between private sector groups (labor and business) in the United States and democratic groups abroad;

3. To promote U.S. nongovernmental participation, especially through the two major political parties, labor, business, and other private sector groups, in democratic training programs and democratic institution building abroad;

4. To strengthen democratic electoral processes abroad through timely measures in cooperation with indigenous democratic forces;

5. To support the participation of labor, business, and other U.S. private sector groups in fostering cooperation with those abroad dedicated to the cultural values, institutions, and organizations of democratic pluralism; and

6. To encourage the establishment and growth of democratic development in a manner consistent both with the broad concerns of U.S. national interests and with the specific requirements of the democratic groups in other countries that are aided by programs funded by the endowment.

There were those in Congress who suspected that any cooperative effort between the major parties was an unsavory form of collusion to divide public funds and patronage. Others saw the Democracy Program as either an extension of the CIA's covert political operations or an instrument of President Reagan's ideological bias. Still others saw the program as a blatant form of interventionism in the affairs of other nations and a presumptuous effort to teach others the forms of democracy that are themselves considered imperfect at home.

However, there were those who were equally convinced that democratic institutions are understandable and transferable through a program that is bipartisan, technical, and informational. They argued that a pluralist civic culture is learned, and learning requires knowledge of the experience of the past and of those nations that have successfully built such a culture. The sponsors expressed no ultimate U.S. formulae for success, acknowledging the achievements of other democracies—British, French, West German, and others. The principal argument was simply that the United States, as the most powerful and affluent democracy in the world, cannot ignore its responsibility for helping make the case for democracy as a political system.

Given the long history of the democratic mission of the United States, only briefly and incompletely surveyed here, the Democracy Initiative of the Reagan administration and the establishment of the NED are simply the latest efforts to implement that responsibility. As this volume will undoubtedly demonstrate, this is complex, delicate, and controversial work. The beacon lit by the Founding Fathers has indeed cast light into many dark corners of the world and has helped many nations build pluralist societies and democratic political systems. But other beacons have since been lit, generating much heat over differences in ideology, institution building, and ways of implementing the mission of democracy, to which the United States remains dedicated. In a shrinking world it would seem that the mission has only begun and has yet to face its most difficult challenges.

REFERENCES

Bartlett, Ruhl J., ed. *The Record of American Diplomacy*. 4th ed., enlarged. New York: Alfred A. Knopf, 1964.

Cole, Wayne S. *An Interpretive History of American Foreign Relations*. Homewood, Ill.: Dorsey Press, 1968.

Crabb, Cecil V., Jr. *The Doctrines of American Foreign Policy*. Baton Rouge: Louisiana State University Press, 1982.

Goldman, Ralph M., ed. *Transnational Parties: Organizing the World's Precincts*. Lanham, Md.: University Press of America, 1983.

Tyson, James L. *U.S. International Broadcasting and National Security*. New York: Ramapo Press, 1983.

Woldman, Joel M. "Issue Brief on the National Endowment for Democracy." Washington, D.C.: Congressional Research Service, Library of Congress, January 17, 1986.

2 ASPECTS OF A U.S. CAMPAIGN FOR DEMOCRACY
Raymond D. Gastil

INTRODUCTION

From the beginning of the Republic, Americans have believed that their model of governance was the natural, rational solution for every country and that all societies would eventually copy it. There was good reason for this belief. Unlike other societies at the time, the United States was founded on a popular document that also incorporated some of the most advanced political thinking of its age. Constitutionally, in the nineteenth century the U.S. model was widely emulated, particularly in Latin America, and honored more indirectly by the progressive liberalization of Europe. This emulation of the U.S. idea of democracy and of U.S. political forms has continued down to today. Countries of all ideological and national colors have in recent years incorporated into their laws our Bill of Rights, our presidential system, our division of powers, or our federal structure—at least on paper. The Universal Declaration of Human Rights is, to a significant extent, a product of the United States and an attempt to universalize its ideals (as of the 1940s).

Yet the simplistic identification of the U.S. political system with political progress had been almost immediately complicated by the experience of the French Revolution. The eighteenth-century Age of Enlightenment passed, to be succeeded by the romantic, nationalist nine-

A version of this chapter appears in Raymond D. Gastil, *Freedom in the World: Political Rights and Civil Liberties 1985-1986* (Westport, Conn.: Greenwood Press, 1986), pp. 199-230, and is adapted here with permission of Freedom House.

teenth, and the economic, technological, and elitist twentieth. The precursor for both these new currents was Rousseau. Implicit in both was the platonic assumption that the few should decide for the many. Romantics, materialists, philosophers, and technocrats were in agreement that only the few could discern the true interests of the "masses." The few who ruled in past centuries did so on the basis of claims of victory or history and admittedly ruled in their own interests. The few who have ruled more recently or will rule in the future do so on the basis of "scientific" claims and ostensibly rule in the interest of all.

For many years the seriousness of the challenge of these alternative visions of the future was obscured for most Americans by the continued progress of democracy at home and abroad and the general unpopularity of elitism in this country. However, as the world modernized and old forms fell away, belief in a scientific or intuitive "right to govern" by the few grew among political groups and the intelligentsia, particularly in Europe. Finally, with the massive breakdown of old political and social forms and structures during and after World War I, the United States lost both its isolation and its easy confidence. The political and military challenge of the 1930s was from highly organized, rigid societies under absolute leaders (or small elites) that had nothing but scorn for democracy. Perhaps only the fortunate fact that one absolutist regime (the Soviet Union) was attacked by another enabled us to deflect the challenge of World War II. The fate of democracy was at issue. If we had lost, the United States would have become an isolated nation and would have eventually succumbed. Democracy in this era would have been over.

After World War II there was a resurgence of democracy and of confidence in the U.S. mission. We had destroyed the racist, parochial elitism of the fascists and imposed upon their peoples (except for Eastern Europe) democratic regimes. Communism emerged from the war as the only legitimate absolutist alternative to democracy. But it was weakened almost everywhere. Unless its adherents or agents were directly supported by a contiguous Soviet Union, they failed repeatedly. In those days of optimism, as new states emerged from colonialism, they initially assumed democratic institutional structures, modeled on regimes already established by their democratic "home" countries.

After World War II and the democratization of the Axis powers, the United States became for the first time in history a truly international power. The great empires of the nineteenth century had vanished, leaving most of the world fragmented, unstable, and militarily helpless. Into this vacuum a united Soviet communist movement began to move. To counter this danger Americans suddenly found themselves everywhere and helping everyone outside the Soviet orbit. Our support for democracy was as automatic as our opposition to communism or concern for poverty. The international communist movement was seen as a limited military and organizational challenge. Evolution to democracy outside its orbit was regarded as a natural process that needed only protection against external influences.

One of the announced purposes of U.S. foreign aid was political development. For most Americans political development was identified with progress toward democracy. U.S. support for political development was based on three related doctrines. The first assumed that economic development led ultimately to political development. The second assumed that security assistance would bring security and that security was an essential requirement for political development. The third doctrine was an explicitly U.S. theory that supporting the emergence of democracies with military and economic aid would bring security and economic development. The first two were the most salient, but all three were significant, in a somewhat circular set of relationships. All doctrines assumed optimistically that what the world needed was U.S. know-how, money, and ideals, and that it was in our capacity to transfer these effectively.[1]

Years later we are wiser, or at least more careful. The struggle has not gone smoothly; the early promise of a democratized world has not been achieved. Even the partial victory of a secure stalemate within a stable balance of power has eluded us. While we must remember, reconsider, and not undervalue our successes in the postwar years, we still must recognize that gradually communism has spread and never retreated. China, Indochina, and Cuba have been added to the hard core; Afghanistan may be in the process of incorporation. Ethiopia, Mozambique, Angola, South Yemen, and other states form an expanding "soft periphery of communism" that now includes Nicaragua and perhaps Guyana in our hemisphere. Beyond this achievement of political control, communist-inspired ideas dominate intellectual thought, education, and often the media in much of the noncommunist world. Procommunist rhetoric and assumptions dominate debate in the United Nations and its agencies.

The communist world is no longer unified, but this gives us little cause for cheer. The Soviet Union, vis-à-vis the rest of the world, communist and noncommunist, is militarily stronger than it has ever been, and most communist expansion remains Soviet inspired and Soviet controlled.

At the same time that communism alternately grows or husbands its strength, much of the noncommunist world has been wracked by enervating violence, tyranny, and brutality. Most of the larger European colonies that emerged as independent states after World War II failed to maintain democratic forms or practices; they lapsed eventually into modified or unqualified despotisms of the Left or Right. Of course, the picture has many shades of gray. In many Third World despotisms the struggle goes on; in most there are still democrats eager to reestablish the rule of law. Recently Latin America has seen a recrudescence of democracy. Yet, withal, the frontiers of democracy are certainly not where we envisaged in the 1950s that we would find them in the 1980s.

In part the failure of democracy in many Third World states has been due to the difficulty of achieving stable political forms without tyranny in uneducated, disunited, and impoverished societies. But this is as poor an explanation as it would have been in the 1920s and 1930s to explain the repeated failure of new democracies. In our time, Chile, Uruguay, and Argentina were not relatively poor or uneducated; Cuba was in fact one of the materially best off and most homogeneous Latin American states before Castro.

It appears that democracy failed to maintain its post–World War II promise primarily because of the renewed acceptance of theories of political legitimacy that deny ordinary human beings their basic rights to say how they are governed. The assumed rights of small elites are buttressed in some societies by a revival of religious fanaticism, in others by modern technocrats who believe that only they can manage development. Democratic forms are denigrated by many leaders as symbols of cultural imperialism, as inimical to authentic national traditions, such as Confucianism in East Asia or "African Humanism" in Africa. Anti-democratic talk of national symbols, group versus individual values, harmony versus conflict, cooperation versus competition has a wide and obvious appeal, especially among the educated youth. It takes a while to realize that the touted harmony and community are generally imposed by brutality and that the group values they express either are those of a few at the top or are idiosyncratically chosen on the basis of ideology.

The military challenge posed by the increase in the armed strength of the Soviet Union compounds the crisis of the democracies in two ways. On the one hand, it forces the United States to spend large amounts for unpopular purposes and to edge closer to the return of the unpopular draft. The imbalances in the defense efforts of the United States and its allies weaken our alliances by leading to recurrent recrimination. On the other hand, the democracies naturally have developed an increasingly pacifistic culture, opposed bitterly (and reasonably) to nuclear war, but also to all war and to the sacrifice of life and blood that war requires. Pacifism is a triumph for democratic individualism and humanism. But it also threatens to disarm democracy faced by a despotic society that grows ever more powerful militarily and in which pacifistic tendencies are more easily countered.

It was in this context that President Reagan announced a "crusade for democracy" in 1982.[2] If taken seriously, such a worldwide effort directly or indirectly must strive to achieve three goals: the preservation of democracies from internal subversion by either the Right or the Left; the establishment of new democracies where feasible; and keeping open the democratic alternative for all nondemocracies. To achieve each of these goals we must struggle militarily, economically, politically, and ideologically.

ECONOMIC AND MILITARY OPTIONS

In regard to the more generally accepted economic and military means of supporting or defending democracy, a critical issue in Cold War debate has been the relative efficacy of the economic alternatives of incorporation or isolation. Do we, in other words, guide a country more effectively toward democracy by punishing its tyranny through isolation or through increasing trade links and thus contacts until the country becomes inextricably a part of our world? This case can be argued as well in regard to South Africa and Haiti as to the Soviet Union or China. Much evidence can be adduced on both sides. Generally, the most isolated states are the most tyrannical, but this does not prove which came first. Certainly Iran imposed its recent isolation on itself as an adjunct of its growing tyranny. On the other hand, trade and aid and superficial openness has not had more than a modest impact on the level of oppression in a society as well situated for change as Yugoslavia.

The use and disposition of the military also must be the constant background, and occasional foreground, of the effort. The use of force can be psychologically costly, and defeat even more so. But we are dealing with ever expanding forces and force capabilities in communist states and with a perception of these as a growing threat to much of the noncommunist world.

Where and how do we make a stand? Here we need consider only three aspects of this question. First, what is the total impact on the struggle for democracy of stationing cr increasing regional forces such as the Indian Ocean force (with bases at Diego Garcia, Oman, Djibouti, Somalia, Kenya, and elsewhere), or Pacific forces (with bases in the Philippines, Japan, and other sensitive areas), or permanent forces in South Korea and Germany? What is the effect on the political-strategic climate as well as the military balance?

The second question involves seeking a new definition of the rules under which we intervene with military equipment, training, or manpower to assist a government we feel is threatened by internal terrorists and guerrillas. What kind of aid do we give or not give countries such as El Salvador and Guatemala, and what is the full scope of the reasoning? Finally, under what conditions and in what ways do we aid guerrillas or any political movement seeking to overthrow a tyrannical government? Do we simply ignore the partisans of Afghanistan, the hundreds of thousands of Iranians, Vietnamese, or Cuban exiles who have been or are oppressed and are struggling in "our cause" as well as their own?

The answers are not at all evident. For many reasons a nonviolent strategy is preferable both at home and abroad. It locks us in less, results in a better press, and results in fewer casualties for the peoples involved. Yet, always to choose this course would be to give away the game, and even in the short run, to condemn millions more to unnecessary oppression. The problem is exacerbated by the asymmetry of press reporting on interventions by an open society and a closed society, by a society primed to doubt publicly the word of its own government, and a society that dares not do so, on pain of prison or worse.

POLITICAL AND IDEOLOGICAL OPTIONS

In a perceptive paper, Maurice Tugwell argues that the essential arms in our current military struggle must be political and ideological.[3] Cognizant of the degree to which we have disarmed ourselves through humanism and individualism and of the inescapable invalidation of war and the military occasioned by nuclear weapons and television's realism, he proposes that we must in this generation move from reliance on political warfare or we will lose the game. To win, and thus to defeat communism and the spread of communist ideas, Tugwell believes that we must surpass the communists in practice and propaganda in three fields: (1) in providing for the world's needs; (2) in the advocacy of peace; and (3) in the promotion of self-determination by all the world's peoples. Since the United States and most democracies can demonstrate their practical superiority to the communists in at least three related areas—higher production, superior technology, and either lower military budgets or fewer men under arms relative to GNP and population—the strategy is to adopt explicitly these principles as the core of our international posture, and then communicate our intentions and accomplishments insistently, and on all levels.

Tugwell does not believe that we should advocate Western democracy or our concepts of rights, as these depart too much from the training and experience of two-thirds of the world. He is wrong. There is much too much evidence from recent events in Latin America and countries such as Poland, China, India, and Nigeria that people everywhere instinctively want, and feel they have a right to, the same political and civil liberties as those we cherish. Of course, there may be differences of detail, and economic systems and priorities will vary, but we cannot oppose the communist vision without a coherent vision of our own as to the nature of humanity and how we think societies should be organized. We cannot show up elitism as the dehumanization of the individual, which it is, unless we make explicit our commitment to political equality.

In any event, the approach Tugwell advocates, coupled with the promotion of the essentials of democratic freedom, could play a critical part in the preservation of democratic societies and the extension of democracy. For on this basis the United States becomes not the defender of the status quo, but the creator of the future.

Tentatively, then, let us suggest for discussion the following five strategic principles that the United States and its allies should adopt for winning the struggle for democracy:

1. Increase our efforts to provide for the basic needs of all peoples—and tell the world about it.
2. Increase our efforts to preserve and secure the peace, particularly in the nuclear area—and tell the world about it.
3. Promote the rights of self-determination of all peoples, large and small—and tell the world about it.
4. Promote the adoption and increasing effectiveness of the political institutions of democracy—and tell the world about it.
5. Promote the guarantee of civil liberties as rights, with respect for human individuality and the maximum economic and social self-reliance of individuals—and tell the world about it.

Each of these principles is discussed briefly below in order that misunderstanding be avoided.

1. For the United States to increase its efforts to provide for *basic needs* does not necessarily mean larger giveaway programs, although it could in some circumstances lead to such programs on an emergency basis. Public health, agricultural technology (particularly for the small farmer through extension services), medicine, and emergency relief are traditional areas of concern, but we could do more. The extent and conditions of providing aid to Soviet-supported or other unfriendly despotisms must be worked out with care, but we should certainly work toward a posture of being willing and able to help any people (as distinct from a government) anywhere.

2. In the area of *peace* we do not have to disarm, but we should be a leader in peace programs and disarmament efforts, and we should decisively shift the burden of blocking such moves onto the Soviet Union or other tyrannies. We should come out resolutely against nuclear war in any form. We should point out that, in spite of their protestations, only the Soviets have rattled nuclear weapons and only they have protected their population against nuclear attack (our mistake, perhaps, but we should make capital of our civil defense weakness). We should let the world know that communist countries form the only bloc of states in which a compulsory military draft is the general practice. The communist states and other tyrannies should also be identified as the ones that do not allow the free movement of people and ideas and thus make possible the national paranoia born of ignorance that besets them.

3. Promoting *self-determination* does not necessarily mean breaking up all states in which territorial minorities have a grievance. It does mean listening to their grievances and probably urging that some degree of autonomy be granted them. We should point to the efforts of the Swiss, Spanish, and other European states, to the federalism of Nigeria and the Sudan, and to the moves of the United States, Canada, and Australia to increase the self-determination of their native peoples. We should popularize the thesis that the only great empire today, in the technical sense of that term, is the Soviet Union, and speak regularly of the Soviets as colonial and imperialist, in regard to both incorporated peoples and satellites. Certainly our approach will not be well received by the present Indonesian regime and a few other quasi allies. However, it can be modulated, and states such as India should be regularly praised for their achievements in this regard in spite of their continuing problems. U.S. efforts in the Middle East that would give a modicum of satisfaction to the Palestinians would, of course, be of inestimable value for this strategic item.

4. We should identify *competitive elections* as the primary means of legitimizing political rule in the modern world. We should remember that the history of all democracies shows an increasing comprehensiveness of elections, eventually incorporating effectively all parts of the adult population. Initial imperfections in new democracies should be expected and admitted as long as movement is in the right direction. Counterproductive rapid change or revolution need not be promoted for the sake of elections, particularly when their likely result is the initiation of a new despotism. But the goal should be to make obvious and defensible efforts to extend electoral and other aspects of democracy.

5. The development of *free media* and effective and *fair judicial systems* is a necessary buttress for democracy. It is a process we can aid. This is especially true for those small, poor countries in which the media remain severely underdeveloped and largey governmental. These are central elements in the promotion of civil liberties, political and economic.

Governments have traditionally not respected the rights and interests of individuals, especially those of poor people or minorities. Democracy compels increasing recognition of these interests. This point must be stressed in any U.S. program, as should the corollary that group interests are essentially the interests of individuals in groups over time.

Along these same lines, the United States believes that economic systems are properly the choice of the peoples concerned, whether through political institutions, private decisions, or voluntary cooperative organization.[4] Self-reliant peoples, deciding on their own futures, live more fully human lives—and, incidentally, often are economically more productive as well. Note that this discussion does not mention capitalism or socialism; in most countries, either would be an imposed, arbitrary system. In making this observation, we would be changing the coin of the global debate—and adopting a more historically and practically defensible stance.

In striving to preserve democratic societies, we must remember the distinction between stable, traditional democracies and newer, more tenuous, democracies. For the former, preservation of economic health is the key to preventing the kind of subversion that appeared threatening in the interwar years. But for less stable democracies such as Spain, Portugal, Greece, India, or Brazil, the economic effort must be supplemented by a continuing struggle for the minds of the opinion-forming classes. This will involve for each country specially tuned versions of the overall Western strategy outlined above. In addition to ideology and information, assistance to these countries will require appropriate aid for unions, parties, news media, courts, and even parliaments. We and our allies must see how we can help institutions of this kind function with a maximum of efficiency and a minimum of injustice. To help effectively in the prevailing climate of distrust and nationalism will, of course, hardly be easy. It will take patience and restraint and a realization that sometimes inaction will be the best choice in the short run.

GROUPING NATIONS FOR POLITICAL AND IDEOLOGICAL ATTENTION

When we consider how we might launch the campaign for democracy in the two-thirds of the world that lies beyond democracy's frontiers, the approaches we should consider become more complex. It will help us to comprehend the problem if we break it down in terms of a classification of nations along the following lines as of 1984:

1. Communist states
   a. The Soviet Union and its closest dependencies—for example, Mongolia
   b. Soviet-supported, but fundamentally anti-Soviet, contiguous states—for example, Poland, Hungary
   c. Soviet-supported, noncontiguous states—for example, Cuba, Angola, Vietnam
   d. Anti-Soviet, liberalizing states—for example, China, Yugoslavia
   e. Anti-Soviet, conservative states—for example, Albania
2. One-party leftist tyrannies—for example, Libya, Tanzania
3. Muslim tyrannies—for example, Saudi Arabia, Iran
4. Rightist tyrannies—for example, Haiti, Malawi
5. Partly free authoritarian states—for example, Singapore, Taiwan, Mexico, South Africa
6. Prodemocratic transitional states—for example, Turkey, Thailand, Bangladesh, Sri Lanka
7. Democracies with insecure democratic institutions—for example, Brazil, Honduras, Argentina[5]

Each of these groups requires a particular strategy, and, within that, each country requires an individual strategy. Obviously the promotion of democracy in some countries will be easier than in others. Indeed, for most countries outside groups 6 and 7, the immediate goal will not be the adoption of democracy, but rather the establishment of a strong basis for democracy by building a pluralism of ideas and institutions that keeps options open.

We should consider in broad outline what each of these areas requires.

The heart of the military side of the problem is the *Soviet Union*, and therefore the blunting of this threat becomes the critical part in any realistic strategy for supporting democracy.

We assume at the outset that: (1) the people of the Soviet Union do not want war and want to reduce the proportion of the national income (and the time of young men) devoted to military affairs and adventures such as Cuba or Afghanistan; (2) that the Soviet people are generally disappointed in communism, especially the form that has been forced on them, and do not really believe in Marxist "science"; (3) that the non-Russian peoples of the Soviet Union desire much more self-determination, to get out from under the Soviet yoke; and (4) that there is no hope that citizens can individually or collectively change the Soviet system.

We also assume that, except for a few with special educational opportunities or skepticism, most Soviet citizens believe: (5) that the United States (or West Germany) is war minded and aggressive; (6) that Western capitalism is unjust and oppressive at home and abroad; and (7) that democracy in the West is largely either sham or anarchy.

Most Russians and many non-Russian Soviet citizens, we may assume, are highly nationalistic and anxious to defend their country both militarily and symbolically against the threats of others. The Soviet people, nevertheless, experience low morale in regard to their own lives and the national future.[6]

It is within these parameters that we need to pursue any effort to revolutionize the Soviet system.

Our strategic task in regard to *contiguous Soviet dependencies*, such as Czechoslovakia, is to weaken the paralyzing assumption that the Soviet Union will be willing and able to intervene against any significant liberalization. At the same time we must strive to use such societies as conduits into the Soviet Union for new ideas and new hopes.

The peoples of Central Europe under communist control are fundamentally anti-Soviet. Beyond nationalistic reasons common to all occupied peoples, these peoples feel a traditional historical association with the rest of Europe and tend to look down on the Soviet peoples as backward. This feeling of distinction and superiority is reinforced by the fact that they continue to have a great deal more contact with the West than the Soviets through radio, television, literature, church association, and travel.

The percentage of people in Sovietized Central Europe immediately attracted by the democratic concepts of political rights and guaranteed civil liberties is certainly much higher than in the Soviet Union (in this regard the former Baltic States are closer to Central Europe). The level of liberalization allowed in Poland and Hungary in recent years has been much greater than in most of the Soviet empire. Interest in these values was evident in the communist leadership of Czechoslovakia that produced the "Prague Spring" of 1968. We should welcome and treasure such partial liberalizations in the area, in spite of their limitations and fragility. Clearly the liberalized Hungarian society of the 1980s is better for its people and less of a militant threat to the West than a more Stalinist Hungary would be.

The limits of abrupt change seem to have been set by Hungary in 1956, Czechoslovakia in 1968, and Poland in 1981. Significant movement away from Soviet domination on both governmental and citizen levels has occurred throughout the area. Most of Eastern Europe is now much more liberal than a generation ago. This movement both weakens the ability of the Soviet Union to project power elsewhere in the world and sends important information into the Soviet Union. It is inconceivable that the Soviet Union would attempt to invade Western Europe as long as its "internal front" in Central Europe is not secured and supportive. The Polish people are our first line of defense—and of ideological offense.

This does not imply that we have the right to use Central Europeans as cannon fodder. The implication is rather that we have a strong common interest in the maintenance and success of opposition in the area. We must carefully consider the best means to support the growing independence and civil liberties of Eastern Europeans without providing an excuse for renewed repression. We must at a minimum conceive and communicate to those opposing repression a credible theory of success. This requires that the Soviet Union be progressively weaned from direct intervention. When General Jaruzelski stepped in to reestablish communist order, this may well have served to preempt a Soviet move and thus to preserve alternatives for a more liberal Polish future while weakening the exercise of the Brezhnev Doctrine.

Noncontiguous communist states offer a different kind of opportunity. If revolution should occur in such a state, the physical ability of the Soviet Union to control the situation is of a different order of magnitude than on the Soviet periphery. In Cuba there is a small Soviet contingent, and in Angola there are Cuban forces, but, for the purpose of containing serious revolts, these contingents might be more irritants than positive factors.

In Vietnam the situation for the Soviets is particularly fragile. Here there are even fewer foreign soldiers to defend the ruling elite, and there is, poised on the border, a powerful Chinese communist force opposed to the government (and sponsoring guerrillas within the country).

It is characteristic of countries in this grouping that the economic situation is desperate. We think of Cuba's economic problems, but in fact Cuba is far and away in the best shape of the group. Ethiopia, Mozambique, Angola, and Vietnam are little short of desperate; and in each case there are guerrilla forces in the field. Vietnam also has to contend with guerrilla forces in an unpopular war in Cambodia.

A program to support democracy should emphasize means of achieving the displacement of current rulers in one or more of these Soviet-supported, noncontiguous communist states. Such revolts would enhance their national self-determination, and, with U.S. support, might lead to progressive improvement in political and civil rights. The ideological and institutional preconditions are, of course, much more favorable for the early achievement of a working democracy in Cuba, less so in Vietnam, least in the African cases. Liberalization would make U.S. and allied aid in the restoration of the economy politically more feasible and enhance the supply of basic necessities. A single success in replacing such a government, particularly an undeniably communist system such as that of Cuba or Vietnam, would do much to destroy the myth of communist invincibility, of communism as the wave of the future, and would give renewed hope to peoples under communist control everywhere.

The first requirement for success in a particular country would be a communications program aimed directly at this result. In order to overcome the sense of isolation of potential opponents, communications should emphasize information on the activities and intentions of those opposed to the regime. It should also facilitate their acquisition of the supplies they need outside the country. Massive military aid is hardly what is required. Even if the struggle is an armed one, as in Angola, the arms for the movement can be obtained within the country. Primarily the question is not one of sponsoring guerrilla wars or coups from outside, but rather the encouragement of rapid change through the increase of information, organization, and confidence in the population, and the decrease of confidence in the ruling elite.

Recent events suggest two models of change: the Dubček model of a communist elite deciding to change radically the nature of their system because of popular pressure and their own changing values; and the Walesa model of popular discontent coalescing into a movement so strong that the official communist leadership shows signs of withering away (until stiffened by Soviet pressure). Obviously, the police and military are critical in either event; they must be ideologically undermined to such an extent that they will no longer use effective, organized force against those who are pressing for change. Reports of demoralization among security forces in communist states are widespread, particularly from Vietnam.

The *anti-Soviet communist states* pose quite different problems. Here the problem for democratic supporters is analogous to that in the noncommunist despotisms considered below. Nations in both groupings are led by political, economic, and media leaders seriously infected with Western values and the legitimacy of democracy. However, the ruling elites do not know how to liberalize without losing their positions completely, perhaps even being swept away in a democratizing tide. The strategic tactic might be to work with the system and its critics in such a way that progressive change can be realized and a modern, relativized Eurocommunism achieved. This strategy fits most smoothly with our other goals, but it must not lead to U.S. justification of the continued suppression of nonviolent dissidents. While we adapt our approach to different contexts and interests, consistency must also be a part of our message.

One-party leftist tyrannies lack the well-worked-out ideologies, the disciplined parties, and the automatic Soviet guarantees that characterize most communist parties. Nevertheless, the control mechanisms in countries of this class, such as Algeria, Libya, Syria, and Tanzania, have been quite successful; this is a stable and even growing classification. In foreign policy, states in this class are generally supportive of the Soviet Union and supported by it, but there is flexibility, and there are important exceptions. Somalia was forced by events to become anti-Soviet, and Guinea under Touré was able to twist and turn in any direction.

Hanging on the coattails of communism and the worldwide tendency to forgive the errors and omissions of the Left, these states generally have ineffective external and internal enemies. At least in part this is because their internationally acceptable ideology makes it possible for them to suppress their opponents at least as ruthlessly as do their communist models and still incur little criticism. Their additional strength is that they offend the nationalistic feelings of their citizens much less than most communist states.

An effective strategy for democratizing these states must be worked out. Perhaps initially the goal should be to isolate the virus of one-party leftism by pointing out insistently to their peoples and their neighbors the true nature of states in this class. Most are economic failures—unless they have a special resource such as Libyan oil. A state's dependency on the aid of nations such as Libya should be viewed as undesirable by the world community and should be penalized in appropriate ways by the United States and it allies.

Muslim tyrannies are those cases in which a royal line rules with the aid and support of an authoritarian religious hierarchy that actively interprets the secular law, as did the Catholic Church in Europe during the

Middle Ages. In this century, Islamic orthodoxy plays the authoritarian role in nearly every country in which it is the dominant religion. Since, however, the purpose of the present classification system is to design a democratization strategy for different sets of nations, the reference to Islam has to do with political rather than religious considerations.

Muslim tyrannies are closer to communist one-party states than to other authoritarian states on the Right. Islam at its most rigid claims to regulate by heavenly decree all aspects of life and, unlike most religious traditions, explicitly claims the right to control the political process. Theoretically, the stance of the democratic strategist toward these states must be the same as toward the left-wing tyrannies.

However, practical objections will be raised to this stance because states in this group can be bitterly anticommunist and thus ignite back-fires for controlling the communist advance. They control important resources, and elites (in the case of Saudi Arabia, at least) may be pro–United States. To undermine the government of such a state in pursuit of a more thoroughgoing prodemocratic strategy would seem self-defeating. (This is, of course, the same argument used against the Carter administration's condemnations of authoritarian "friends" of the United States.)

A compromise is to treat pro-U.S. states in this group with relative passivity. At best their progress toward democracy will be halting. Groups pressing for change in these societies should receive encouragement from the United States as long as they are at least intentionally democratic. We should communicate to them general news and the preference for rationality, science, and equality (but not necessarily liberty) that has become nearly universal in the West. We can condemn the most egregious human rights violations. But in the short run we need not explicitly attack the governments for their nondemocratic political forms.

Other *authoritarian rightist tyrannies*, such as Haiti in the final year of Duvalier rule, are under increasing pressure from the international community. Few people take states in this category as models, sometimes not even their ruling elites. Some are traditional societies, but many fewer than is often claimed. Most are temporary solutions to the problems of order and stability or temporary solutions to the personal power needs of their rulers. In such states, the United States can use its considerable leverage to achieve some liberalization, as President Carter sought to do with the Shah and Somoza. But the Carter administration did not solve the problem of achieving substantial liberalization without initiating violent swings toward yet another despotism of the Right or the Left.[7] It is insufficient to rely on repeated messages to both incumbents and opponents (or potential opponents) that we desire fundamental change and that we will support any democratic or even potentially democratic alternative that emerges.

At this level another part of the U.S. strategy starts to emerge, that of institution building. This is the first group of countries for which it becomes conceivable that public U.S. support for business and labor organizations, or even political party organizations, becomes feasible. For only at this level can the foreign policy interests of a target country be such that the United States can act as a shield for an institutionalization that may eventually support democracy.

Partly free authoritarian states offer more scope for U.S. influence. Governments, elites, and the general public often know what a functioning democracy is like and yearn for it. There is a steady flow of outside information and a great deal of travel by people from Western democracies and by their own citizens.

It is true that these states often have more institutionalized and stable social and political systems than the one-party tyrannies. They nevertheless accept in theory the idea of democracy as we know it. The goal of communications and political leverage would be to get the process of democratization started again. Often this will mean working out interim power-sharing agreements between present rulers and opposition leaders, similar to that worked out between the conservative and liberal parties in Colombia.

The last two groups—*prodemocratic transitional states* and *democracies*—may be treated together. Countries such as Brazil, Thailand, and Honduras have in common a strong affinity for democracy and repeated experience with its workings. In these countries there is no powerful antidemocratic ideology, although institutions such as the armed forces may have a record of repeated interventions.

The job of political elites in these countries is to build gradually more unshakable democratic institutions among party structures, unions, farmers, professional organizations, courts, the media, schools, and churches. Eventually the military forces must become so integrated with the rest of society that they serve as the guardians rather than the usurpers of democracy.

The United States' role in these societies is perhaps more critical than at any other point on the spectrum. While being sufficiently sensitive to the nationalistic feelings of societies in this group, we should at the same time make clear our realization of, and respect for, the dedication their elites have to democratic values and calibrate our various aid programs so as to promote the society's progression toward democracy. We should endeavor to provide private as well as public assistance in the many practical affairs that make democracy work.

ORGANIZING THE EFFORT: COUNTRY COORDINATORS AND PROGRAMS

The campaign for democracy will eventually require a substantial bureaucracy dedicated to its purposes and able to represent its interests vis-à-vis competing foreign and domestic interests. We can hope that the greater attractiveness of democracy will allow the campaign to perform satisfactorily with hundreds of employees rather than the thousands routinely assigned by the Soviet Union to the task of promoting communism internationally. U.S. electoral experience suggests that good candidates and good causes may, with modest campaign efforts, defeat undesirable candidates or causes that spend lavishly. But good causes do not win without a carefully organized and directed effort and a reasonable level of funding.

Since the United States does not now have a tightly organized, internationally involved political party in any way comparable to the Communist party of the Soviet Union, and since we cannot yet organize what amounts to party branches throughout the world, the structure of our effort cannot be matched directly to this central aspect of the Soviet effort.

In order to improve the efficiency of our support for democracy, we should make a renewed effort to record and consider the history of the activities the United States or other democracies have already undertaken toward that end. Even those cases where democracy was imposed —as in the former Axis states after World War II and, more recently, Grenada—should not be forgotten. Sometimes these efforts have been rewarded, as in Costa Rica, Venezuela, and (at least recently) the Dominican Republic. We have also used our leverage with remarkable consistency in Bolivia—with mixed but not entirely negative results. The continued and positive struggle for democracy in Thailand may owe much to U.S. efforts. Vietnam offers a rich fund of experience; even when ultimately unsuccessful, our past attempts certainly should be reviewed.

Inconsistency must be remembered as the plague of much of U.S. policy. One of the most searing and egregious examples has been Afghanistan. Here the king established a constitutional democracy with U.S. political help in 1963. He persisted with the new system, imperfect but the best the country had ever had, for ten years. Yet, in spite of Afghanistan's extreme poverty, U.S. economic aid steadily declined during these years and was greatly outdistanced by that of the Soviet Union.[8] U.S. policy cannot be said to have been economical or effective.

In assessing our role in the world, it is particularly important to note how important the United States is in the consciousness of peoples everywhere, especially in Latin America. The opportunities and problems this gives us have never been adequately assessed, yet those responsible for developing a strategy for extending and institutionalizing democracy must understand and exploit this factor. Sometimes it will mean shifting responsibility for the campaign to more local actors or other Western allies. Other times we might conclude that a direct effort by the United States would be particularly effective.

Regional loyalties and anti-Western attitudes loom large in some societies. In Asia it might be particularly desirable to increase interest in, and knowledge of, Japanese democracy. Japan is widely accepted as the economic model for Asia. This may lead to a rapid transition from grudging admiration to enthusiastic emulation. If this tendency could be applied to political systems, it would constitute a critical breakthrough for the democratic cause. How to encourage the Japanese to view themselves as potential exporters of democracy and have others share this perception is a major challenge.

Parts of the campaign for democracy are already in place, particularly in functional areas such as the information services of the United States Information Agency. These are being and must continue to be expanded. More time needs to be devoted to both planning and broadcasting, and more languages should be employed. A massive translation and book distribution service should be developed, at least sufficient to begin to compete with the Soviet effort.[9] Much is also being done in other functional areas such as union organization, often by U.S. labor unions. The Human Rights and Humanitarian Affairs Bureau performs an important service in direct support of many of the goals of the campaign. Institutes for the study of democracy could be developed on a continental basis to help train cadres of leaders familiar with democracy and to study the problems of developing and maintaining modern civil societies and democratic institutions. Certainly the State Department, Foreign Service, and Central Intelligence Agency perform supporting functions in other areas.

Paralleling such functional efforts, and perhaps under a general supervisory office, individual programs for every country should ideally be developed, with coordinators specifically responsible for the promotion of democracy in or through that country.

The goals for country programs will vary widely. In stabilized democracies goals will include developing or increasing both private and governmental efforts in support of democracy in Third World countries and reducing or eliminating counterproductive support for nondemocratic regimes. Every democracy has certain other countries in which it takes a particular interest. We may be able to shape this interest more positively—for example, Sweden in Tanzania and Ethiopia, Italy in Somalia and Ethiopia. We must struggle in every country against an interpretation of the world that describes most nonindustrialized countries in essentially Marxist and antiimperialist terms. This is important, in addition, because of the influence of the climate of opinion of developed countries upon resident exiles or other Third World nationals.

In prodemocratic transitional states and fragile democracies, the ideological and foreign policy struggle will occupy less of the coordinator's time. The main tasks will be discovering ways to advance the functioning of democratic institutions and sounding alerts when economic or other trauma threaten to overwhelm these institutions. Here it will be particularly important to have someone specifically responsible for democratic analysis and thoroughly knowledgeable about what works and does not in that particular country.

Democratic campaign coordinators for other nondemocracies will be faced with another set of problems, whose solutions will be no less country specific. They must be prepared to work along at least three tracks: (1) assisting in the provision to the people of the country of information about democracy, the state of the world, oppression in the country and opposition to it, and democratic alternatives where such information is not otherwise obtainable; (2) influencing the policies of government elites so that they move the country in a more democratic direction; and (3) improving the effectiveness and/or democratic promise of ostensibly democratic groups actively working for a change of government. Multitrack approaches of this kind are commonly pursued by both Soviet and anti-Soviet communists and, with care, can be emulated.

Special coordinators might be appointed to represent and coordinate the interests of particular nationality groups by working closely with the coordinators for the countries affected. For example, South African blacks, Kurds, Tibetans, several of the Soviet nationalities, and the Indonesian, Burmese, and Indian dissident minorities might have such specialists. It is important that *all* peoples come to appreciate the democratic campaign as potentially meaningful for them and that they not, by inadvertence, be left to see communism as their only hope.

The message, the vision, we offer must be modulated in relation to each country's situation and possibilities. For example, in a recent discussion of liberalization in the Soviet Union, the discussants generally agreed on the "principle of proximate criticism," that is, that the ideas most likely to promote democratic change in the minds of Soviet citizens are those not too far from the assumptions of the socialist world they know (although this would vary with class and region). This implies that our ideological offensive should begin with emphasis on the many historical and contemporary Marxist critiques of the Soviet Union and descriptions of successful socialist aspects of the West.

It was also recommended that we promote relatively objective information services to a society thirsty for real news, and that we expand support for religous dissidents. (Many would also give support to nationality dissidence, but some believe this leads only to greater repression.) Emphasis on religious dissidence was considered to be especially important because there existed a constituency for this effort in the United States—a critical consideration for the long-term effectiveness of any U.S. policy.[10]

Supporting democratic tendencies in a country such as Iran poses an entirely different set of problems. Does "proximate criticism" make sense here, or should we instead campaign for the secularization of society, as in Ataturk's Turkey? Are Islam and democracy fundamentally antithetical? Is it possible for modernized Islam to lay the basis for democracy? Does it make sense to support a dissident movement of an essentially Westernized elite when that movement seems so thoroughly rejected and its leaders are in exile? Should democracy mean increased autonomy for the Baluch, Kurds, Turkomen, and others when their movements offend many Persian nationalists? Before we consider democracy for Iran, should we promote the evolution of a modern civil society, and, if so, over what period of time and in what manner?[11]

A primary task of the country coordinators in nondemocracies will be to open an informed dialogue with opposition or resistance groups in order to assess their strengths, weaknesses, and depth of commitment to democracy. On the one hand, country programs should be developed on the basis of these contacts; on the other, the contacts will help coordinators discover what can be done to strengthen the effectiveness or democratic fiber of such groups. It may be that in some countries these groups will be found to be so weak and disassociated or so weakly dedicated to democracy that coordinators will plan to limit the campaign initially to working with incumbent elites and upgrading U.S. information services.

Where groups or individuals with democratic leadership potential are discovered either within or outside a country, it should be a major goal to develop attitudes of conciliation, compromise, and moderation. Not only are these essential to any democratic, and therefore pluralist, society that emerges, but they are also absolutely necessary for the incorporation of those many leaders even among ruling elites, who will be needed if change is to occur. It is also important to realize that the more peaceful and incorporative the means by which a democratic system comes to power, the more magnanimous to their opponents will the new power holders likely be and the more likely that the new incumbents will be able to achieve a modern and stable pluralism.

The example of Iran also suggests the necessity for country coordinators in a particular region to develop among themselves regional programs. Democratic elements within nondemocracies must necessarily exist internationally. They must work with similar groups across borders. They must hear approximately the same messages from the United States and its allies. Moreover, groups of countries generally evolve together; democracies exist only with difficulty in isolation or when surrounded by hostile states.

The campaign for democracy will not, of course, be only a governmental effort. Many organizations, such as Freedom House, are already in the field. The National Endowment for Democracy (NED) is a semi-private, federally funded attempt to achieve many of the purposes of the campaign. Its efforts have already made an important contribution. However, NED suffers from the push-and-pull of the domestic political forces that brought it into being, the continuing fragility of its political position, and inadequate funds for the development of a coherent program. This is particularly so since its funds are largely allocated to groups outside its direct control. If it achieves some organizational stability, there are signs that it may be able to overcome these obstacles.

EXPANDING THE DEMOCRATIC COMMUNITY OF NATIONS

An important aspect of a national policy to support democracy is the further development and exploitation of alliance relationships. Clearly it is past time for the United States to extend or reformulate its alliance structure. The spectacle of allied lack of interest in, or even sabotage of, U.S. policy in regard to Israel, Vietnam, Poland, Afghanistan, Central America, and elsewhere weakens both defense and deterrence, gives aid and comfort to our detractors, and ultimately lays the basis for the dissolution of our military alliances. The natural gas pipeline controversy of the early 1980s certainly proved again, if proof were needed, that our international obligations and special relationships should be reexamined.[12]

If we are to maintain our alliances, we will need to take our traditional allies more fully into partnership, ask their advice earlier and more consistently, and more often accept their judgment for the sake of preserving unity. We may also find it advisable to reach out globally for new alliance relationships.

The importance of this approach may be seen when we look beyond immediate goals to the construction of an ever widening community of democracies. Ultimately, what the campaign for democracy should envisage is a new internationalism and the growth of truly democratic international institutions. The UN, the Organization of African Unity, and other ideologically mixed organizations are failing either to handle the problems for which they were designed or to advance the interests of the peoples they were purportedly established to help. Meanwhile, more uniformly democratic organizations such as the Council of Europe are able to play more positive roles in extending and incorporating a sense of international and democratic law within their spheres.

The sense of an institutionally unified, democratic Europe played an important role in extending and defending its "frontier of democracy" in the last decade. This role was an important one in returning Greece to democracy and in creating democratic, noncommunist regimes in Spain and Portugal; it will be critical in holding these countries to the democratic tradition. If, as planned, Turkey reestablishes its democratic institutions, it will be in large part because it wishes to maintain its identification with democratic Europe.

Neighboring democracies support and help to maintain one another, as in North America, in Australia–New Zealand–Papua New Guinea, and in the island worlds of the South Pacific and most of the Caribbean, and, recently, in the Andean states of northern Latin America. The British Commonwealth offers a model of a similar set of democracy-reinforcing relationships that is not based on geography. It should be U.S. policy to encourage these groupings, and at the same time to encourage an international community of democracies with an increasingly overlapping and dense set of relationships.[13]

The nonaligned movement satisfies certain ideological needs, but it has come to be used primarily as a means of spreading the anti-American virus. New sets of relationships can be developed to supplement and perhaps replace those based on ignoring the difference between oppressive and free societies, between tyrants who rule through fear and those leaders who rule only at the pleasure of their people.

In the light of these considerations it has recently been proposed that an intergovernmental association, the Association of Democracies, be established on the model of the Council of Europe.[14] The organization would be devoted primarily to the development of democratic institutions and the expansion of human rights. It is not assumed that the association would initially campaign actively for the establishment of democracy in authoritarian states. Rather, it would actively support democracy where it exists and wherever it comes to exist.

Through cooperation on issues of common concern in this limited institutional arena, there might be developed a sense of mutual interest that would allow for later cooperation on economic and other development issues as well as questions of self-determination. Since the world's most modern and wealthy states would form half of its membership, the Association of Demcracies would symbolize the relationship of democracy to progress. It is hoped that many countries now on the democratic periphery would eventually see their future best secured by identifying with the association and its ideals. Since this would require the institutionalization or preservation of full democratic rights, the association should by its very existence operate to increase steadily the number of democracies in the world.

OVERCOMING EDUCATIONAL AND IDEOLOGICAL BARRIERS

The struggle for democracy begins at home, and, specifically, on U.S. campuses and in the cultural media. The United States is viewed by many of the politically aware in U.S. higher education as the enemy of democracy in the Third World as well as the exploiter of the resources of Third World countries and the deliberate opponent of their development. These views often spread beyond Marxist circles to affect the intellectual environment generally. The United States itself is widely, though less commonly, viewed as repressive in U.S. and West European intellectual-academic communities. Unfortunately, these are the communities that write the books and teach the courses directly or indirectly consumed by the rest of the noncommunist world. U.S. information programs and other forms of intellectual warfare outside the United States can perhaps do no more than offset a part of this larger and unintended effect of education and other forms of cultural communication within Western states.[15]

This burden on the campaign for democracy can never be entirely lifted. It is in fact partially a by-product of the teachings of democratic dissent and reformism. However, it will help to recognize the burden and try to work around it. One approach would be to publicize, for example through refugee speakers, the extent of oppression in the world that can clearly not be ascribed to "U.S. machinations." Another is to develop educational programs for foreign students on U.S. campuses that foster understanding of our political and party systems, our different levels of government, the meaning of consensus and compromise in the context of the United States, and other values. Most foreign students do not take political science or government courses and leave with only a "street knowledge" of what goes on here. Similar programs could be developed on campuses in other democracies.

It is equally important to modify those actions of the U.S. government that affect perceptions of our role and purposes. For example, we must more fully consider the ideological losses incurred throughout the West as well as in the regions affected whenever we appear to befriend a repressive regime such as those of South Korea, South Africa, or Chile. We may have good reasons, even reasons that benefit the people directly affected, but we must also fully realize the losses that we must accept in the struggle over images and ideologies.

The war for the minds of men will continue to face many obstacles. Intellectually, two of the more important of these are the arguments that the campaign is an example of cultural imperialism or cultural naïveté. We must overcome these interpretations through explaining the limited but universal nature of the change we support, as well as the irreversibility of most of the change that is occurring with or without our support.

Obviously, we must understand differences among cultures, the difficulty of cultural change, and the pain that enforced change inflicts when it forces people to abandon values and practices with which they identify their lives. Our trivial fads and fashions are not the only true ways; we must be sure we do not foist them on others when they do not want them. On the other hand, *all* our culturally determined actions, technologically and morally, are not trivial; we may have good reason to believe that selected aspects of our culture should become universal parts of civilization, and, in a free world, it is our privilege to propose them.

We approach other cultures with the understanding that the world is changing rapidly, that many people are not satisfied with their pasts, and that they wish to change both the structure and the details of their lives. For good or ill, attaining one wish inevitably generates others. For example, everyone wants people to have good health and babies to survive, but, as this wish becomes realized, the old wish for large families is progressively set aside, and, finally, one-child families are promoted, as in China.

Specifically, in politics and in economics, old ways are changing, and people everywhere are adopting new models or radical revisions of old models. In this situation we would be unfair to ourselves and others not to promote what we have found, or have reasoned to be, the best models. Of course, for any model to work, it must be adapted to its local situation.

We must remember that nearly all systems of belief or organization in the world today were imposed on, or copied by, the peoples with which they are now identified. Arab imperialism imposed Islam on Khomeini's Iranian ancestors just as surely as Spanish imperialism imposed Catholicism on Latin America. After World War II, we imposed democracy on West Germany, Italy, and Japan. They have no reason to complain, nor do we feel guilt. The Universal Declaration of Human Rights is an imperialist document—primarily a liberal, Western, Christian document. The Africans had little to do with it (there were precious few in the U.N. in the late 1940s). But is it any less applicable today to Africa? All powerful contending leaders in the world—from Khomeini to Qaddafi, from Castro to Gorbachev and Nyerere—are imperialist in the sense of actively trying to get their patterns adopted by other nations. This is a responsibility of all who think they have something others should also have.

In development and Marxist literatures—by no means identical—U.S. advocacy of democracy has often been criticized as superficial. For example, Owens and Shaw write:

In a number of countries the democratic system has served merely to confirm and legitimize the precolonial power structure. Elections reflect the influence of ruling groups rather than the wishes of the people. Parliaments have been established, but have little power. . . . In these countries the democratic system lacks one of its crucial characteristics—choice.

In some countries, however, there has been an illusion of choice—much of Latin America and Asian countries such as Ceylon and the Philippines. There is more than one party, and governments have been changed peacefully in accordance with election results. However, these parties represent a division among ruling groups rather than alternative choices for the nation at large. In addition, the competition among immature parties has often led to grossly unrealistic promises to the electorate, pledges that could not be redeemed by any party in power.

In both situations—no choice or an illusion of choice—there is a lack of effective participation by the people. And in both situations, the failure of the transplant to become a viable political system has led to a series of military coups, dictatorships, and one-party states.[16]

In some degree, these accusations might be made (and are often made) against any democratic system. To a large degree they are simply overstated; poor people do participate meaningfully in most Third World democracies. The fact that their interests, and thus their votes, remain too conservative in the eyes of Western critics does not invalidate their participation.

The final remark of Owens and Shaw that coups and dictatorships result from the "failure" of democracies should alert us to this common misunderstanding of system failure; it falsely suggests the greater desirability, or at least viability, of the successor regimes that replace "failed" democracies. It is well to remember that the developing democracies of the 1920s in Germany and Japan did not so much fail as fall before the superior forces of their opponents. It is likely that in most Third World countries the reason for the periodic collapse of democracies is not that the majority turns its back on democracy, but rather that an armed minority (often a section of the military or the army as an institution) is more interested in power than democracy and grasps the opportunity during a period of societal malaise. It is the more intense inculcation of democratic values in such minority power groups that distinguishes stable from unstable democracies.

Nevertheless, there is an initial air of unreality in many new democracies. A major goal of any campaign for democracy must be to increase the perceived reality of the choices offered to the electorate and to make it possible for all groups of any size to use the system. A first step is to recognize openly the impediments to true democracy that exist in formalistic democracies such as Singapore, Malaysia, Mexico, or Paraguay—impediments that make it next to impossible for opponents to threaten the power of incumbents. Such states should not publicly be called democracies by U.S. officials. The campaign for democracy should not ignore such problems but rather work within the limits of our knoweldge of nationalistic sensitivities so as to overcome them more successfully.

While we may be justified in our cultural imperialism, we may still be wrong in our optimism. But here we need only be clear that there is no fixed timetable for all states. We realize that the basis for stable democracy, or even the possibility of adequate group self-determination without anarchy, is simply lacking in many states. The fact that India,

Botswana, and Papua New Guinea are democracies and Chile a despotism suggests that this is not simply a matter of levels of modernism and development. Many factors are involved. We must work with these, never forgiving leaders who unreasonably deny elementary rights, and expecting repeated setbacks in many countries.

CONCLUSION

The effort outlined here will not be inexpensive or completed quickly. But there is little choice. The proposed campaign for democracy must be conceived in the broadest terms and must weave together a wide range of superficially disparate aspects of U.S. foreign policy, including the efforts of private groups. The defense effort of the United States and its allies is the ultimate guarantee of democracy; the democracy campaign should become an increasingly important and highly cost-effective component of that effort. U.S. foreign policy serves primarily the multitudinous public and private interests of the country; yet, if this policy ignores the struggle of systems and images that forms its context, it will ultimately fail.

The campaign recognizes that U.S. and allied interests are more than pragmatic; they are also idealistic and ideological. Continuity of policy is indispensable if we are to serve these interests successfully. President Carter's human rights policy attempted to serve the idealistic side of the national character; President Reagan's campaign for democracy serves another but overlapping aspect of this character. Only if the campaign expands to cover the full spectrum of these related interests will it be supported through successive administrations. The successful campaign for democracy will be informed, self-critical, and broadly focused. It will be anticommunist, antifascist, antiracist, for the self-determination of individuals and groups, for human rights, for development, and for the provision of basic necessities for all. It will be a campaign for peace, antitotalitarian and antiauthoritarian. It will be a campaign for people and the dignity of individuals.

NOTES

1. See Robert A. Packenham, *Liberal America and the Third World: Political Development Ideas in Foreign Aid and Social Science* (Princeton: Princeton University Press, 1973), esp. pp. 4-6.

2. President Reagan's June 8, 1982, speech to the British Parliament, *New York Times*, June 9, 1982.

3. Brig. Maurice Tugwell, "The War of Ideas and Ideals," in G. S. Stewart-Smith, ed., *Global Collective Security in the 1980s* (London: Foreign Affairs Publishing Co., 1982), pp. 111-23.

4. This political-economic concept of freedom is developed by Lindsay Wright

in "A Comparative Survey of Economic Freedom," in Raymond D. Gastil, *Freedom in the World, 1982* (Westport, Conn.: Greenwood Press, 1982), pp. 51-90. The mixed and incomplete nature of economic systems in the real world is also indicated by tables at pp. 34-35 and 78-83.

5. This categorization is based in large part on the categories and experience of the Comparative Survey of Freedom. See Raymond D. Gastil, *Freedom in the World, 1984-1985* (Westport, Conn.: Greenwood Press, 1985), and previous editions of this annual.

6. Much of the evidence for this view of the Soviet Union can be found in Raymond D. Gastil, *Freedom in the World, 1979* (New York: Freedom House, 1979), part 3, "Supporting Liberalization in the Soviet Union," pp. 85-200.

7. On the effects of President Carter's human rights policy on Iran, see the discussion by Richard Cottam in Raymond D. Gastil, *Freedom in the World, 1981* (Westport, Conn.: Greenwood Press, 1981), pp. 95-110.

8. See Louis Dupree, *Afghanistan* (Princeton: Princeton University Press, 1980), pp. 629-31. I believe this point was first made to me by Zalmay Khalizad.

9. See U.S. Congress, House, Permanent Select Committee on Intelligence, Hearings, December 1977, January and April 1978, "The CIA and the Media," (Washington, D.C.: Government Printing Office, 1978), p. 546; on the more general Soviet information effort, pp. 532-627.

10. See Gastil, *Freedom in the World, 1979*, pp. 194-97, for a summary of the discussion.

11. For further discussion of these and other issues, see Gastil, *Freedom in the World, 1981*, pp. 81-312.

12. See Myer Rashish, "Digging Beneath the Pipeline Affair," *New York Times*, September 8, 1982.

13. As are outlined for the older democracies in James Huntley, *Uniting the Democracies: Institutions of the Emerging Atlantic-Pacific System* (New York: New York University Press, 1980).

14. See R. D. Gastil, "Affirming American Ideals in Foreign Policy," *Freedom at Issue*, November-December 1976, pp. 12-15, for the concept of a "Council of Free Nations." R. D. Gastil, "Toward a Long-term Strategy for Human Rights," *Journal of Asian-Pacific & World Perspectives*, Winter 1982-83, pp. 39-46, introduced the term *Association of Democracies*. An association is now a major project of the Committees for a Community of Democracies.

15. The pervasiveness of the leftist interpretation of the U.S.-Third World relationship can be found in the works of otherwise quite conservative authors. See, for example, Gen. Sir John Hackett, *The Third World War: The Untold Story* (New York: Macmillan, 1982), pp. 234-49.

16. Edgar Owens and Robert Shaw, *Development Reconsidered* (Lexington, MA: Lexington Books, 1972), p. 151. This was, of course, before Marcos changed the system in the Philippines.

3 THE DONOR-RECIPIENT RELATIONSHIP IN POLITICAL AID PROGRAMS
Ralph M. Goldman

If political parties, trade unions, cooperatives, business associations, and civic groups are to be truly democratic, the members of these groups must choose their leaders as well as select the basic policies of the organization. If outsiders, even sympathetic and well-intentioned ones, were to become heavily involved in these decisions, this would clearly be undemocratic. Even if the outside involvement were welcomed by the local group, it would still constitute what in less congenial circumstances is called "interference in internal affairs." A U.S. program to promote democracy abroad would be self-defeating if it led to even benevolent control of foreign private groups by U.S. organizations, such control being, by definition, undemocratic.

"He who pays the piper calls the tune," and foreign aid donors often have generous sums of money available for aiding domestic groups. How can such aid to democratic political development be given without shifting control of domestic democratic groups significantly from their members to the foreign donor, however benign the latters' intentions? If recipient groups become dependent on foreign funding, they may be subject to foreign influence in their choice of leaders and policies. Aid can create dependency, dependency can invite outside involvement, and such "interference" is undemocratic.

From the experiences of U.S. and Western European groups working in developing countries with business associations, student groups, trade unions, cooperatives, and citizen associations, it is possible to identify a number of factors in foreign aid relationships that increase the danger of dependency. As these are reviewed in the following pages, it should be kept in mind that issues of dependency and interference cannot be avoided in the political aid relationship. The problems are inherent in the relationship itself. They can only be managed and minimized.

PATRON-CLIENT RELATIONSHIPS

In many developing countries the prevailing political culture has been formed in a traditional rural society and is based on long-established patron-client relations.[1] When people in these cultures have a problem, their first instinct is not to marshal their own resources and deal with the problem through their own independent efforts, but, instead, to seek a rich, powerful, influential patron to provide a solution. They will offer their loyalty and support, in return for which the patron is expected to arrange to have their problem solved. There are mutual obligations in such patron-client relationships: the client owes loyalty, and the patron owes services. (This kind of political relationship is by no means confined to developing countries, as can be attested to by anyone who has worked in the United States in a big-city political machine, or handled constituency relations tasks for a congressman, or played office politics in any corporation, government bureau, or university faculty.) In patron-client political cultures, the clients must devote considerable time and energy to forming and maintaining their relationships with patrons. Contrary to the touted Yankee ideal of "rugged independence," clients can be said to be "ruggedly dependent." They work at it.

Foreign donors of aid for democratic political development tend to be rich and powerful. They are excellent candidates for becoming useful patrons for struggling democratic would-be client groups in developing countries. There is thus considerable danger that democratic groups abroad may simply transfer their normal domestic political habits to the relationship with their foreign donor. With a dependency relationship of this kind, the donor may end up—willy-nilly—with considerable influence over the recipient group's selection of its leaders and its policies. Such influence, of course, undermines the democratic principle that the group should be controlled only by its own members and should serve *their* interests.

When local democratic groups do build up dependency relations with foreign patrons, these relationships can become quite turbulent. The leaders of such groups in developing countries have more than one strain in their political culture. In addition to their patron-client instinct inherited from their rural, traditional past, they are also usually modern nationalists. As patriots they are wary of their nation becoming dependent on foreigners, and especially a foreign superpower. They feel it important that their country "stand up to" the United States, for example, and not "sell out" to foreign interests. Local democrats in a developing nation are thus in a difficult position. Their traditional political instincts tell them to defer to the foreign patrons, offering them loyalty and support. Their modern instincts tell them to assert their independence of the foreigners. These conflicting impulses explain the often wild swings in the behavior of aid recipients toward aid donors. One minute they are in their "patron-client mode"—deferential and cooperative. The next minute, horrified at their own tendency to sell out, as they see it, to a foreign patron, they seek to regain self-respect by hurling some "non-negotiable demand" at the donor, thus asserting their independence.

DISPROPORTIONATE RESOURCES

The money and resources available to donors of aid may be excessive in relation to the usual scale of budget and program to which local democrats may be accustomed. Showering programs costing hundreds of thousands of dollars on people who may never have dealt with more than five hundred dollars at a time can produce "gold poisoning" in the recipients. Donors in such situations should reflect on how they would react if the Martian Institute for Democratic Development were suddenly to provide their own organization with programs valued in the hundreds of millions of dollars. Might not one become more interested in the largess than in the goals of the programs? Could one be blamed for thinking that a few thousand dollars diverted to support a needy uncle would be of no consequence to a program of such huge scale? The scale of resources with which the aid recipients have prior experience sets a limit on the size of foreign-supported programs that can feasibly be undertaken. Going beyond that limit is almost certain to produce dependency, leading to an increase in foreign interference and a decline in the democratic character of the recipient group.

In addition to dependency, gold poisoning may also produce disunity. Factions within the recipient groups may become pitted in ferocious power struggles over what they consider huge resources. Many local groups that had managed to work together in reasonable cooperation before the foreign donors arrived often begin squabbling once the donors are on the scene. The stakes simply become too great.

Money is not the only resource that may be disproportionate to the scale to which local groups have been accustomed. An airplane ticket to a foreign country to attend a course or a conference may seem to the foreign donor like a simple logistical detail. But what if only one ticket is available to a group of people who can expect no other opportunity in their lifetime for travel abroad? In such a case, the stakes have again expanded beyond any normal human being's capacity to retain perspective, equanimity, and cooperativeness. The group may split wide open in the struggle over who—or whose client—will get the ticket.

The above considerations regarding gold poisoning assume that the leaders of the local group are initially fairly decent, responsible souls. Naturally, once the word gets out that large resources are available, every opportunist, con man, and wheeler-dealer in town will swarm to the organization—most of them speaking perfect English and possessing an uncanny understanding of the psychological make-up of the well-intentioned foreign donors. In democratic development, throwing money at problems not only fails to solve them but often aggravates them. A sense of scale and proportion must be maintained on the part of the donor.

DIFFERING PRIORITIES

Another factor that increases the danger of dependency is that the donors and the recipient democratic groups may have different program priorities but may not be aware of the differences. The foreign donors may be enthusiastic about an idea for a project to help the local democratic group, but this project may rank only third of fourth among the group's own priorities for use of its limited resources. The foreign donors propose the project, often with the idea that they will pay the initial costs and the local group will gradually pick up more and more of the continuing costs until the project is fully turned over to it on a self-sustaining basis.

Needing all the help it can get, and not wanting to look a gift horse in the mouth, the local group may readily agree to the project. However, when the time comes for transfer of the continuing costs to its budget, the local group's leaders may realize that they have much more important things on which to spend their own money. The donors then have a dilemma: close down the project, admitting failure, or continue to subsidize indefinitely a project that was expected to become self-sustaining. This is not a happy choice.

Typically, foreign donors prefer projects that are appropriate for foreign support and that they feel competent to undertake. The foreigners' proposals are thus most often for training courses, research, publications, conferences, and exchanges. However, local groups' top priorities are often in areas where foreign contributions tend to be most controversial: salaries for additional paid staff, campaigns to recruit new members to the organization, and costs of election campaigns within the organization itself as well as on the national political level.

A bit of reflection on the part of the foreigners often leads them to the conclusion that the local group's priorities are in fact correct. If an organization is having trouble serving its affiliated local groups because it is woefully understaffed, then hiring two or three more full-time activists certainly *is* more important than maintaining a research department. This is usually true regardless of whether the central organization's affiliates are cooperatives, trade union locals, business associations, or district committees of political parties.

The danger that differing priorities may produce dependency is greatest when the foreign donor's project involves creating a new organization, such as a regional confederation of cooperatives or trade unions, or a joint training center for several pluralist political parties. The local democratic groups may initially participate energetically, assuming that if the foreigners are enthusiastic about the project, then they are obligated to support their patron's concept. Client groups also assume that the foreigners will pay for the new organization indefinitely and that the new organization will provide some new jobs that can be handed out as patronage, thus strengthening the local group, not to mention its incumbent leadership.

Unfortunately, the new organization may have no other constituency or life of its own, and it may not have a high priority for the local democratic groups. In this case, when the foreigners later try to turn the continuing costs of maintaining the organization over to the local groups, nothing will happen. The difference between a new organization that the foreigners want and one that the local groups want is analogous to that between a baby and a doll. A baby, if given some support while learning to walk, may learn faster and will eventually walk off alone. A doll, no matter how often it is supported, will never walk; it has no life of its own.

UNINTENDED FUNCTIONS OF AID PROJECTS

Another factor leading to dependency is the recipient's use of aid programs for purposes quite different from those envisioned by the foreign donors. Local groups may become dependent on the aid programs to support those alternative functions. For example, many donor programs to aid democratic development involve sending mid-level leaders of local democratic groups to training courses in Europe, Japan, or North America. The purpose of such trips in the donor's mind is to provide needed training. The purpose in the eyes of local group leaders may be to provide "grease" for their political machines, as they dole out trips to their supporters and deny trips to those who have supported their rivals. The recipient organization may not be very dependent on the training, but the local leaders may well become dependent on the patronage involved.

To cite another example, the local democratic group may describe to the foreign donor an urgent need for a local training course in a certain province capital. The wise donor will investigate why this need has come up in that particular town at that particular time. It may be that the local group is to hold its provincial congress in that town that week but lacks funds to bring delegates to the province capital. Perhaps the foreign donor will pay the delegates' travel to participate in the proposed training course. It may also turn out that the person proposed by the local democratic group as the course instructor happens to be an officer of the group expecting to be challenged in the group's next election; this officer-instructor may need to get out to that province capital to do a bit of political fence-mending. In programs of democratic political development, as in any other part of life, it is always useful to know what is really going on, not just what is ostensibly happening. Such knowledge is crucial to prevent aid programs from creating dependency.

In several ways, then, the very nature of aid to democratic groups abroad incurs risks of creating dependency. There are donors and their money, patron-client systems, disproportionate resources, differing priorities held by donors and receivers, and the unintended functions, any or all of which may produce dependency. As was stated at the outset, dependency can lead to interference, of which there are several kinds, to which we must now turn.

STRENGTHENING POLITICAL BOSSES

It is clear from the above discussion of unintended functions of projects that considerable patronage can become available to local democratic leaders through aid programs. This can mean that foreign interference may promote bossism (*caciquismo*) in the aid-receiving organizations. The leader of, say, a local political party branch, business association, or trade union may have built up a personal political machine in that group, putting political clients in various offices within the group and maintaining their loyalty through judicious distribution of favors. These clients also know that they hold their positions only because of the boss's influence. If they were to fall out of favor or if the leader were to fall from power, they would lose those positions. Often, to underline the point that they are dependent in their incumbency, the boss will appoint persons who are unqualified for the positions, so that only the boss's influence can keep them in place. This style of politics, involving the colonizing of lower organizational levels with one's clients, is found in many settings: in hierarchically organized bureaucracies, in single-party political systems, and also in some private democratic organizations in developing countries.

Foreign aid for democratic political development must aim not only at strengthening political democracy for the nation but also at building internal democracy at other levels of organization: business associations, trade unions, cooperatives, and democratic political parties. This internal democracy is the necessary foundation for the long-term maintenance of a democratic culture and government in a developing nation. When parties, unions, cooperatives, or business associations are boss-ridden, they may fail to produce leaders with the skills necessary to win popular support for needed programs. For example, talents needed to build a sturdy patronage network within one of these organizations may be very different from those required by a national leader who must rally people to cooperate in, say, an economic austerity program. In addition, if a party boss succeeds in getting elected president of the nation in a free, contested election and then decides to become a dictator once in office, there will be no restraints on this ambition from within the leader's own party; most of its officials will be the new president's firmly controlled political clients. An authoritarian political party or interest group cannot develop or sustain national political democracy over the long term. This is why any U.S. program to promote democracy abroad must work as diligently in support of what we here have called internal democracy as it does in building a competitive national politics.

If foreign political aid strengthens bossism within the recipient organization, this is a kind of interference. It displays favoritism, possibly inadvertent, by the foreigners toward certain leaders and violates the democratic principle that only the organization's own members should choose its leaders. If the organization's boss becomes the client of the foreign donors and dependent on them, then the purpose of the group is diverted from serving its members' interests to serving those of the foreigners. Even when these two sets of interests are highly congruent, as fortunately they often may be, the strengthening of bossism, by weakening the group's internal democracy, is in the long run counterproductive to the aid program's goal of promoting democracy. A strong, dynamic leader does not have to be a boss. The support of the members can be won through effective performance and charisma, and that support can be used to put the leader's personal imprint on the organization.

The purpose of the foreign donor is to strengthen the recipient organization, not to strengthen the hold of some particular leader on that organization. However, if distribution of the donated resources among the group's members is firmly controlled by the incumbent leader, then it is very difficult to strengthen the organization without, in the process, also strengthening that person. The boss will assure that all of the training courses, trips abroad, project funds, and so on will flow to supporters and none to adversaries. When the boss firmly holds the drawstrings to the bag of goodies then foreign assistance cannot build up the organization without also entrenching the boss as its leader.

SHOWING FAVORITISM AMONG COMPETING FACTIONS

Even when local democratic organizations do have flourishing, competitive internal democracy, foreign political aid programs can nonetheless result in interference by favoring one faction in the organization over others. Foreign donors are not omnipotent. Just because a local group receives foreign aid, it does not follow that it can be manipulated by the donors. However, through the allocation of the aid resources, the donors can obtain some degree of influence. In a close election within the recipient group, for example, that marginal influence could well swing the balance between factions.

At first glance it would appear that such foreign influence in the group's internal affairs will always be unethical and improper. When cooperativists, trade unionists, or party members are asked if foreign donors should try to intervene in their group's internal affairs, the initial response is always a resounding "No!" Unfortunately, life is not so simple, and aid recipients can easily employ a double standard, in which foreign aid to their competitors is "interference" while foreign aid to themselves is "international solidarity."

Circumstances can also arise in which the aid donors, for their part, may feel morally obligated to take sides in the internal politics of a recipient group. Suppose that the donors have incontrovertible proof that one faction contesting an election in a cooperative, local party unit or similar group is hopelessly corrupt, while the other slate of candidates appears reasonably honest. Should the donor remain scrupulously neutral between the scoundrels and their honest competitors? Or should the donor throw a few more trips, training courses, and projects to the honest group, so they can deliver more services to the organization's membership and thereby win more votes? When such a moral dilemma is posed to members of democratic groups in developing countries, their responses are typically ambivalent: some say that the foreigners cannot in good conscience remain neutral between good and evil, while others contend that aid recipients have the responsibility to clean house in their own organization and should do it without foreign help.

Suppose that an internal election in a local democratic organization is being contested by two factions, both of which are honest, but one of which favors a dictatorial movement striving to come to power in the country concerned. (It matters not for purposes of this example whether the dictatorial movement is of the pro-Soviet totalitarian Left, the pro-West authoritarian Right, or simply the vehicle of an opportunistic, personalist caudillo.) If the donor's purpose is to further democracy, both within the local organization concerned and in the national political system, what purpose would be served by remaining impartial in the allocation of projects and resources to the two factions? In such a circumstance, the local democrats usually see the donors as obligated to help the democrats and to deny assistance to the prodictatorial forces.

Suppose that elections in a local democratic organization are being contested by two slates, both honest and both democratic, one of which tends to offer loyalty to the foreign donor-patron, while the other is more nationalistic and remains aloof from and somewhat critical of the foreigners even while welcoming their aid. In this circumstance, it would seem clearly improper for the donor to play favorites in the allocation of assistance. But, given normal human feelings, the donor will be under considerable temptation to favor those who offer praise rather than those who accept help while criticizing. Unfortunately, because of the internal conflict between their feelings as clients and as nationalists it is quite common for some of the most democratic, honest, and capable aid recipients to appear ungrateful and even rude in their relations with donors. Gratitude is almost the only emotion that plays no major role in donor-recipient relations.

The above examples make clear that the dependency of local democratic groups on foreign aid gives donors the capability to play favorites. Whether this is moral or not is a complex matter. There can be both "good" and "bad" interference.

FINANCING ELECTION CAMPAIGNS

Along with financing bossism and playing favorites, another kind of interference that dependency can engender is the financing of electoral campaign activity by foreigners. Especially in developing countries, few political parties have adequate campaign funds, and few interest groups such as business associations, trade unions, or cooperatives can easily generate from their own resources the funds needed to campaign effectively on behalf of the parties and candidates that they may endorse. Because foreign donors do have money, they may receive urgent appeals from local democratic groups for contributions to the direct costs of campaigning.

In most countries, foreign financing of campaign activities, whether by political parties or their interest group supporters, is generally considered to be illegitimate. It is viewed as an extreme form of interference in internal affairs. This public aversion to foreign campaign financing makes sense in that the funding allows foreigners to play a role in determining who comes to power in the country concerned. This means a diminution of control by the people of that nation over their own political destiny.

The contradiction between democratic principles and foreign funding of campaign activities explains why such funding, though common, is usually done secretly. Neither the donors nor the recipient groups want the existence of the funding known. Typically, the funds flow through the intelligence agencies of foreign governments, not because spies know anything about running election campaigns, but simply because spies are specialists in doing things secretly. Accounts appear periodically in the press of both Eastern bloc and Western bloc funds flowing freely into election campaigns in key countries. Though covert funding of campaigns is most often handled by governments, funds also sometimes flow from private groups such as political parties in the richer countries to their ideological colleagues in other nations. West European social democratic parties are generally thought to have subsidized their counterparts in Spain and Portugal during the transitions of those two nations from autocracy to democracy.

The Iberian cases raise some doubts about whether foreign funding of campaign activities is always immoral—the results of this practice in Spain and Portugal have been very positive for democracy. Three caveats come to mind regarding the assumption that foreign funding is wrong. First, what if foreign dictatorial governments or private groups are pouring covert funds into the campaigns of rightist or leftist dictatorial movements in certain countries where democracy is threatened? If the world's democratic governments and movements maintain their purity of democratic principle by not providing campaign funds to the democratic parties, and the dictatorial forces thereby win the election and snuff out democracy in the nation concerned, the cause of democracy will be set back, not advanced, by the observance of democratic norms. Is it moral to remain aloof from such a deleterious process?[2]

This dilemma is a common one. The Soviet Union is widely thought to pump substantial amounts of money into the campaigns of Moscow-line Communist parties. Elections in postwar Italy and in Chile in 1970 are said to be prominent cases in point. In 1984 the Western press carried many reports that right-wing Salvadoran oligarchs, from exile in Miami, were secretly funding the presidential campaign of Roberto d'Aubuisson, a leader of the terrorist far Right in El Salvador. Had foreign democrats adhered scrupulously to the rule of no foreign funding for democratic campaign activities, d'Aubuisson's financial advantage might have allowed him to win, a result that would have been disastrous for El Salvador's efforts to evolve toward democracy. According to published reports, the U.S. government did not stand aside: funds were provided covertly to the Christian Democratic party's campaign.[3] There are thus many instances in which democracies are caught between conflicting democratic obligations: support beleaguered fellow democrats but do not fund election campaigns in foreign countries.

A second doubt about the immorality of foreign funding of campaigns stems from another practical consideration. It is generally agreed that the richer democratic countries *should* provide democratic political parties and interest groups in developing nations with training courses on how to organize campaigns, use consultants on opinion-polling techniques, and similar practical political aid programs. However, what good does it do to train party, trade union, or business association activists how to campaign if they never expect to have the money actually to do it? Campaigning requires money as well as training courses and consultants. If the money is not forthcoming, there may be no payoff from the approved, overt, democratic development programs.

The third consideration regarding foreign funding of campaigns results from the modern institution of transnational political party groupings—the Socialist International, the Christian Democratic International, the Liberal International, and the International Democratic Union.[4] Is it necessarily wrong for these transnational entities to move campaign funds across national borders? Within the United States the national Republican and Democratic parties each maintains analogous interstate funding units, such as the Senate campaign finance committees. These committees collect funds nationally and then allocate them to the state-level senatorial campaigns most in need of funding and with the best prospects of winning. If it is not thought a serious breach of democratic principles in the United States for national parties to distribute funding across state lines, some observers question why it would be any worse for transnational parties to distribute funds to their cobelievers without regarding to national boundaries. In purely logical terms the distinction may be hard to see, but in the Iberian cases, the Western European social democratic parties certainly felt constrained to provide their campaign subsidies covertly to their Spanish and Portuguese colleagues. Obviously, the question is still a controversial one and turns more on nationalistic feelings than on abstract logic. Even if many people in developing countries cannot explain the difference, they do feel the difference.

In various ways, then, the dependency of local democratic groups on aid from foreign donors can result in various kinds of foreign interference, the propriety of which is controversial.

WAYS TO MINIMIZE DEPENDENCY AND INTERFERENCE

It should now be clear from the above analysis why problems of dependency and interference can only be managed, not eliminated. No universal rules can be set down for managing each category of dependency or interference. These issues involve contradictory moral obligations and controversial judgment calls as to what is right or wrong in various situations.

For every general rule, three will be frequent exceptions. Keeping these cautions in mind, let us turn to a discussion of some general rules and give consideration to possible responses in some of the exceptional cases. These rules are derived from the experiences of business, cooperative, labor, and civic aid organizations as to what has been most effective in dealing with the problems set out in the preceding pages.

Provide Goods and Services, Not Money

In assisting democratic organizations abroad, experience has shown that one good rule of thumb is to try to provide them with goods and services rather than awarding grants of money for projects. If the recipient group needs a training course, the donor could organize and finance the course. If a consultant on polling techniques or political advertising is required, the donor could hire the consultant whose services would then be given to the recipient group. If local democrats need some typewriters and mimeograph machines, provide the machines themselves.

This practice can serve in several ways to diminish problems associated with the political aid relationship. First, it is somewhat more difficult to misappropriate or make off with goods and services than with cash, and thus the projects are less attractive to corrupt elements and flimflam artists. There will be a better chance of having responsible democrats with whom to deal. Second, in relationships with an honest and responsible group, the allocation of goods and services, because of their nature, is more likely to be related to real project objectives and less to the extraneous patronage needs of the local leadership than would be the case with cash. A local boss will gain little by providing a mimeograph machine to some loyal client who doesn't really need one. Everyone, however, always needs money. Third, the problem of disproportionate resources is somewhat diminished if the resources are goods and services. The psychological effect on a local political party or business association activist of using a $3,000 computer is different from that of dispersing $3,000 in funds.

Do Not Subsidize Administrative Budgets and Staff Payrolls

Foreign political aid programs have found it most effective to provide services to local democratic organizations, not support the basic existence of those organizations. Organizations tend to serve the interests of those who pay their bills and salaries; democratic organizations should serve only their members' interests. While the two sets of interests may be congruent in many respects, in other respects they are not. Political parties, trade union political action committees, business associations, cooperatives, and others grow real political roots best when their office rents, staff salaries, and national congresses are not subsidized by foreigners. When local democrats, even in poor countries, really feel the need for an organization, they manage to create one. It may consist of cramped and scruffy offices, not much of a staff, and elections conducted by postçard ballot, but it is theirs.

When foreign donors perceive the need for an organization that does not yet exist and sponsor its birth by subsidizing its basic administrative budget, the stage is set for helping a doll, not a baby—the organization often will have no life of its own. The new group may well end up in permanent dependency on the foreign donors. Funding the existence of a group that would not exist without foreign support is the ultimate error in handling the problem of differing priorities. Most aid for democratic institution building will be provided in very nationalistic settings. What young nationalist will respect the secretary-general of a political party or business association who is on salary to a foreign government, especially if that government is the dominant superpower in the region? An artificial organization created and funded by foreigners can seldom grow real political roots among the local populace. All too often, administrative subsidies, intended to strengthen recipient democratic groups, end up weakening them by creating dependency instead of self-reliance and by putting the foreign donors in the role of permanent patrons to the local democratic clients.

Though foreign subsidies for local groups is commonplace, and "everybody does it," it is indicative of the inherent weakness of the practice that nobody admits to doing it. The newsletters and annual reports of Western European and U.S. aid organizations trumpet the virtues of projects that provide services—training courses, medical equipment, technical consultants—but they have nary a word about what "everybody does," namely, provide the administrative subsidies and the salaries of officers of local democratic groups. Even when the subsidy is not secret, it is never given publicity. Both givers and receivers tend to feel they have something to hide. In democratic assistance work, a good rule of thumb is to limit projects and funding to items for which you want publicity.

The general rule against administrative subsidies has, of course, some exceptions, primarily in cases where there exists dictatorial repression of democratic groups. If the dictatorial regime denies permits for importation of newsprint for a free newspaper and sends goon squads around to intimidate businessmen who might place advertising in the paper, then the paper cannot sustain itself from its normal sources, even at a modest level. Either it will cease publication, or it must find outside subsidies. In such a case, the principles of democratic international solidarity require a subsidy, which, in normal circumstances, should be avoided.[5]

Similarly, when dictators prevent trade unions or political parties from collecting dues or holding fund-raising events, there is good reason for foreign democrats to step in and sustain the beleaguered groups until political conditions allow them to resume self-support. The level of foreign subsidy in such cases should be held to what the indigenous group has been able to generate on its own in the past or can reasonably be expected to generate in the future, after repression eases. In this way the creation of permanent clientelism and dependency can be avoided. It is noteworthy that funds for providing subsidies to repressed organizations are sometimes raised through public drives, with maximum publicity: television and newspaper ads, celebrities appealing for public support, and street-corner collections. Such practices are an interesting contrast to efforts to prevent publicity about subsidies to democratic groups that are not suffering repression. Obviously, both the public and the participants in the process regard the two sets of circumstances quite differently.

Don't Let Local Political Bosses Control Allocation of Aid Resources

The purpose of foreign aid in democratic development is to strengthen democracy within the recipient groups as well as democratic pluralism among them. However, as has been shown above, if a local group is firmly controlled by a political machine and its boss becomes the loyal client of foreign patrons, then dependency may become permanent and internal democracy weakened. The donors' goal must be to strengthen the democratic organization as a whole, not just its incumbent leadership.

Experience in labor, business, and cooperative programs has shown that this goal is best met when allocation of aid resources among the group's member units is on the basis of need, merit, and programmatic factors. Aid should not be awarded by the group's *cacique* to clients and denied to adversaries. Allocation must therefore be in the hands of an impartial body, created for this purpose, and designed to avoid favoritism. Suppose the aid program involves some scholarships to send group members abroad for training. If the boss has full authority to choose the participants for the course, they will be selected on the basis of personal loyalty, and often persons may be sent who do not really fit the requirements.

Selection for courses must be assigned to a committee that is indifferent to the factional rivalries within the local democratic group. The committee might be composed of representatives from several units within the group (not all of which may be staffed by the boss's clients), plus one or two representatives of the foreign donor agency and some disinterested parties from the local community (perhaps university professors or retirees who are no longer taking sides in local political maneuvering). Mixed selection committees are used in some countries by the U.S. Fulbright scholarship program as a way of keeping selection based on merit rather than clientelism.

Another device for maintaining some impartiality in the selection process is to have the foreign donor announce to the local democratic organization's various chapters that any one of them is free to nominate prospective participants. The choice from among the various nominees could again be made by an independent, mixed committee. A competition open to proposals from any of the organization's chapters can also be used in awarding projects for clinics, consultants, purchase of equipment, and other purposes.

Naturally, the incumbent leaders of any local democratic group would much prefer to keep their hands on the drawstrings of the bag of goodies and will fight tooth and nail against impartial ways of allocating aid resources. They will cite the fact that they are the elected leaders of the organization and have the responsibility for policy-making. They will rail against foreign interference in the internal affairs of their organization. They will feel that using foreign aid as grease for their political machine is one of the legitimate advantages of incumbency: to the victor belong the spoils. They will tell the donor group that either the aid allocation will be done solely by the incumbent leaders, or else the foreign donors can take their aid and leave. Standing up to such pressures is what executives of donor groups are paid to do.

There are two ways in which foreign donors can minimize friction with local democratic leaders when denying them sole control over resource allocation. One is to point out that the local organization, as a whole, is obtaining foreign aid and is being strengthened. The leaders can, and should, take credit for obtaining that aid, and the donors can facilitate that process. Let the leaders announce the grants, award the scholarships, lay the cornerstones, and cut the ribbons. Such steps are indeed legitimate advantages of incumbency, which leaders earn by winning elections.

The second way of minimizing friction is for representatives of various foreign donor groups—from Europe, North America, and elsewhere in the democratic world—to get together informally in each recipient country, exchange notes, and assure that they are not played off against one another by the local leadership. If they are confident that if they break with the North Americans, then the Europeans will pick them up, or, if they break with the Social Democrats, the Christian Democrats will pick them up, then local bosses can indeed tell one foreign donor either to give the aid the way they want it given or to take their aid and leave. However, if the various foreign groups were all to insist on impartial allocation of their resources, this would put the leverage in the hands of the donors, whose resources local groups desperately need. In the final crunch they will take the resources any way they can get them, even, as a last resort, with impartial allocation. Unfortunately, divisions among donors are often so deep that they do end up being played off against one another by skillful local leaders.

(None of the above is meant to imply that leaders of democratic groups in foreign countries are any more ambitious, unscrupulous, devious, or autocratic than are their counterparts in the donor nations. Quite the opposite; the point is that they are very much like us. Responsible, decent, committed people are not blinded by those virtues when it comes to their own interest and advantage. Men and women of integrity are still men and women, not angels.)

Require Self-Help

This is one of the oldest rules in the field of technical assistance programs, and still one of the best. That it is often honored more in the breach than in practice does not mean that it is not a good rule, any more than violations of the Ten Commandments vitiate their utility. The basic idea behind requiring self-help is that if local democratic groups must contribute some of their own resources to a project, then they will not commence projects unless they are serious about them. By putting something of their own into a project—time, materials, labor, or money—they will have a stake in it, and they will become emotionally committed to it.

The self-help requirement diminishes the problem of differing priorities. The local group will not contribute its scarce resources to a low-priority project. Self-help also helps deal with the problem of unintended functions. If the project costs them something, too, local groups will be less likely to undertake a project merely to piggy-back their own purposes onto it.

When self-help requirements are framed in terms of a percentage of the project's total cost, this may reduce the effects of disproportionate resources. It limits the total scale of a project to, at least, some finite multiple of what the local group can itself afford.

Self-help requirements also lessen the danger of donor aid strengthening bossism. They compel bosses to expend some of their own resources, not merely spread the foreign largess around among their loyal clients.

Self-help requirements can have their intended beneficial effects only if they are enforced. One way to do this is for the donors to make each increment of foreign aid contingent upon completion by the recipient group of a previous portion of its promised self-help. For example, if the agreement on a construction project is for the local group to provide labor and the foreigners materials, the bricks and boards should be provided only in stages, as the labor materializes, weekend by weekend. This may slow the project but, in the long run, will build not only the school or clinic but also a stronger local democratic institution.

Give Subsidies and Campaign Contributions Openly and Multilaterally

In those special situations in which subsidies to the administrative budgets and political campaign costs of the democratic groups are not only ethically permissible but morally obligatory, it is often both more politically effective and more supportive of probity and democracy to provide the money openly. The most obvious advantage to overt transactions is that if one is not hiding anything, one is not subject to exposure. Both the foreign donors and the local democratic recipients can be open in their dealings with the press, with their own members, and with other interest groups. Openness is healthy for democracy; secrecy and deception are corrosive. In their relations with communist or far-right adversaries, democratic groups funded openly need not worry that their foes may embarrass them with a dramatic exposé. On the contrary, the democrats can more righteously try to expose the covert outside funding activities of their nondemocratic enemies. It is then the prodictatorial enemies who must undergo the agony of initial denials, subsequent admissions, and public obloquy for having tried to deceive the nation.

The overt route for foreign subsidies and campaign funds in special cases is feasible. Foreign funding is indeed a practice that is seldom now admitted, but one that "everybody knows about." Thus, making such funding instances public will not reveal anything that was actually unknown. It is less discrediting for a recipient democratic party, business association, or union to have everyone know that it acknowledges foreign funding than to have everyone know that it is in fact receiving it but is dissembling and deceitful as it tries to hide the truth. When foreign funding is hidden, rumors will exaggerate the gift to proportions far beyond the actual modest amounts that are usually involved.

As was mentioned earlier, funds for democratic groups suffering from repression are often collected by foreign donors openly in public campaigns. The public accepts the propriety of funding in such special circumstances. What must be kept secret, of course, if the recipient group must work clandestinely in its country, is informaton about the names of recipients, their location, and the channels through which the funds are delivered. During World War II, the United States and Britain publicized the fact of their aid to the Free French resistance fighters but avoided providing Nazi intelligence with names and addresses. While U.S. provision of campaign funds across national boundaries has not yet been conducted with similar openness, the situation is analogous; everybody knows about it, public opinion accepts it as proper in special circumstances, so why not do it openly and save all the sneaking around and dissembling?

Both the propriety and the effectiveness of giving administrative subsidies and/or campaign funds are strengthened if the money is given through multilaterial channels. Neither type of funding is proper under normal circumstances because democratic groups should be controlled only by their own members. But he who pays the piper can call the tune. If the donor is from a single country, and especially if it is the government of that country, and most especially if that country is a superpower, then the public may have good reason to fear that the recipient group will end up serving merely as a tool of foreign interests. That these interests are compatible with those of the recipient nation may be of little solace to people in small, weak, nationalistic countries. However, if the money is provided by an international democratic organization, such as the Christian Democratic International or the Liberal International, or by a consortium of democratic countries, then the influence of any one country over the recipient group will be considerably attenuated. It is much better to be perceived as being under the influence of the democratic world community than as being a paid puppet of the U.S. State Department or the Quai d'Orsay.

Provision of administrative subsidies and campaign funds to democratic groups under these special circumstances could best be done by an international fund, created by contributions from democratic governments, controlled by a consortium of the world's democratic private organizations, and distributed openly, with procedural secrecy maintained only to protect recipients working clandestinely against dictatorships. Given the national rivalries and ideological divisions among the Western democracies, such a common endeavor would be difficult to sustain. However, there probably was sufficient consensus among the democratic nations that such a fund could have openly and effectively funded democratic parties in Spain and Portugal in the 1970s, campaign costs of the Christian Democrats in El Salvador in 1984, the underground apparatus of Solidarnosc in Poland after 1981, or the democratic trade unions and parties opposing Chile's Pinochet in 1985.

A MODEL STRUCTURE

Are there structures that are propitious for the application of the general principles set out above, that can deal with dependency-creating problems such as patron-client psychology, disproportionate resources, and unintended functions, and that also can keep donors from strengthening bosses, playing favorites, or improperly financing election campaigns? Obviously, there can be no standardized, all-purpose aid structure able to fit every country's situation. The fashioning of donor-recipient aid relations must be done on a case-by-case basis, taking into consideration a myriad of factors.

To show that it is possible to devise appropriate structures, we present here an illustrative example that would have a number of advantages for strengthening democracy while minimizing dependency and interference. Given the vicissitudes of practical politics, it is not realistic to think the model presented here could always work, even in those particular country situations to which it would be well fitted. Our purpose here is to set out principles and goals to which those involved in the political aid process should aspire. The degree to which these principles can be implemented will vary in each situation.

Let us suppose that, through one of those happy coincidences of circumstances that have actually occurred in the 1980s, the developing nation of Surlandistan, after years of military rule, has held free and honest elections that produced a democratic civilian government.

No one can be confident of the future of Surlandistani democracy. Vigorous measures are needed to strengthen the democratic system. This is a task in which all democratic elements in the country have a common interest. To pursue that interest, let us assume that these pluralists form the Democratic Coalition of Surlandistan. Within the coalition are groups from the professional, middle, and working classes; from conservative, Social, and Christian democrats; from business, labor, and the peasantry; from urban and rural areas in both the coastal plain and the interior hills of Surlandistan; from different religions; and from both adult organizations and youth and student groups. The common denominator among these disparate member groups is the determination to strengthen democratic pluralism in Surlandistan.

The creation of a civic coalition for democracy is not farfetched. Such groups have been formed in several developing nations in recent years. In Nicaragua the Coordinadora Democratica united to oppose the Sandinistas' moves toward totalitarianism. In Chile the Catholic Church in 1985 brokered a common opposition front—the National Accord for Transition to Full Democracy—to oppose the Pinochet regime. The National Endowment for Democracy (NED) has encouraged the efforts of three Chilean academic institutions—the Centro de Estudios Publicos, the Centro de Estudios del Desarrollo, and the Facultad Latino Americano de Ciencias Sociales—in support of the National Accord. NED has also provided assistance to similar centers: the Paraguayan Institute for International and Geopolitical Studies, the Haiti Institute for Research and Development, and the Centro de Estudios Politicos Institute in Guatemala. In South Korea a similar civic coalition was created briefly during the political thaw of 1979-80. In all these cases political and economic antagonists joined together to pursue their common interest in a democratic pluralist system within which they could play out their adversarial roles under rules protecting their organizational rights and preventing violence.[6]

Let us further suppose that the Democratic Coalition of Surlandistan sponsors the Democratic Action Center to provide logistical support for the activities of the coalition's member groups. Many of their activities could be conducted more cheaply and more effectively through a central staff. Editing and printing of written materials is best done centrally, not separately on a small scale by each group. Many topics of importance in training volunteers for the various member groups' activities are of common relevance, for example, the method of organizing a meeting, basic democratic principles, fund-raising methods, accounting, and public speaking. These topics could best be covered in joint training courses planned, organized, and taught by the Democratic Action Center, open to staff and volunteers from any of the coalition's constituent groups. The center could also organize the coalition's joint activities: conferences on national issues, publication of a monthly magazine on development of Surlandistan's democracy, and similar projects.

The Democratic Action Center, let us suppose, has a small full-time staff of persons with prior experience in civic organizing. These professionals would be prohibited from favoring any particular member party or interest group in the coalition. The staff's services would be provided on an impartial, professional basis to all coalition members. The center would need physical facilities including offices for its staff, a small printing and duplicating facility, storage space for materials, a conference room, and some classrooms. The center would also need two or three vehicles for transporting its staff into provincial towns and rural areas.

Under this hypothetical structure, the center could be controlled by an executive committee of the Democratic Coalition of Surlandistan, which would select the center's director and staff to work under the committee's direction. The center and its staff would adopt no policy positions; policies on Surlandistani issues would be enunciated only by the parent coalition. Funds from foreign donors would go to the center acting strictly as a technical and logistical group.

The proposed coalition-center structure would be conducive to the implementation of the four general principles set out above to guide foreign aid to democratic gorups. First, the center would be well structured for providing services—not money—to Surlandistani organizations. Training courses, editorial services, publications, and conferences could all emanate from the center for the benefit of those local pluralist groups that join the coalition. Second, the rule against subsidizing the administrative budgets and staff salaries of local organizations, except in unusual circumstance, could easily be observed. It would be well known in Surlandistan that the editors and program coordinators on the center's staff were receiving foreign support, yet no one of the coalition's constituent groups could be charged with receiving center funding for their own staff salaries. Center staff could be made available to local democratic groups, but everyone would be clear who was foreign funded and who was not.

This separation of what is "ours" from what is "theirs" is of great psychological importance in preventing dependency on foreigners. It would also allow a politically important division of labor between the coalition and the center. The coalition, even if operating out of a shabby little office, issuing press releases on cheap newsprint, would be an entirely

Surlandistani entity, taking positions on issues of democratic development in Surlandistan. The center would take no political stands. As a
creature of foreigners, it would limit itself to technical services.

This division of labor could facilitate provision of foreign funding
while minimizing the danger that foreigners could choose leaders and
policies in organizations that should be controlled only by their own
members.

The third principle, namely, that foreign donors not let bosses of local
democratic groups monopolize the allocation of aid resources, could also
be applied effectively under the coalition-center structure. Admission to
training courses offered by the center for participants from various
democratic groups could be granted by a multigroup selection committee, forcing the bosses of various groups to compete by proposing strong,
qualified candidates. Access to the center's editorial services or
consultants would be controlled by the center and its board, not by any
one group leader. Finally, with foreign funds going directly to the center
to provide only in-kind services to local groups, local leaders, be they
bosses or otherwise, would seldom have foreign funds to dole out to their
supporters.

The coalition-center structure would also aid observance of the fourth
general rule, that is, the rule requiring self-help. Assuming that the
demands of local democratic groups for the center's services would
exceed its resources, the center would be in a position to allocate its staff
time and facilities on the basis of the quality of various proposals of the
local groups. The center would thus be in a strong position to enforce
self-help requirements.

In addition to being conducive to the application of our four general
rules of democratic development aid, the coalition-center structure
would facilitate the collaboration of various foreign donors in democratic
aid programs. Because the center would aid all groups within the democratic spectrum, foreign governments or foundations could grant funding
to the center to support Surlandistan's democratic system in general,
without backing any particular party, political outlook, or interest group.
The greater the number of foreign countries giving funds to the center,
the less dependent it would be on any one of them.

This multilateral, nonpartisan, impartial aspect of the center concept is
particularly attractive for a U.S. democratic aid program. As a superpower the United States is particularly suspect among nationalistic
democrats abroad. The latter need U.S. help but fear dependency on and
possible manipulation by the United States. The center structure would
help assuage such concerns. Also, the U.S. political system, with its non-
ideological and poorly disciplined party structure, is better suited to give
general, nonpartisan support for democracy than aid to a particular

democratic party or interest group. This is evidence from the difficulties of the Republican and Democratic parties' international affairs institutes in seeking congressional financial support in 1984 and 1985 as part of the funding of the NED.

General funding of the center by various governments and private groups abroad would in no way obviate complementary programs in support of a particular political party, interest group, or ideological position. Progressives and conservatives could still aid their counterparts in Surlandistan. So could Christian Democrats, Social Democrats, and Liberals, as well as business and labor groups. U.S. democratic aid could be expected to put more emphasis on the nonpartisan approach through the center, while Western European governments and foundations could put greater stress on what they are especially well equipped to do, namely, help particular parties or interest groups that are colleagues or cobelievers.

Another advantage of the coalition-center structure would be the contacts arising among local democratic groups as they participate jointly in center training courses, conferences, and study groups. These contacts would show the competing parties and interest groups that they share common democratic ideals that bridge their differences. The center's joint programs would thus strengthen "family ties" within the democratic sector.

More importantly, in joint programs each interest group would be obliged to address the concerns of the others. In modern polities, all too often each interest group seeks only to protect its own members from costs involved in solving a national problem but offers nothing to help in its solution. By studying and discussing together, democratic adversaries are compelled to address each other's problems, an experience that can help build a national consensus on what needs to be done. In many developing countries, there is virtually no forum where labor and business, or Social Democrats, Liberals, and Christian Democrats, can sit down and discuss these issues. The coalition-center structure could provide such forums.

The coalition-center structure suggested here will not be applicable in many countries. It is offered illustratively. It *is* possible to devise other structures for aiding democratic development by applying the general rules or principles presented here.

The degree of collaboration among adversarial democratic groups assumed in the above coalition-center structure will usually be present only in the face of very acute challenges to democracy—a civil war, a tyrannical regime, or the anticipation of a military coup. In general, however, foreign donors to aid programs must remain aware of the factors that contribute to dependency, be alert to the dangers of excessive interference, and consciously design aid structures that fit the local situation and promote healthy donor-recipient relations in the interest of advancing the cause of democratic development.

NOTES

1. See René Lemarchand and S. N. Eisenstadt, *Political Clientelism, Patronage, and Development* (Beverly Hills, Cal.: Sage, 1981).

2. John Stuart Mill's comment on this issue has been widely quoted recently. He wrote in 1859: "The doctrine of nonintervention, to be a legitimate principle of morality, must be accepted by all governments. The despots must consent to be bound by it as well as the free states. Unless they do, the profession of it by free countries comes but to this miserable issue: that the wrong side may help the wrong side, but the right may not always help the right."

3. On outside funding for both d'Aubuisson and the Christian Democrats, see Joanne Omang, "CIA Channeled Millions into Salvador Elections, Panels Told," *Miami Herald,* May 12, 1984.

4. See Ralph M. Goldman, ed., *Transnational Parties: Organizing the World's Precincts* (Lanham, Md.: University Press of America, 1983).

5. On funding for the beleaguered *La Prensa* newspaper in Nicaragua by the NED, see David K. Shipler, "Missionaries for Democracy: U.S. Aid for Global Pluralism," *New York Times,* June 1, 1986.

6. On Chile, see *Freedom at Issue,* March-April 1986, p. 12. On Nicaragua and South Korea, Michael A. Samuels and William A. Douglas, "U.S. Political Interests in a World of Party Transnationals: How Does the U.S. Promote Democracy?" In Goldman, op. cit., pp. 280-81.

4 PROMOTING DEMOCRACY IN AUTHORITARIAN COUNTRIES: PROBLEMS AND PROSPECTS
John R. Schott

If the United States is to embark upon a more organized and systematic effort to promote democratic institutions abroad, nowhere could the focus of its activities be more appropriately directed than toward countries subject to an authoritarian regime.[1] What is it then that diverts or restrains us?

PROBLEMS OF ACCESS

The problem of access is the principal roadblock erected by those who discourage a concerted U.S. attempt to promote democracy in authoritarian countries. Normally this roadblock is the authoritarian regime itself, which is presumed, sometimes correctly, to be adamantly opposed to the provision of assistance to any democratic forces or institutions within its borders. Two equally daunting roadblocks, however, can be the intended beneficiaries themselves, who often distrust U.S. assistance, and we ourselves, who traditionally fear foreign entanglements. Yet the obstacles are not as insurmountable as some would lead us to believe.

In any authoritarian milieu there are interstices of relative autonomy in a government's network of control. Activities in such areas of relative autonomy—in specific geographical areas, within particular established institutions, or among various associatons or quasi-organized groups— may be severly circumscibed, but they provide the bases upon which nascent democratic processes can be built. These interstices may persist by inadvertence, by design, or simply because the regime's limited resources are insufficient or inefficiently employed; whatever the cause, they often permeate a country and provide foreign donors with potentioal points of access to various societal levels.

Although frontal assaults on the popular or institutional underpinnings of an authoritarian regime will normally not be tolerated, opportunities can almost invariably be found for discussing quite openly with the incumbent regime's leaders the prospects for democracy or ways in which nascent or corrupted democratic institutions can be strengthened or reformed. Such discussions are sometimes enthusiastically engaged in at the highest policy levels of government as well as among its supporters in particular sectors of the economy. Three principal reasons account for this toleration of discussion about democracy.

1. A significant number of authoritarian regimes legitimize themselves on the basis of one or both of two arguments: (1) theirs is an interim government providing a period of tutelage during which, à la colonialism, the people are gradually prepared for the responsibilities of democracy; or (2) theirs is to provide honest, efficient, and determined government as the country extricates itself from the throes of some continuing crisis, and it will remain in power until the crisis is resolved and politicians can again be put in charge. Under both rationalizations, the strengthening of some democratic processes must, at least ostensibly, be promoted during the regime's incumbency.

2. No authoritarian regime can long subsist without providing escape valves for public dissent, economic or other incentives that indirectly instill democratic values, and some popular control over local governing officials; it must also permit some organizations of a social, religious, or economic nature, which are necessary to the cohesiveness and cultural identity of both state and society. Each of these requisites of an authoritarian regime may provide an external, democracy-promoting organization possible points of access to the society.

3. Few authoritarian regimes have had sufficient time or possess sufficient resources to exercise a full measure of political control over the entire country, even if it were their desire or intention to do so. There are certain geographical areas or segments of a society that appear less threatening to an authoritarian regime than others. The regime considers it a waste of resources to seek control over them; they are best left alone: "Control the radio station, but don't mess with the pulpit."

A second problem of access is created by the ultimate beneficiaries themselves. Sadly, ambivalent Third World attitudes toward the United States often simultaneously cause a recipient to view U.S. assistance as both welcome and a kiss of death. Antiregime groups and institutions attempting to lay the foundations of democracy have two oft cited problems in dealing with the United States: (1) they cannot fathom the variety of supportive individuals and organizations of differing hues and interests that purportedly represent the United States—ranging from a congressman to a private volunteer organization (PVO) to an intelligence agency contact; and (2) they are befuddled by the lack of continuity of U.S. assistance and the bifurcation of visible U.S. support provided simultaneously both to them and to the regime they oppose. When aid is openly extended to democratic groups, it is usually by project and hence with narrowly defined objectives and limited time frames. These groups may be courted and perhaps supported, but they often very soon hear of some new loan or military shipment to the regime they oppose. Access may therefore be difficult because of the reluctance of the intended beneficiary to receive our largess.

There are many instances, however, where a trust engendered by a donor's personal representative and the relevance and continuity of the assistance provided have enabled external assistance from the United States in support of democratic institutions to be both welcome and successful. Access, then, is in part a function of the recipient's interest in receiving our aid (not just whether and how it is provided). We are not universally liked among the proponents of democracy in the Third World; nor are we—sometimes for good reason—trusted.

The basis for this distrust constitutes the third major obstacle to access, that is, the way the United States comports itself. Any U.S. program in support of democracy abroad is likely to have trouble winning the approval of a broad section of the American public, their congressional representatives, or the administration's ambassadorial spokesmen and official agencies overseas. Despite the emotionally catalyzing nature of racism and widespread condemnation of apartheid, this country remains profoundly fragmented with respect to devising an appropriate national response to Botha's repugnant South African regime.

When the Agency for International Development (AID) was first mandated by Congress in 1965 to promote democratic institutions abroad, through Title IX of the Foreign Assistance Act, profound opposition arose from a variety of powerful and influential sources within the United States. Title IX called upon AID, inter alia, to maximize the participation of local peoples in the development process, encourage the growth of democratic private and local governmental institutions, and help provide civic education in aid-recipient nations. Opponents declared it presumptuous of the United States to promote any form of political (versus social and economic) development.[2] Such a program, it was argued, would unconscionably interfere in the internal affairs of other countries. It would involve us in influencing processes about which we knew too little. It would entangle us in more Vietnams. It would undermine official diplomatic relations and the role of our ambassador. It would taint AID with the scent of the Central Intelligence Agency.

It was soon clear that unless this congressional mandate were interpreted in the most innocuous way possible by subsuming under the rubric of democratic political development virtually all the activities save relief then being undertaken by AID directly or through its PVO intermediaries, important forces both within and outside the U.S. government could be marshaled to subvert entirely the legislative intent of Title IX.

Lacking a knowledgeable, profoundly committed, broad-based, or powerful domestic constituency, a U.S. agency seeking to promote democracy in countries under authoritarian regimes can therefore be effectively denied access to a country by the U.S. ambassador, the White House, or a congressional committee. Its work can also be undermined by the U.S. intelligence community and military establishment. Why? To assist democratic forces in an authoritarian milieu is often to assist destabilizing processes in that country. Instability is often contrary to the perceived interests of many U.S. corporate and governmental entities. When the author, then an AID official, was asked by Afghanistan's minister of interior in the late 1960s to review a proposed local government law then being considered by a parliamentary committee, the U.S. ambassador became livid with rage; to respond to this informal but serious request was not only to "meddle" in the domestic politics of Afghanistan but would also contribute to a destabilizing, albeit democratic, direction for the country, and this was considered contrary to U.S. interests at that time.

It is possible for an agency, when faced with such circumstances, either to build a U.S. constituency or to compromise its overseas objectives or modus operandi. Supporters can be gained by co-optation: providing funds to politically influential U.S. intermediary organizations, research establishments, grant-making institutions, universities, and so on, whose interests may be allied with those of the democracy-promoting program and that can provide a supportive constituency with political clout. Indeed, with imagination, both liberals and conservatives can be enamored of the concept of democracy promotion; however, they may balk at the specifics, particularly with respect to recipient country or group.

When Title IX was enacted, it constituted, in a politically somewhat unusual way, congressionally initiated legislation rather than legislation responding to outside pressures. As such, it became a legislative mandate in search of a constituency. With AID and the State Department hostile, PVOs attached themselves to this legislation as if it were their own, hoping thereby to compel a positive response to their next requests to AID for grants or increased project support. By defending Title IX before Congress, PVOs did in fact receive from a reluctant AID much of the responsibility and the benefits of implementing it, although they did little differently than they always had done, except for doing it under a new label: Title IX.

Superficially, therefore, AID responded to Title IX not because it wanted to but because it had to. A beleaguered agency need always support its supporters. For example, the AFL-CIO-s American Institute of Free Labor Development (AIFLD) for years operated overseas with public monies from AID not because AID thought the labor programs important or even appropriate for an economic development agency to fund but because of the political clout in Congress and the White House of the powerful interest group that was behind it.

Major PVOs have traditionally been virtually sacrosanct within the halls of AID because they effectively testify before Congress in favor of the foreign aid program and have popular (CARE), organized (Catholic Relief Service), or homespun populist (Cooperative League of the USA) constituencies that can cause AID more trouble than a few million dollars annually are worth. Title IX made millions more available to these organizations.

A White House constituency is a transient and ephemeral base, subject to the vagaries of domestic politics. What, for instance, has happened to one small legacy of Title IX, the Carter administration's human rights initiative? Congress is of the same ilk. The effectiveness of the profoundly dedicated, knowledgeable, and highly respected congressmen who sponsored Title IX, Bradford Morse (Republican, Massachusetts) and Donald Fraser (Democrat, Minnesota) lasted only so long as they remained in office. It was widely acknowledged that AID's ostensive response to Title IX was largely to placate a couple of congressmen so as to preserve two votes on the House Foreign Affairs Committee. The interest of AID's senior officials went no further than that.

Access to a specific country or to all Third World countries in order to promote democracy can be frustrated in several ways: by the regimes to which the program wishes to counterpose an alternative, by those in the country who seek to keep alive the hopes of democracy but who distrust the United States, or by forces within the United States whose immediate interests are not likely to be served by the replacement or tempering of a reputedly stable, "pro-American" authoritarian regime and who see such prodemocracy programs as bothersome or expensive democratic "experiments."

ACCESS BY SUBTERFUGE

In certain country contexts, access may require a confluence of varied interests—host government (authoritarian regime), beneficiary (democratically disposed group or other recipient), and donor (the United

States)—which is difficult to muster. This, understandably, gives appeal to the potentially dangerous notion that a democracy-promoting institution need resort to covert or clandestine methods in order to circumvent the regime's administrative network, gain direct and unencumbered access to intended recipients, and protect the donor from disclosure at home.

Strong arguments can obviously be made for dealing with certain recipient groups covertly. For instance, there are occasions in most authoritarian countries—most recently in the Caribbean and Latin America—when the frustrations of the dispossessed reach such a point that only by resorting to violence can they hope to achieve redress of legitimate grievances within a reasonable period of time and otherwise reduce the regime's excesses. It is at such times that proponents of democracy are placed in the age-old quandary, When do the ends justify the means? Should a democratic nation such as ours, founded in violence and revolution, refuse to support that route when taken by others? To support violence can undermine diplomatic efforts to effect gradualist reforms (or promote other interests of the United States); not to do so suggests, by implication, that when the going gets toughest, we withdraw or somewhat reluctantly support the powers that be, fearing the specter of communism. Should we, 200 years later, be the Lafayette of our own Revolution or limit our support to nonviolent democrats only?

The diversity of U.S. interests abroad renders it far more complicated to deal with authoritarian regimes today than in far simpler times when nations were not so inextricably interdependent and fears of retaliation were not so profound. Yet, whom should we support, where, in what ways, and why? Supporting a group that resorts to violence can exacerbate the passions of certain U.S. interests opposed to any meddling with the status quo in a particular country. If support is given covertly (as, in such circumstances, it often must), and if it is then discovered and made a matter of public record, the entire democracy-promoting program can be brought into jeopardy, here and abroad. Access in all countries could become closed to the initiating agency. Violence may be justified in support of democracy, and covert means may be appropriate to facilitate such efforts when access is not otherwise possible. The only question is whether an agency that supports violence and/or conducts business covertly should be one and the same as an agency that lends publicly accountable assistance to groups and organizations engaged in democracy-promoting activities of a nonviolent nature.

In an authoritarian country there can be no clear line of demarcation between acceptable and unacceptable democracy-supporting organizations. Recipient local organizations and groups may change direction or splinter. Foreign access to a group or institution may open or close. Apolitical professional organizations can become politicized overnight.

Unanticipated events can feed the frustrations of moderate democratic groups, sending them over the edge into violence out of sheer desperation. Some activities can be supported openly and forthrightly; others only by indirection, with circumspection and a low profile. In some cases assistance can be extended over many years, whereas in others it may be terminated abruptly by unforeseen events.

A democracy-promoting agency must therefore display not only acute judgment but also a large degree of agility in determining the appropriate type and timing of aid so as not to discredit its entire program by a particular ill-considered decision or bad guess. Two judgmental considerations must therefore be paramount in determining whether or not to extend aid: the prospects for programmatic continuity and the degree of program relevance for the particular country.

PROGRAM ANALYSIS AND PLANNING

The development of democratic institutions is not a short-term undertaking in which the quick fix or any series of them will be appropriate. Promoting democracy is a long, arduous process with an abysmal success rate. Even the succession to power of a democratically disposed group, no matter how charismatic and committed its leader, scarcely ensures its longevity or prevailing democratic character unless certain preconditions are met. Regimes throughout sub-Saharan Africa demonstrate the fragility of democratic experiments and the awesome power of aged governing traditions and propensity toward authoritarianism. Even Indira Gandhi, despite all that the Congress party has stood for over many years, saw fit to abrogate fundamental democratic liberties to retain personal control over India's fissiparous tendencies. Assistance to a democracy-promoting group or institution must presume its continuity and longevity, while allowing aid to be rapidly withheld or withdrawn as the recipient's changing predilections and host country conditions decree.

It is also necessary to consider the relevance of aid, recognizing that in any country all activities are not of equal merit or importance. Priorities must be established. Because of the exigencies of the situations and difficulties of access, it is easy to fall prey to the notion that doing something is better than doing nothing. This has been a major failing of the U.S. foreign aid program. "Moving money" to protect mission jobs and effect large capital resource transfers has often been given greater priority than the relevance of specific programs and projects for a country's economic development. When objectives are vague, as in "the promotion of democratic institutions," relevance can easily be misguided by a "targets of opportunity" approach. This can sometimes mean "Wherever you can spend the money, place it; we can always make it sound good in Washington."

The Title IX experience is instructive in this regard. In the first few years following Title IX's enactment, the most frequent claim of AID bureaus and missions was "We've been doing it all along." To display continued and sincere interest, they declared in the following fiscal year that "because of Title IX, we're going to do more of it." This led to a scatteration of project activity (an endemic disease in AID that might be known as projectitis) that minimized Title IX's impact on a country program while giving AID increasing numbers of project tidbits to report to Congress. This attitude totally missed the point made by Title IX's congressional sponsors, who sought an overall change in the thrust of U.S. aid policy. Nevertheless, the AID claim and reports wre relatively effective from a funding point of view. How, after all, could a congressional committee staff indisputably show that individual projects enumerated in these long lists of projects were not "Title IX oriented"?

It must, of course, be understood that AID or any other large donor agency is mainly in the business of making capital transfers, that is, moving money. It is therefore uninterested in perceiving its role, and ill-equipped to do so, in terms much different from that of the Army Corps of Engineers upon their discovery of a river without a dam—namely, build one. Gradual recognition of this form of response, together with a belief that many of the most consequential Title IX activities could be best and most easily accomplished at the micro level, led to (1) the establishment of the Inter-American Social Development Institute (now the Inter-American Foundation); (2) the use of a few thousand dollars here and there out of a mission director's special projects fund for "doing" Title IX; and (3) increased reliance on PVOs. That this was to a large degree an abdication of AID's responsibilities did not seem to bother anyone very much.

Thus arrived tokenism and the dispersion of project activity devoid of an overriding policy objective possessing significant programming consequences. The declaration of any specific policy objective, except perhaps the most innocuous (e.g., "assisting the development of agricultural cooperatives") was anathema to AID and the State Department, the latter fearing negative repercussions in the recipient country.

The lesson is clear. To avoid one of Title IX's major pitfalls, it is necessary to develop a clear and explicit policy framework and a set of realizable objectives within which priorities for a country can be established. Democracy-promoting program activities ought not simply to consist of an uncoordinated medley of largely uncontroversial good works that, in the long run, add up to very little of consequence. In this regard it may be instructive to consider the work of the Inter-American Foundation. Despite its deep commitment to building democratic community organizations and its many successes in the Caribbean and Latin America, there are serious limitations to what any single agency can accomplish

with a broad social and economic program approach that does not specifically address the potential political dimension of its funded activities.

To avoid scattered good works and to define realistic objectives, establish priorities, and ensure relevance, it is necessary to engage in a type of
program analysis significantly different from that of most foreign aid
donors. In some of the more accessible authoritarian countries, this
involves nothing more special than the ability to ask questions that
foreign aid donors usually neglect. For instance, when asked to assess
their programs according to Title IX criteria, AID officials have often
resisted examining any program in terms of its implications for political
and social development, focusing instead on what they consider the
agency's macroeconomic mission.

These macroeconomic objectives, however couched, tend to be short-
term and quantitative, and so, therefore, were their criteria for success.
AID would ask not how many wells were dug and pumps installed that
were being maintained by regular collection of rates through elected
village committees, but, rather, how many wells were dug and pumps
installed. A loan was judged successful by its magnitude in dollars and
visible physical size, for example, $50 million for a new 75-mile irriga-
tion system. There would be no attention to strengthening existing democratic procedures by which water would eventually be allocated at local
levels. The question was not whether participating trainees might be
launched upon significant political or other careers by their training, but
simply how many participants had been trained properly in their particular specialty. The question was not asked whether AID-assisted agricultural cooperatives were operating as independent business enterprises serving their members' interests through elected boards or committees, but simply how many new cooperatives had been established or
strengthened in gross output or revenue. The question asked of humanitarian relief agencies was simply how much food had been distributed,
with no attention to the political consequences of distributing food to one
group rather than to another. Nor was there interest in whether a local
administrative network, with a modicum of democratic organization,
had been established to assist in the distribution of the food.

In brief, only occasionally, and even then only in certain geographical
regions, have questions of process and sociopolitical consequences been
considered as part and parcel of AID's project planning repertoire and,
hence, of the evaluation criteria used to adjudge the success of these
projects. Yet it is precisely these questions that any program seeking to
promote democracy anywhere, whether in authoritarian or other country contexts, needs to address.

In less open authoritarian countries, where access is more circumscribed, analysis can become a more delicate task, requiring intimate
knowledge and broad-based awareness of the nuances of the local situa-

tion or, at least, an ability to sense them. Delicacy is required in knowing with whom to speak, about what, and within what limits. To press beyond such limits, which may be difficult to comprehend except intuitively, is to invite trouble.

A coordinated program to promote democracy in authoritarian countries therefore must have its own analysts. This requires an important choice: whether the program's funding agency will use, or be used by, any part of the U.S. intelligence community, or whether it will gather its own information and perform its own analyses. If the latter, will the findings be made available to the general public, be made quietly available to certain elements within the U.S. government, or be wholly private and secure (a virtual impossibility)?

Whatever the case, information concerning the prospects for democracy in any given country will be of some value to the U.S. intelligence community and, by that fact alone, render the donor agency both suspect to those it seeks to help and liable to misrepresentation. Are its analysts, advisers, and representatives engaged in intelligence-gathering or program-assisting functions? A relief agency's field-worker in a refugee camp may fearlessly discuss many delicate political topics with a wide variety of people because he is doling out needed food, blankets, and medicines. May a democracy-promoting agency's field representative also do so?

The type of political analyst most useful to the work of a democracy-promoting agency is likely to be one who is on the spot, can perceive trends without being distracted by immediate issues, and is openly representative of the donor agency. An unusual example is a former well-known overseas representative of a politically astute U.S. PVO who was a U.S. citizen, Harvard Ph.D., former Peace corps volunteer in the country, married to a local woman, fluent in the local language, and not only *sympatico* with the local peoples but also enjoying highly placed contacts, having lived in the country for more than 15 years. Such individuals are obviously rare, but the qualities portrayed are of the type that render local credibility to the organization they represent, provide a visible and personalized point of contact for those institutions, groups, and individuals seeking assistance, and enable a U.S.-based agency to maintain a reliably interpreted understanding of what, within any single person's purview, is actually happening in the Third World country.

Such persons are as much use to the intelligence community as to others. This suggests that they will be hard to locate and harder to recruit. It also means that, however far removed they may be officially from intelligence gathering, they will be suspected of engaging in it or be asked to do so. If the operations of the democracy-promoting agency are to be conducted openly, then a major problem may be to determine a way of insulating its personnel from suspicion of being used for ulterior and covert purposes.

APPROACHES TO PROGRAM IMPLEMENTATION

Overt aid to proscribed political parties or underground leadership groups should, of course, for practical purposes, be eschewed. Also to be avoided are covert activities and the support of groups advocating or engaged in the use of violence. These are likely to precipitate more problems than useful outcomes. By-passing quick-fix opportunities— everything from local demonstrations to the violent overthrow of the regime, perhaps leaving these for other agencies—in no significant way diminishes the opportunities available in most authoritarian countries to help build the foundations for a future democracy. If sound analyses of local situations are available, a significant variety of democracy-promoting and fundable activities becomes evident and justifiable.

In all authoritarian countries there is a variety of individuals, groups, organizations, and institutions with serious political concerns that go beyond the economic, yet to whom foreign assistance is often denied. To others, however, despite their obvious political dimension, aid is often given for primarily economic reasons: an agricultural or multipurpose cooperative, a local leadership training institute, a labor union, a barrio council or community organization, or an agency organizing local self-help groups. Then, too, there are individuals, past or prospective leaders, who have only a local coterie of supporters, but to whom various forms of assistance have been given in an effort to advance the cause of democracy in however small a way.

Some of these organizations have legal status, for, in virtually all authoritarian regimes, a partial framework for democracy is allowed to exist openly. "Responsible" labor unions are permitted to represent the workers of the nation in many Latin American countries. Government-controlled rural and urban cooperatives are encouraged in Thailand and Indonesia. Professional associations and interest groups are allowed to assemble, as in the Philippines under Marcos. Even hotly contested local government elections sporadically take place, as in places such as Nyerere's Tanzania. Controlled as they may be by informers or in-place officialdom, or circumscribed by legal constraints or self-imposed moderation, these organizations provide the latent seeds of either gradual change or violent revolution.

Providing assistance to such potential recipients normally requires the employment of indirect rather than direct approaches if the aid is to be of continuing and telling effect. Assistance must be extended with the realization that aid is normally long-range in its results, seldom demonstrable (with the donor unlikely ever to receive kudos), and seldom very exciting or dramatic in its visible impact. Building an impressive bridge, dam, or expressway, feeding thousands of starving Kampuchean refugees or Ethiopians before the TV cameras, or winning a firefight with U.S. weaponry is usually far more gratifying to the American public and its representatives than anything a democracy-promoting organization in an authoritarian country is ever likely to do. Foreign political aid will be damned by the beleaguered or outgoing regime and publicly dismissed by a triumphant opposition as incidental to its success. A case in point was U.S. involvement in the February 1986 overthrow of Ferdinand Marcos in the Philippines. Marcos was left angry and bewildered even as Corazon Acquino's defense minister, Juan Ponce Enrile, was stating, in response to U.S. claims to credit for the revolution, "We owe them nothing."[3]

Indirect aid implies two facets of the proper donor-recipient relationship. First, the donor agency needs to maintain a low profile, seeking little or no credit for the assistance extended or the results achieved. Second, the donor must not expect specific results but rather encourage democratic institutions and processes to evolve or flow out of foreign-sponsored developmental undertakings. For example, a significant indirect approach involves piggybacking onto other major sectoral economic development projects funded by large bilateral or multilateral agencies such as AID, the International Bank for Reconstruction and Development, the European Economic Community (EEC), or the Asian Development Bank. Such piggybacking provides entry to a specific economic sector, group, or geographical area and enables the democracy-promoting agency to provide these projects with an additional political dimension while reinforcing the project's distinct economic objectives.

There is probably no senior foreign aid official or field technician who cannot recount examples of projects gone awry because a needed political dimension was purposely or inadvertently neglected in a project's formulation, implementation, or evaluation. A dam-building/irrigation scheme, for example, affords an opportunity to help transform or strengthen traditional local organizations responsible for the allocation of water and the enforcement of water rights. These may be informal and/or traditional institutions that nevertheless possess a more potentially democratic character than any others in the country. Unfortunately, they may have become perverted in their objectives and controlled by wealthy or better-connected landowners and government officials. An indirect approach must therefore focus on ways to strengthen their potentially democratic character. The tactics of such an effort could include reuniting a village fragmented by political events, pulling together groups of villages within a larger democratic framework and purpose, and developing a new local leadership. Yet, over the years, even in a country of such potentially critical importance as Indonesia, our aid programs have not systematically or consistently sought to do so.

Recently, for instance, ambitious national plans were prepared, with the assistance of foreign experts, for the development of agricultural and multipurpose rural cooperatives in Thailand and Indonesia. These plans involved changes in the banking and cooperative laws of the countries, the establishment of new supply and marketing channels, the construction of storage, processing, and transportation systems, and the education and training of managers, officers, and members. The plans also called for the further democratization of these nationwide membership institutions by the removal of central government officials from control over their day-to-day operations. Various foreign funding agencies have supported—and are currently considering further support of—discrete facets of these plans. Yet, when the plans were being divided up among various foreign donors, no agency was inclined to help orchestrate an integrated implementation effort at the national level or directly help reorganize, and hence democratize, local cooperatives. Such activities were considered by these funding sources, including AID, as too political. Yet, in fact, these same donors have provided massive support of politically significant activities clearly designed to secure the status quo and shore up the political base of the current regimes in these two countries.

Another example may be drawn from transmigration schemes where, as in Indonesia, the unsettling effects upon the peoples involved are as much political as social and economic. Despite huge sums expended to effect these schemes, wherever they are implemented, foreign donors decline involvement in helping to develop the political foundations upon which a new village in a transmigration area can become an organized, viable, working entity. Instead, donors concentrate on the politically neutral clearing of the land, building of roads, constructing of houses, and provision of agricultural extension services, even when these donors fully realize that failure to address the organizational and political problems of these displaced persons adds their infrastructural maladjustment to the growing list of the West's foreign aid failures in the Third World.

Experts knowledgeable about ways to strengthen democratic processes set in motion by economic development projects could be invaluable adjuncts for the eventual success of these projects. But few foreign aid donors utilize such expertise. Were a credible organization capable of providing such experts, both foreign donor and country recipient might welcome them. An economic development agency might be encouraged to use its leverage to involve such experts in implementation schemes; so, too, might recipient governments recognize that the success of a project depends as much on social and political—that is, organizational—elements as on the economic ones. The donor agency need not declare that it is promoting local democratic institutions. It is, quite legitimately, helping to establish viable institutional foundations, based upon traditional institutions already in place, that will enable an economic development project to be successful. One feature of implementation could call for helping to organize the active participation of the local populace in maintaining improved irrigation systems, health clinics, clean water supplies, footpaths, and feeder roads. This indirect approach enables the funding agency to promote democracy as an inextricable part of economic development projects and to do so in an inoffensive way.

The above examples emphasize the economic side. The organizational and participatory side promotes democracy by helping to strengthen the institutional underpinnings of a democratic society and by strengthening the commitment of individuals or groups to the concept of a prospective democracy in their country. This type of indirect approach can draw upon a wide variety of activities. It can subsidize the writing, translation, and publication of locally appropriate, technically oriented political texts as well as local language periodicals for party or interest group functionaries (as distinct from partisan political leaders) on organizational and electoral procedures, the conduct of meetings, record-keeping, minutestaking, fund-raising, financial structuring, and membership recruitment. Similarly, it can provide foreign technical advisers to trade unions (as AIFLD now does) or professional associations (as has the League of Women Voters) in connection with these same organizational matters. Advisers can assist quite forthrightly in these politically neutral technical issues. Quietly, over beer in the evening, the same advisers can have a most extraordinary democratic political impact.

Another line of attack is to focus on legal development and judicial reform, that is, assistance in the drafting of laws, a new commercial code, cooperative law, or the development of a legislative service or reference library. These require knowledge of Western law and procedures for translation and adaptation to local conditions.[4] As a noneconomic but essential component of a democratic state, legal and law enforcement development have been matters that, with few exceptions, were until recently almost totally neglected by foreign aid programs.

Largely because of the uncritical and static nature of law in most Third World countries, where law is often seen as an incidental adjunct to society rather than its binding element, foreign assistance in the field of legal development is seldom viewed as unacceptable or even particularly sensitive by host country governments, except with respect to obviously untouchable topics. Ironically, difficulties in undertaking work in this field more often arise from projections by donor nations of their own culture-bound sensitivities than from Third World countries frequently anxious to modernize their legal systems.

Localized Approaches

Localized approaches constitute another way to promote the foundations of democracy in an authoritarian country without provoking excessive controversy. Externally supported activities with political implications at the local level are generally not considered threatening by national governments. These activities are often negotiable when larger economic development projects are being broached. A broad range of activities under the rubric of popular participation have in this way been promoted by foreign donors under all sorts of governments, including staunchly authoritarian ones. Access at this level may also be facilitated by the fact that such assistance, while popular in the United States, is often so dispersed in the host country that the sum total of promoted activities adds up to very little.

It is possible, however, for local-level, foreign-assisted activities to have a significant political impact if properly entered into and intelligently executed. This is realized by an increasing number of U.S. PVOs, although the results of such local initiatives may initially be viewed as transient. The very act of organizing groups, for whatever narrow purpose, establishes a procedure for group problem-solving that may carry over into other activities.

Successful group action—for example, providing medicines to a remote village, demanding road repairs of a local government, managing a communal water sysem, or forming a small credit union, consumer cooperative, or joint marketing organization—often begins a highly politicized, democratically based process. If properly designed, small self-help projects that emphasize the organization of local people with shared interest in the pursuit of common goals can result in a village-level institutional infrastructure that can both spread to and link with adjacent villages. This paves the way for more effectively seeking redress of local grievances and response to local demands for important government services.

The International Institute of Rural Reconstruction and its affiliated movements, which ring the globe (Guatemala, Columbia, the Philippines, Thailand, India, and Ghana), have addressed this issue successfully through a fourfold integrated approach to rural development. The crucial element of their fourfold program is "self-government" (together with health, livelihood, and education). By helping to organize village-level democratic groups to meet specific, locally identified primary needs (from dealing with land reform issues to establishing a health clinic), the fundamentals of democracy through interest group formation are quickly learned. When several such groups are formed within a single village, they obviously become competitive and hence mutually reinforcing and self-perpetuating, expanding concentrically outward from each village.

Successful group action can also lead to potentially violent confrontations with legal and administrative arms of the central government or with wealthy, politically powerful landowners over, for example, tenancy rights and land confiscation (a frequent, volatile issue). Effective local organization cannot be carried very far, however, before linkages need to be forged between localities. This is the point at which the interest of an authoritarian government usually becomes threatened, engaged, and obstructive. A village-level meeting is less threatening than one at the provincial level.

Similarly, as an organized village group gains self-respect and confidence, it tends to involve itself in more and more contentious issues. At this point, the foreign sponsor finds itself in a major dilemma no better articulated than by a very intelligent young man in a recent (1985) confidential report to an international development organization operating in the Philippines. "If we do the right thing and support the people in their just struggles, important officials of the local and provincial governments will be enraged because their vested interests are at stake; if we do not support the people in following through on these issues we will lose credibility with them and be escaping from our responsibility of encouraging a genuine people's development process." The local approach, however, if systematically undertaken with a clear eye to the development of democratic decision-making organizations at the village level, can gradually produce politically effective organizations involving larger groups and covering larger areas.

Effective control mechanisms of many authoritarian regimes do not reach very far into the countryside. Whole provinces or federated districts exist in which local democratic experiments are genuinely welcomed. A resettlement area, for instance, whether in Ethiopia, the Sudan, or Indonesia, often begins as an institutional tabula rasa upon which both the government and the resettled peoples wish to see self-governing, democratic institutions organized, often for purposes of sheer survival of the resettled people. Frightened by their new surroundings and released from traditional sanctions governing their former lives, they are particularly amenable to revolutionary, that is, democratic, ways of reorganizing themselves under new forms of leadership. Some of the most effective and unquestionably the most democratically organized multipurpose cooperatives in Indonesia are found in remote places and in resettlement areas—areas farthest removed from frequent government supervision and control mechanisms. By-passing central government channels to the extent possible and consciously focusing on local-level organizational promotion of democracy in carefully selected areas can produce a concentrated and mutually reinforcing effect.

This outcome is quite different from the dispersed local-level project activities of the early Peace Corps or the work of many AID-funded PVOs. The danger to the donor and its implementing agency is clearly seen by the author of the report quoted above. It suggests a third approach that relies primarily on nongovernmental agencies (NGOs), in part as a way of protecting the donor agency from the processes it has set in motion.

The Nongovernmental Approach

By working through reliable foreign or indigenous intermediaries, a democracy-promoting donor may enhance its access to certain countries. A major advantage of working through many of these democracy-promoting organizations is their ability to gain access to a country under a quasi-humanitarian umbrella, even when engaged in development as distinct from relief activities. Yet, despite notable exceptions, NGO/PVO capabilities and country programs are usually so localized, so politically innocuous and unsophisticated, and so fearful of donor nation and host government conflicts that they may make poor bedfellows for an organization seriously committed to promoting democracy, especially in an authoritarian milieu.

Many of these organizations, at one time focused on varying forms of relief, have metamorphosed into development-oriented agencies with some well-trained field staff. However, their headquarters officials tend to become politically timid, often merely posturing when faced with politically sensitive issues in host countries, overly focused on helping only the poorest of the poor, determined to maintain an image of political neutrality, and overwhelmed by conditions of poverty that they perceive as demanding immediate responses rather than long-range solutions. Such officials tend to be ill equipped to undertake difficult systematic, coordinated, and focused efforts to promote democracy in an aid-recipient country.

It is nevertheless true that some NGOs are now undergoing a further change as their success rate, however judged, continues to decline and as they work more collaboratively with and through indigenous organizations. The latter are more acutely cognizant of the political nature of the problems they seek to address and the growing need to eschew economic palliatives in favor of political action. A democracy-promoting agency may significantly contribute to this emerging reorientation as much by funding the training of NGO personnel for the authoritarian political milieu, with its opportunities and ramifications, as by direct funding of the field activities some NGOs may be eager to undertake.

Some U.S. PVOs (notably the Maryknoll orders and, less dramatically, the aid arms of two Protestant denominations) are in fact already engaged in supporting structural (particularly political) reforms in the Third World, recognizing these reforms to be essential if their work in a country is to be of lasting account. Providing training to PVO management and field staff and offering consultative assistance to PVOs at the project formulation stage of their work on a complimentary basis could open a major indirect entrée to authoritarian countries.

PVOs that are willing to be involved in politically relevant work, or are pressured by their constituencies to do so, seldom have on their staffs persons who are technically able to perform political impact studies or systematically design programs with a democracy-promoting dimension. AID's Development Program Grants of the 1970s sought to shore up the institutional capabilities of PVOs for their economic development work. This grant program could be revised to award similar assistance to PVOs for training staff in the political analytical and managerial skills they must increasingly employ in the 1980s and beyond. A difficulty arises in first identifying those nonprofit agencies truly capable of undertaking useful work in support of democratic institutions and then encouraging them to develop programs and staff suitable for such financial support.

Another important nongovernmental approach may be made through indigenous organizations. These may be PVOs of an international character or, more appropriately, various types of voluntary (and partially government-controlled) organizations that survive despite the authoritarian nature of the regime. In some countries they are not easily identified. The donor's search for a local representative to identify and recruit them therefore may be crucial. Indeed, the Asia Society's success rate in doing so has been the exception. Such indigenous organizations may be political, charitable, religious, developmental, special-interest, or social/ traditional, each serving as a small but significant unit in the pluralistic society that must provide the context for a democratic political system. Such indigenous organizations can provide greater access to many Third World countries where locals increasingly look askance at foreign nationals "intruding" upon work that locals are able to do. Direct assistance to these organizations can also be far more cost-effective and programmatically focused than if a timorous or ill-informed U.S. intermediary agency engages directly in this work.

In dealing with or through indigenous private sector voluntary agencies, any democracy-promoting organization must be fully conscious of the dangers and possible setbacks. Voluntary agencies come and go, amalgamate with one another, or unexpectedly change course. One day they operate with the government's blessings; the next day they are proscribed. It is necessary only to recall the mortality rate among not very troublesome leaders of rural cooperatives in Guatemala or Indonesia to appreciate the vulnerability and transience of voluntary groups operating in Third World private sectors.

Individual Approaches

The least troublesome way to assist the prospect of democracy in authoritarian countries is to identify and support individuals whose interests and concerns may now or in the future serve the cause of democracy in their country. Access is facilitated if the individual's visibility is low. As in the case of the long shot in a horse race, the payoff can be surprising and exhilarating. While political exiles are, of course, easily identified and their political predilections are often a matter of all too public record, they constitute an easy group with which to open this discussion.

Unfortunately, the individual approach has its drawbacks. The history of AID's participant training programs, for instance, suggests that the identification of worthy candidates for support requires a higher degree of perceptivity and culture-bridging understanding than is possessed by most U.S. officials. On the other hand, delegating the selection process to host country committees frequently encourages the use of inappropriate selection criteria, which makes a mockery of the process. Furthermore, individuals who choose to live in exile usually constitute a highly frustrated breed whose impatience produces a predilection for violence and a precipitate interest in fomenting dramatic but short-lived coups.

The support given in the past by the United States to exiled individuals, when exclusively overt, has largely been confined to training or other education, usually in the United States and, regrettably, less often in third countries (purportedly for balance of payments reasons). Usually this training has had only the most remote relevance to the political roles that participants may perform upon return to their country, even when their selection has been based upon expectations that they will perform such roles. Aside from the military training of some, potential future leaders have been provided with technical skills, including managerial, undergraduate liberal arts education, or graduate work in an academic specialty. None have been specifically and overtly provided training in the political techniques needed to establish, build, or maintian political parties, mass movements, or other politically pertinent organizations at the national, provincial, or local level in their home country.

Support of a local, politically oriented training school in an authoritarian country is normally out of the question, unless the intended result is to reinforce the effectiveness of the regime in power or unless it is conducted under another guise. The latter may include elected leaders of cooperatives or trade unions in their circumscribed administrative roles or persons involved with local foundations or organizations engaged in charitable, educational, literary, and sometimes developmental work.

It would be far more useful to establish a training institute, preferably in the United States, where carefully selected participants could receive practical, if not ideological, theoretical, or historical training, in political and organizational techniques and procedures. A feature of this training could be professional help in planning ways in which they could apply their knowledge and skills in their own country situations and cultural contexts. These programs need not be propagandistic, but rather technical in orientation, reaching a broad clientele in the Third World, including not just potential civic leaders, but also current organizational functionaries and administrators.

A democracy-promoting agency could help establish such an institute and even contribute to its operating budget through trainee scholarships without actually operating the institute. Such an institute could also be the locus from which nonpartisan technical advisory services could be provided to selected political parties on request and to other indigenous democracy-promoting organizations and groups. Even U.S. organizations, including multinational corporations, could be assisted in coping with politically sensitive Third World situations. Linked with ancillary and complementary activities, such an institute could provide, quite openly, a distinguished alternative to those with contrary interests now operating elsewhere.

To ensure its credibility in the eyes of both supporters and participants, such an institute needs to be insulated from any appearance of engagement in conspiratorial activities. Political fallout could probably be minimized and the interest of prospective trainees encouraged if

- participants from authoritarian countries were intermingled with those from more open societies;
- the institute's curriculum avoided propagandistic overtones and focused on fundamentally technical matters, for example, the ways in which the needs and desires of people in a particular situational context can be most responsibly articulated, aggregated, organized, and nonviolently realized;
- participants were selected on the basis of openly and widely promulgated criteria that emphasized the long-term interests and career hopes of participants; and
- the institute were initially given some academic or nongovernmental credibility.

In many authoritarian countries, there is an often considerable contingent of grateful persons who have received subsidized training or education in the United States. Yet many feel abandoned by this country once they return home. It is truly appalling how little the United States subsequently does for them. However enamored they may be of our life-style of freedom and democratic liberties—and not just our affluence, as some would allege—we know neither who they are nor where they are, and we do precious little to retain, let alone reinforce, their linkages to what the United States may represent for them. Alumni associations, for example, are seldom promoted to help our foreign graduates. Instead, if promoted, such associations are undertaken for what they might do for the United

States or their U.S. alma mater. Has this country, for instance, given selected students/trainees from developing countries a central clearing-house through which to enjoy an opportunity to purchase a broad range of books published in the United States—novels no less than political and economic texts—at significant discounts so as to make them affordable in Third World countries? How immense the benefit of such an initiative at how small a cost!

CONCLUSION

If we are to encourage actively and forthrightly the growth of democratic institutions and attitudes in Third World countries, as our political heritage calls for, it is necessary for this country to acknowledge and accept three basic postulates concerning our present international role and responsibilities. First, whether or not the United States con-sciously seeks to affect the political situation in any particular Third World country, its influence can be either decisive or devastating to the interests of democracy by doing nothing or by doing something. How-ever burdensome it may be, it is impossible to avoid having an impact—real or as imagined by others—on the dictatorial regimes with which this country must continually deal in a variety of ways.

Second, powerful interests in this country, within both the public and private sectors, often have a far greater interest in maintaining the status quo of authoritarian regimes in Third World countries than in seeking their replacement. As a democracy, we must be responsive to such inter-ests while recognizing the need to be far more conscious than hitherto of the long-run ramifications of catering to short-term domestic interests.

Third, whatever our intended objectives, and however they may be sought, the results of our aid may be vastly different from what we anticipated or sought. For example, well-meaning humanitarian relief may save lives but leave in its wake brain-damaged children, with whose needs Third World countries must subsequently cope. Or a leadership training program may produce a country's next Amin-like dictator or Marxist-oriented rebel no less frequently than a democratically elected future prime minister.

Although results are still largely unpredictable, it is nevertheless possible to undertake a systematic effort to mitigate the forces of authori-tarianism and to help lay the bases for more democratic regimes to follow. Indeed, authoritarian countries often provide just as many oppor-tunities to support democratic institutional development as do more openly democratic ones; it may require only more knowledge and fi-nesse to provide assistance effectively.

If the United States chooses to reestablish its image abroad as a beacon of hope to which the oppressed and the neglected of the Third World may turn for help as their responsible future leaders chart a more benevolent and democratic course, then much that is do-able must be done, not just in words but by deeds.

NOTES

1. I am grateful to William A. Douglas for the opportunity to discuss aspects of this subject with him.

2. For a more thorough analysis of the policy issues and negative responses this legislative mandate raised, see John R. Schott, "A New Dimension in U.S. Foreign Aid?" *Foreign Service Journal*, March 1970, pp. 19-24.

3. *Manila Times*, March 6, 1986.

4. It may, of course, be recalled that AID officials, with the help of U.S. police chiefs, once rationalized AID's public safety assistance programs on the principle that democracy without security can not survive. This meant providing the Third World's police forces with predominantly military largess rather than legal and organizational models.

5 TRANSNATIONAL PARTIES AS MULTILATERAL CIVIC EDUCATORS
Ralph M. Goldman

Americans of the eighteenth century were the first to create political parties capable of implementing popular sovereignty and building democratic institutions. Americans of the twentieth century seem to be the last to appreciate the place of political parties—in this case, transnational parties—in the promotion of democracy worldwide. Transnational parties such as the Christian Democratic International, the Socialist International, the Liberal International, the defunct Communist International, the International Democratic Union, and others are organized collaborations among like-minded national parties, groups, and individuals across the world. They are multilateral associations and probable precursors of a transnational party system. Yet, the major parties of the United States have, until recently, remained aloof from these associations, thereby denying U.S. foreign policy a major instrument for the promotion of democracy abroad.[1]

Thomas Jefferson, James Madison, Andrew Jackson, Martin Van Buren, Woodrow Wilson, and other students of the relationship between party systems and democracy agreed that the correlation between the two is close: the more representative and stable the political parties, the more sturdy the democratic system. What has been true for party systems within nations may well become true for parties among nations. As will be described below, West Germans, through their distinctive political foundations, have already recognized the analogy and are working closely with certain transnational parties.

Transnational parties are legitimate and significant organizations with great potential for helping democratize the politics of nations and the world. Yet, the case for U.S. participation in their multilateral civic education activities still needs to be made. Many in Congress and the press oppose Democratic and Republican participation. The analysis that follows will examine the reasons for this resistance, the actual and prospective role of transnational parties in democratic institution building, and ways in which U.S. parties may contribute to the development of a transnational party system and, through it, the growth of democracy worldwide.

POLITICAL PARTIES AND DEMOCRACY

Over the past 300 years, political parties have been central institutions in the mobilization of large populations into governable communities. Where party systems have been constitutional and competitive, democracy has thrived. Jefferson and Madison anticipated as much, and their vision and prescience continue to amaze us. It has also been true, but not widely recognized, that party systems have often provided the institutional alternative to domestic warfare as a method for political conflict and elite competition. For example, it is common knowledge that, after centuries of recurrent internal warfare, certain nations—two specific cases are England and Mexico—ceased having civil wars. This happy development tended to occur soon after their political party systems emerged and became stabilized. In each case the evolution of a stable party system as a principal system of conflict management provided the political context within which it became possible to build other enduring institutional components of democracy.

The democratic form of government, in its many versions in the United States and elsewhere, is notable for its effectiveness as a system of conflict management. Before a democratic system can be established, the participants, explicitly or not, must agree that disagreement is inevitable and functional. They accept dissent as legitimate. This is perhaps the most fundamental difference between pluralist and totalitarian systems, the latter being intolerant of dissent.

The next problem for democracy builders is the designing of economical procedures for carrying on disagreements and for measuring consensus through such devices as majority rule, comprehensive systems of representation, rule of law, open judicial process, bills of rights, and so forth. Those democracies that are most cost-effective in the management of conflict are usually the most enduring, particularly if they are able to eliminate the need for costly violent forms of change. As a means of nonviolent change, political parties are probably the most effective institution available.

Another traditional function of political parties is particularly pertinent. Politicians and philosophers since Plato's day have been aware of the fundamental importance of civic education. Civic education is a basic function of governments, usually supplemented, if not entirely implemented, by political parties. In the United States, for example, Democratic and Republican campaigns, rhetoric, and debates, not to mention organizational activities, are among the principal sources of civic knowledge. In the Soviet Union, the Communist party exercises a civic education monopoly.

As most civic educators will testify, a classroom, a textbook, and a lecture have to be the dullest and least effective way to carry on civic education. Whether the political catechism is about democracy or totalitarianism, rote learning of civic roles, responsibilities, and privileges appears to guarantee lack of citizen interest. What best teaches civics is personal participation in and personal experience with the political affairs of the community. Civic education is best when it is on-the-job training through citizen participation in the political process, particularly through its political parties.

The participative aspect of civic education is perhaps the great secret of the civic good health of most democracies. This is accomplished by operating through open political parties, frequent elections, competititve political campaigns, and open recruitment of new party and interest group leadership. Americans know how all this is carried on in their own domestic political life. Americans have yet to apply this experience and knowledge to civic education for a democratic world.

TRANSNATIONAL PARTIES AT THE GLOBAL LEVEL

Transnational political parties are a new phenomenon for most U.S. leaders and citizens, typically considered "foreign," "subversive," "incompatible" with U.S. political mores, and, in general, suspect. The best known of the transnationals have been the communist internationals—the "Red Menace"—that have for the past century propounded the violent overthrow of bourgeois governments. Americans have given practically no attention to the emergence of Christian Democratic, Liberal, Social Democratic, and Conservative internationals.

From a theoretical perspective, the Marxist movements have been the only ones explicitly to make the analogical leap from national to global party development. The Communists see theirs as a *world* party movement and precursor of a world government in the Marxist-Leninist mold. For most Americans this is reason enough to consider transnational parties anathema to "the American way." Only very recently has it begun to occur to U.S. policymakers that the democratic transnational parties—Christian Democrats, Liberals, Social Democrats, Conservatives—

may provide an effective channel for a multilateral approach to the promotion of democracy.

Defining Transnationals

A brief definition may serve as a reminder of the institutional elements with which we are dealing. In the Western tradition, a political party is usually defined as an organization that has as its principal goal the placing of its avowed representatives in governmental offices. Party organization is formal, with officers, headquarters, rules of operation, and the like. Numerous activities are related to that of placing party leaders into public office: the proposal and implementation of programs of public policy, the teaching and reinforcement of community political values, and the distribution of public resources. Party nominations are the typical procedure for confirming connection between party and avowed representatives. In the pursuit of these activities, political parties engage in election campaigns, the formation of coalitions of organized interest groups, and mobilization of funds and rank-and-file supporters.

Marxist usage of the term *political party* differs from the Western concept. In the West, party is organizationally subordinate to government (even in the case of the city political machines of old) and competition for leadership positions and programmatic objectives are legitimate both within and between parties. In orthodox Communist states, ideological principle requires that the party be senior to the government and that the party serve as the organizational agent for the "dictatorship of the proletariat." Various bureaus of the Communist party have the responsibility for defining and maintaining the ideological purity of the membership. Leadership recruitment involves an elaborate system of promotion from rank-and-file to candidate status, and then to full membership in the party's ruling committees.

Political parties become transnational when they develop supra-national organizations that cooperate in a variety of ways across national boundaries. Transnationals meet several of the definitional requirements of political parties generally: formality (officers, central headquarters, etc.), overtness, program, for example. The membership of the major transnational parties consists of national parties, national and international observer groups, and individual persons. The formal names of the major transnationals are: the International Socialist Conference, the Christian Democratic World Union, the World Liberal Union, and the International Democratic Union. The Communists do not at present have a formal transnational party organization as such.

Marxists

The oldest of the transnational parties have been the Communist and Socialist internationals. The International Working Men's Association came to be known as the First International after 1864. Over the next decade the International organized trade unions and party affiliates in several countries, disbanding, however, in 1877 as a consequence of severe factional rifts. In 1889 a coalition of trade unions, reformist Marxist parties, and revolutionary groups merged to become the Second, or Socialist Worker's, International, which reached into 23 countries by the time it disbanded because of the outbreak of World War I.

The Bolshevik Revolution of 1917 in Russia created the first Communist-controlled government. The founding congress of the Third International (referred to as the Comintern) convened in Moscow in March 1919, and the Communist Party of the Soviet Union (CPSU) became the world organizing center for the new transnational party. The Bolsheviks declared themselves the vanguard of a movement that would eventually establish a Communist world order.

After years of advocating the overthrow of capitalist governments throughout the world and coping with domestic strife in the Soviet Union, the goal of world revolution was shelved by Joseph Stalin in order to establish firmly "socialism in one country." The Comintern was dissolved in 1943 in response to requests from the Soviet Union's World War II allies. However, the gesture lasted only until 1947, when a Communist Information Bureau (Cominform) was established by representatives of Communist parties in nine countries of Europe.

Over the next three decades the world communist movement suffered fluctuating fortunes. Tito of Yugoslavia was expelled from the Cominform in 1948 for advocating "separate roads" to socialism. A decade later a breach between the Soviet and Chinese parties initiated an era of Sino-Soviet tension that continues to this day. In 1956 the Cominform was disbanded even as unsuccessful popular uprisings took place in Poland and Hungary. In 1957 the Soviet Union made an unsuccessful attempt to reestablish the international or some equivalent. By 1960 Maoism became a leading force in the Third World. By 1975 Eurocommunists in Italy and France were distancing themselves from Moscow-centered programs.

In response to the growing polycentrism of the communist movement, the CPSU devoted increasing resources to its International Department, establishing country and regional desks for most of the countries in the world. Moscow also gave attention and support to the World Peace Council, its principal front organization. The Comintern may not exist as a formal organization, but the transnational character of the communist movement persists in a well-organized fashion, supplemented by various forms of direct Soviet military, economic, and political aid.

Socialists

Although the Socialist international regards itself as the direct successor of the Second, or Socialist Worker's, International, a wholly new organization was inaugurated after World War II. Specifically, on March 5, 1945, at the invitation of the British Labour party, the First Conference of Social Democratic Parties, with 13 parties represented, gathered in London for the purpose of planning the founding of a new international. By 1951 a new Socialist international came into operation.

According to recent count, the Socialist international claims a membership of 47 national parties, 15 consultative parties, 3 fraternal organizations (e.g., the International Union of Socialist Youth), and 8 associated organizations. There are 22 Socialist parties in Western Europe, another 11 in Latin America, 5 in Asia, 3 in the Middle East, 3 in Africa, and 3 in North America. World headquarters are in London.

In the early years of this revival, a major concern of Socialist parties was containment of the spread of communism. Historically, most social democrats and laborites have advocated nonviolent change within the context of parliamentary systems and have been staunch in their opposition to totalitarian political methods. Some socialists have from time to time preferred collaboration and "united fronts" with all fellow Marxists, on the dubious assumption that governmental power could be shared and that shared power might even serve as a moderating force among the more revolutionary factions. This issue was and remains a divisive one among socialists.

In 1969, under the leadership of Chancellor Willy Brandt, West Germany adopted an *Ostpolitik* strategy of rapprochement with the Soviet Union and Eastern Europe. This weakened the anticommunist stance of West German Socialists and carried over into Brandt's leadership of the Socialist international in the 1970s, during which there prevailed a kind of detente between socialists and communists. In most recent practice, the Socialist international has favored firmness in dealings with Eurocommunists but united fronts with Communists in the Third World.

Christian Democrats

Christian democracy emerged in the nineteenth century as an antagonist of liberalism, the dominant ideology of that era, and in opposition to the centralizing tendencies of nation-states. The movement was steeped in its Catholic theological origins and active in local politics. During the early years of the twentieth century, as Christian Democrats gained stature and office in many European countries, significant modifications began to appear in the orientation of Christian Democratic parties. After World War II these parties set aside their Catholic orientation, were elected to governmental office throughout Europe, began to gain organization and influence in Latin America, and gave substantial attention to the task of strengthening their own transnational organization.

First efforts at international Christian Democratic cooperation were initiated by Don Luigi Sturzo in 1919 shortly after the founding of the

Italian People's party. The First International Congress of People's Parties was held in Paris in December 1925. Successive congresses were held during the 1920s and 1930s but without the benefit of effective transnational organization.

In 1936 Don Sturzo once again took up his campaign to create a transnational Christian Democratic party. By 1940 the International Democratic Union was organized and included many European governments in exile. In July 1947, an international congress established the International Union of Christian Democrats. Today, Christian Democrats have a world union, and three regional organizations—in Western Europe, Central Europe, and the Americas. World headquarters are in Rome.

Liberals

Liberals were the major ideological force in Europe during the nineteenth century, representative of commercial and industrial interests in particular. International conferences of liberals made their first appearance in 1910, but not until April 1947 did liberals take steps toward transnational organization. On April 14, 1947, representatives of 19 liberal parties and groups, mainly European, signed the Liberal Manifesto in Oxford, England, which became the basic document of the World Liberal Union, or Liberal International. Headquarters were established in London.

The International was mainly European in its membership and policy concerns until the Canadian Liberal party joined in the early 1970s. Thereafter, the leadership of the Liberal International began to focus on issues from a global rather than a Eurocentric perspective and also began to reach out to organized liberals on other continents. Nineteenth-century ideological doctrines were either dropped or modernized by the Declaration of Oxford in 1967 and the Liberal Appeal of 1981. Growth in the number of member parties has been slow but steady, handicapped by the minority status of Liberal parties in most countries.

Conservatives

The most recently instituted transnational is the International Democratic Union (IDU), an outgrowth of the European Democratic Union of Conservative parties. The principal of the European parties is the British Conservative party, whose leader, Margaret Thatcher, is that country's prime minister. Encouraged by Vice President George Bush, the Republican party of the United States joined, and a new transnational organization was formed. The IDU held its first international conference in Dallas at the time of the Republican National Convention in 1984. A second conference was held in Washington in July 1985, attended by 250 officials of approximately 40 parties worldwide. Richard V. Allen, former national secruity adviser to President Reagan, characterized those in attendance as "mainstream conservatives" and "classical liberals."

Republican membership in IDU is evidence of a growing consciousness of transnational party development among U.S. political practitioners. It remains to be seen to what extent Republicans find the transnational affiliation useful in the promotion of democracy abroad. As of this writing, the Democratic party has yet to make a commitment to a transnational party, although it has sent observers to the conferences of the Socialist and Liberal transnationals and its National Democratic Institute for Internaitonal Affairs has acquired observer membership in the latter.

Transnational Activities

Generally speaking, in what kinds of activity have these contemporary transnational parties been engaged? Without attempting to attribute particular activities to specific transnationals, one can see that the roster is typical of pluralist political parties at all levels of community, and the democratizing influence of their activities may be readily inferred.

1. *Election of party leaders to public offices.* This activity was pursued supranationally in the first and second direct elections of representatives to the European Parliament, during which most of the transnationals ran coordinated campaigns throughout Western Europe. Election work was also manifest in assistance provided by the transnationals to colleagues seeking national office in particular countries, for example, the Socialists in Portugal and Spain and the Christian Democrats in El Salvador.

2. *Coordination of transnational party programs.* This has been most explicit in the manifestos and other programmatic declarations produced by transnational party congresses. Issues of ideological posture and purity are, of course, articulated during intraparty debates over the specific content of manifestos, declarations, and campaign pitches. On a less intermittent basis, transnational party policymaking has been the work of party groups serving the membership of the European Parliament. Each major European transnational party represented in the Parliament—Socialists, Christian Democrats, Liberals, and others—has its own caucus-type organization and staff whose principal function is the preparation of research and policy positions on the issues before the European Parliament.

3. *Development of global party organization.* Each of the major transnational parties has operated at its own organizational pace. The Communists have been the most systematic, assiduous, and experienced, providing training and other resources to party cadres in countries throughout the world. The results to date include the existence of almost 100 Communist parties worldwide, some 16 of which control their governments.

Running a close second in organizational experience and success are the socialists, moderately constrained by their policies of peaceful change and national self-determination. Christian Democrats stepped up their attention to transnational cooperation and organizing over the past quarter century, scoring significant successes in Europe and Latin America. Liberals, burdened by minority status and a penchant for independence, have been the slowest to mobilize their transnational membership.

4. *Supranational centers of operation.* Transnational parties, like other organizations, acquire formality and vitality as a consequence of regular activity. For political parties such activity usually relates to operations within legislative assemblies, the management of executive bureaucracies, civic education, constituency service, and the conduct of electoral and propaganda campaigns, to name a few. In the case of most transnational parties, centers of political activity vary in formality from the well-organized party groups in the European Parliament to the informal collegial consultations at the United Nations. Transnational party representatives are in evidence in a number of supranational and regional organizations, often collaborating with one another on an informal basis. In matters large and small, the programs of transnational parties have had a growing impact on the course of world politics.

U.S. ANTIPARTY ATTITUDES

This is hardly a propitious time for suggesting new projects for the major parties of the United States, least of all a significant role in the implementation of a U.S. foreign policy. The traumas of Vietnam and Watergate have rubbed off on the party system. The major parties have been in disrepair. Yet, antipartyism is a condition that must be dealt with if the parties of the United States are to make a contribution to the promotion of democracy abroad.

The antiparty trend is readily observed. There has been a significant rise in the proportion of unaffiliated or independent voters, that is, voters unwilling to identify with either major party. Opinion polls have recorded a declining public confidence in our political and economic institutions, with the parties among the lowest on this roster. Many of the functions performed by the parties—such as nomination, platform building, fund-raising, and campaigning—have been assumed by other institutions: the press, political action committees, public relations consultants, single-issue interest groups, personal political machines and others. These attitudes and trends have been reflected by those members of Congress who have been adamant that the parties should have nothing to do with the work of spreading democracy around the world. This opposition has been most pointedly expressed in congressional objections to the award of funds by the National Endowment for Democracy (NED) to the National Democratic Institute for International Affairs (NDI) and the National Republican Institute for International Affairs (NRI).[2]

These antiparty attitudes should come as no surprise. They are part of tradition in the United States. Their persistence is in many ways ironic. Political parties have been a very special U.S. contribution to human institutions for nearly two centuries. The first modern *parliamentary* party system emerged in England in the seventeenth century, but the first modern *electoral* party system was a U.S. creation in the eighteenth. Yet, there has been a strong antiparty feeling in the U.S. civic consciousness from the earliest days, influentially expressed in President Washington's farewell address.

"Let me warn you in the most solemn manner," he said, "against the baneful effects of the spirit of party generally. This spirit . . . exists under different shapes in all government, more or less stifled, controlled, or repressed; but in those of the popular form it is seen in its greatest rankness and is truly their worst enemy."

Most leaders of the Federalist party shared Washington's opinion to the point of refusing to refer to their organization as a political party. Consequently, they declined to support Alexander Hamilton's efforts to improve the organizational structure of that party. As the history books testify, the Federalists disappeared as a political party within a generation. To this day the press, antiparty intellectuals, reformers, and even some party politicians employ an antiparty rhetoric that keeps in constant question the legitimacy of the parties.

There is another view, to which Jefferson and Madison subscribed. Their view is aptly expressed in modern terms by contemporary students of parties. "Parties are as natural to democracy as churches to religion" (James Q. Wilson). "Political parties created democracy . . . and modern democracy is unthinkable save in terms of the parties" (E. E. Schattschneider). There is no reason to confine these assessments to national party systems; they could also be said of transnational parties.

Most Americans, with so little confidence in their domestic parties, have less confidence in transnational parties. Most still believe, from experiences with the Comintern and the Cominform, that all international party movements are Marxist, subversive, and anti-American. Views in the United States about transnationals continue to be hamstrung by nonintervention policies that were nurtured in times of less global interdependence. Nor have U.S. party leaders and their staffs been quite sure just how to design and implement programs that connect themselves advantageously with transnational parties.

As a consequence, many members of Congress have been unwilling to write blank checks for national party participation in the promotion of democracy abroad, and, more specifically, in activities related to the operations of NED. Many objections are offered. The Democratic and Republican national committees have been weak agencies even within our own national parties; why give them so significant a task in world politics? The national committees have no track record with which to demonstrate strategy or competence in the creation and management of prodemocracy transnational projects; why should Congress expect them to acquire strategy and competence overnight? In response to concerns over conflict of interest, why should Congress give funds to an agency—NED—that simply redistributes these funds among the interests, including the party national committees, represented on its own board of directors? Will not the politicians' penchant for travel lead to excesses of international junketing and boondoggling? The expressions of doubt have been intense.

As a consequence, in the several congressional negotiations regarding the mandate and funding of NED, the designation of the Democratic and Republican national parties as statutory recipients of endowment funds has been opposed and deleted. The endowment's board of directors has not regarded this omission as a prohibition and has allocated funds to the national committees as it would to other nonstatutory groups according to its own best judgment.

The endowment initially awarded $1.5 million each to the NDI and the NRI. These agencies were especially created by the party national committees in order to separate overseas promotion of democracy from the domestic activities of the parties. Each of the institutes has acted as both a grant-making and an operating organization.

The NDI, whose president is J. Brian Atwood, has awarded grants for a Western Hemisphere leadership conference, a workshop in democratic development, a conference on democratic pluralism in Africa, consultations in Washington with foreign democratic leaders, and numerous graduate fellowships. Particularly notable have been NDI-hosted conferences of opposition party leaders of the democratic center in Haiti, South Korea, Taiwan, and Liberia. These conferences provided unique opportunities for these leaders to consult among themselves about ways to pursue a pluralist politics without succumbing to the violent tactics of their respective nations' extreme Left or extreme Right.

The NRI, headed by Keith Schuette, has funded a series of international meetings to help establish a regional association of conservative and moderate democratic parties in the Americas, responded to requests for training, voter education, research, and technical assistance from political party and civic groups in Columbia, Bolivia, Grenada, Guatemala, Chile, Costa Rica, and Portugal, and planned specialist conferences on totalitarianism, political environment and economic growth, and similar issues of institutional development and public policy. Of particular relevance to the transnational party focus of this chapter are NRI's efforts to strengthen the organizational links between the International Democratic Union, that is, the Conservative international, and its affiliates in the Western Hemisphere and the Pacific Basin. In this regard, steps have been taken to coordinate institution-building projects with the Pacific Democratic Union and to establish the Caribbean Democratic Union.

Both party institutes were represented on the observation teams in the controversial Philippine elections in which Corazon Aquino displaced Ferdinand Marcos.

Congressional antipathy toward the parties' role led to a report on the NED, prepared by the General Accounting Office at the request of Senator Malcolm Wallop. This report provided further grounds for skepticism. However, little congressional attention has been given directly to the relevance of the party institutes for a multilateral approach, through the transnational parties, to global civic education for democracy.

Thus, a program of potentially major importance for the conduct of U.S. foreign policy and for the future of democracy in the world has been in jeopardy because the case has not been convincingly made that the national parties can contribute significantly to the promotion of democracy. It is as though the case had never been made that churches serve and promote religion.

In West Germany, however, on the basis of German political experiences prior to World War I and World War II, that nation's leaders acknowledged the key role of parties in the development of democracy and designed a uniquely practical way of assisting the parties in this function by creating special political foundations.

STIFTUNGEN: THE WEST GERMAN APPROACH

In Germany after World War I and West Germany after World War II, civic education became a serious concern of public policy. Despite a long tradition of philosphical and cultural freedom, the German people had not had substantial experience with democratic institutions—in fact, quite the contrary under the Bismarckian empire (1871-1918) and the Nazi dictatorship (1933-45). Political leaders of the Weimar Republic (1919-33) and the Federal Republic of Germany (after 1949) were determined to do what they could to teach the citizenry the ways of a pluralist polity. To this end they assigned primary responsibility to the German political parties. In doing so they created a unique organizational device: the *Stiftungen*, or party foundations.

At the present time there are four *Stiftungen*, each of which is affiliated with one of the four major parties of West Germany: the Friedrich Ebert Foundation (Social Democratic Party); the Konrad Adenauer Foundation (Christian Democratic Union, or CDU); the Friedrich Naumann Foundation (the liberal Free Democratic party); and the Hanns Seidel Foundation (Christian Social Union). The Green party has been taking legal steps toward creation of a fifth *Stiftung*.

In most countries that permit private nonprofit foundtaions, there is an almost universal requirement that they be apolitical in purpose. In West Germany, however, the *Stiftungen* are essentially auxiliary organizations of the parties. Their boards of directors are drawn from the leadership of the respective parties. Also unique is the fact that the principal financing of these foundations is from public funds appropriated by the West German Parliament (Bundestag).

The oldest of the foundations is the Ebert Stiftung, established in 1925 in order to provide instruction in "the spirit of democracy," promote understanding and cooperation between nations, and give financial and intellectual support to talented German and foreign students. Thus, the Ebert Stiftung set the pattern of both domestic and overseas activities that were to be imitated by the other *Stiftungen* after World War II.

The Ebert Stiftung was banned by the Nazis in 1933 but reestablished soon after the war ended. The Naumann Stiftung was created in 1958. The Adenauer Stiftung came along in 1964. The Seidel Stiftung was established in 1967. The four have since become principal agencies of civic education at home and important instruments of West German influence abroad.

The activities of the West German party foundations tend to be of three types: domestic civic education; political research; and foreign operations. Civic education efforts consist mainly of courses, seminars, conferences, and colloquia on political topics, broadly defined. These include such specific activities as seminars for senior citizens, workshops for staffs of school newspapers, conferences on technical political topics, and brochures with general civic information. Course content is almost always compatible with party ideology, but not blatantly so.

The research programs usually involve scholarship programs for university students (with an eye to recruitment of future party leaders), archival functions pertinent to party history and development, and research institutes dealing with politically relevant issues in the behavioral sciences, for example, public opinion, economic trends, development of political systems.

Approximately half of the attention and resources of the *Stiftungen* is devoted to foreign operations, primarily development aid projects in Third World countries. It is estimated that the four foundations, with a total of about 300 advisers overseas, are involved in about 400 aid projects on 5 continents and that these are financed almost exclusively by the West German Ministry of Development Assistance. There is little doubt that a partisan political dimension rides on these projects. This partisanship is particularly manifested through the transnational party affiliations of the West German parties, that is, the Socialist international, the Christian Democratic international, and the Liberal international. In a more nationalistic sense, however, the foreign operations of the *Stiftungen* represent a West German investment in the long-run future of the developing nations of the Third World and therefore constitute a significant aspect of West German foreign economic and political policy.

Domestically, the four foundations share a strong consensus with respect to the growth and reinforcement of West German democratic institutions. For these objectives they consider it legitimate to articulate the ideological foundations of their respective party programs, to recruit and instruct potential future leaders, and otherwise keep the West German citizenry informed about political values and processes. While civic education is usually left to traditional educational institutions in other countries—with the notable exception of the Soviet Union, where the Communist party performs this function—in West Germany the Nazi experience has apparently made political leaders wary about leaving this activity to the public schools, where it could become difficult to resist the influence of particular regimes. Civic education seems better conducted in the competitive arena of a multiparty system.

In international politics, however, the consensus among the foundations tends to disappear. Confrontations are common. In El Salvador, for example, the Adenauer Stiftung has lent substantial support in several forms to the Christian Democratic party of President Jose Napoleon Duarte. The Ebert Stiftung has given aid to the leftist opposition. It may seem incongruous that the West Germans should be expending public moneys to support both sides of a revolution, but those who are familiar with campaign fund-raising in the United States will recognize the merits of giving to both parties as a guarantee of subsequent access regardless of which side wins. Furthermore, the *Stiftungen* enable West Germany to "intervene" in the domestic politics of another country at a nongovernmental level and without interfering with government-to-government relations.

The financing of the *Stiftungen* has been characterized as "a jungle," "a secret operation," and worse. Such negative assessments have been related to an inability to comprehend a complex accounting system or accept the sometimes ambiguous legal status of the foundations. The West German Bundestag debates and appropriates basic funds for the foundations chiefly in connection with two ministry budgets: the Ministry of Home Affairs and the Ministry of Development Assistance. The overall *Stiftung* appropriation is based on specific rules and the calculation of 5 marks per potential voter, that is, an approximate total of 200 million marks in recent years. Of this, the Ebert and Adenauer Stiftungen receive about 70 million marks each, the Naumann and Seidel about 35 million each.

The official relationships among the various bodies are semiautonomous, open, and sometimes subtle. Rather than conduct direct oversight of the *Stiftungen*, the Bundestag relies upon the programmatic assessments and foundation budget recommendations of ministry officials. Ministry officials review foundation programs and activities but cannot explicitly direct or constrain them. Foundation officers design their own programs but endeavor to be sensitive to the needs of both private and governmental donors. At least three of the foundations receive fairly substantial grants from private individuals and private corporations; the Ebert Stiftung receives outside funds chiefly from trade unions.

As was noted earlier, approximately half of the collective resources of the *Stiftungen* are devoted to foreign operations. This is the feature most pertinent to U.S. efforts to promote democracy abroad. Over 40 percent of the foundations' public funds for overseas operations is spent on projects in Latin America, more than 30 percent in Africa, and the remainder on projects in the rest of the world. Each approaches its overseas work with somewhat different emphases.

The Naumann Stiftung sponsors institutes that provide professional training in the physical and social sciences. It organizes international conferences around themes of community and national development and the organization of democracy. These educational activities inevitably encounter delicate situations in countries with authoritarian regimes and aspiring opposition parties. Naumann representatives often must work with groups other than political parties. The Naumann Stiftung is particularly interested in those overseas projects that provide young West German specialists with experience in the affairs of developing countries and that help gather research data for foundation publications about those countries.

The Ebert Stiftung pursues somewhat different overseas objectives, in substantial measure influenced by the unfortunate past experiences of German Socialists, namely, the demise of the Weimar Republic and the encounters with the Nazi and Communist totalitarians. The Ebert Stiftung maintains a close relationship with West Germany's highly organized trade unions and hence is intimately involved in the training of union leadership at home and abroad.

Ebert programs tend to give major attention to defensive tactics, that is, ways of coping with communist and fascist organizational and propaganda tactics. The research enterprise of the Ebert Stiftung is perhaps the most extensively developed of the several foundations. Further, the foundation is particularly attentive to the technological aspects of mass media projects overseas. Consistent with Willy Brandt's *Ostpolitik* approach to relations with Eastern Europe, Ebert representatives overseas have cooperated with indigenous Communist and other revolutionary parties in the Third World.

Long accustomed to their association with the former ruling party of West Germany, namely, the CDU, the Adenauer Stiftung is in effect the "opposition" *Stiftung* at this time, with a budget second only to that of the Ebert Stiftung and with overseas operations that are comparable in scope. The Adenauer Stiftung carries on its work mainly through six "institutes": a political academy at Eichholz, where scores of seminars are conducted; the Social Science Research Institute, which concentrates on the study of political attitudes, problems of political communication, electoral analyses, and similar investigations of social behavior; the Institute for the Sponsorship of Talented Students, which awards scholarships and fellowships to West German and foreign students; the Institute of Local Politics; the Archives of the Christian Democratic Union; and the Institute for International Partnership, which engages in overseas operations. The activities of the last of these institutes tend to concentrate in countries where Christian Democratic parties are significant political actors, and this is mainly in Latin America.

The Seidel Stiftung, an offshoot of the Adenauer Stiftung, is the last and smallest of the four foundations. During the late 1960s and early 1970s, most of its activities were domestic in orientation. Work in the international field began in the late 1970s and appears to be focusing on transnational collaborations with congenial parties in southern Europe.

One activity that has been common to the three major *Stiftungen*— Naumann, Ebert, and Adenauer—has been the foundations' close ties with their respective transnational parties: the Naumann with the Liberal international; the Ebert with the Socialist international; and the Adenauer with the Christian Democratic international. The foundations have helped finance international conferences of their associated transnational parties, jointly coordinated Third World projects, and otherwise supported multilateral ideological and civic educational programs of the transnationals.[3]

INVOLVING THE UNITED STATES IN
GLOBAL CIVIC EDUCATION

If the promotion of democracy continues to be a basic foreign policy of the United States, there are substantial reasons for improving U.S. participation in transnational party affairs. One obvious reason is that it is increasingly difficult to understand political events in many parts of the world if one ignores the role of the transnational parties. In the case of El Salvador, for example, the Socialist international and the Christian Democratic international have been deeply involved in the politics of that unhappy community. To cite another example, despite the absence of a formal Communist international, the International Department of the CPSU has successfully coordinated its own efforts with those of the approximately 120 Communist parties throughout the world. Communists are skilled in the use of the "organizational weapon." This fact, for example, lends special importance to the recent promotion of the Soviet ambassador to the United States, Anatoly F. Dobrynin, to the director-ship of this department. Who better understands U.S. vulnerabilities among the capitals of the world?

Another reason for improving U.S. involvement in transnational party developments is the dramatic growth since World War II in the number and reach of transnational nongovernmental organizations (NGOs). NGOs are in effect transnational pressure groups. Well over 3,000 NGOs exist and have substantial memberships. Hundreds are registered with such supranational bodies as the United Nations and the European Commission. They include international trade unions, international chambers of commerce, and other NGOs of almost every type: religious, professional, scientific, humanitarian, agricultural, academic, and many others.

The relevance of these NGOs for transnational parties and the promotion of democracy would have been clearly apparent to James Madison, who pointed out that organized interest groups are an inevitable and essential component of pluralist societies. Further, political parties, when at their best, are organizers of coalitions of such interest groups. The prospects for transnational party development and the advancement of democratic institutions throughout the world are likely to be greatly enhanced by party-led coalitions of NGOs.

Finally, transnational parties and NGOs provide opportunities and means for a global civic educational enterprise. From this perspective, the democracy-promoting programs of the United States should be nothing less than a major Point Four type of program of technical political aid and civic education for all who wish to share the political freedom and vitality that the United States and other democracies enjoy. The national Democratic and Republican parties, working in large part through the agencies of the democratic transnational parties, are the most appropriate organizations to implement such a program.

In what ways may transnational parties facilitate the U.S. effort to promote the development of democratic institutions throughout the world? One way is to "entrap" totalitarian parties and regimes into democratizing practices, as suggested by the eminent historian, Frederick Jackson Turner. Turner's renown was derived from his analysis of the impact of the frontier upon the political development of the United States. In 1918 he wrote a memorandum for President Woodrow Wilson to take with him to the peace conference at which the creation of the League of Nations would be the key Wilsonian proposal. Turner's memorandum discusses the advantages and disadvantages of bringing the Moscow-dominated Comintern into the league.

Is it better to try to exclude these international political forces from the organization of the new order, or to utilize their internationalizing tendencies by enabling them to operate upon an international legislative body, responsive to the play of parties? . . . In the reconstruction and the ferment which will follow the return of peace [after 1918], there will be doubts about the existence of Edens anywhere, and the Bolshevik serpent will creep in under whatever fence be attempted. May it not be safer to give him a job of international legislation rather than to leave him to strike from the dark corners, and with no sense of responsibility?

Turner's recommendation remains pertinent. The political practicalities at the U.N. and other agencies of the international system have enveloped the Soviets in both the constraints and opportunities inherent in pluralistic politics. Unable to control the U.N., totalitarian and authoritarian regimes have acquired some of the habits and civility that are antecedents to tolerance and democratic conduct.

With respect to the promotion of democracy as a U.S. foreign policy, the United States has exploited and should continue to exploit the U.N. as a platform for expounding democratic principles and for constructing the institutional components of democratic global politics. The Universal Declaration of Human Rights is a prime example of expounding democratic principles. Most of the debates and votes of the General Assembly, whether favorable to the United States or not, have followed the institutional patterns characteristic of democracies. If the United States and other democracies created a consultative caucus of democracies at the U.N., as is suggested elsewhere in this volume,[4] a more coherent multilateral approach to global democratization would undoubtedly ensue. If such a caucus were encouraged by the United States and others working through one or more of the transnational parties, the constraints of formal diplomacy could be ignored and the democratic principles and institutions more vigorously promoted.

A second U.S. approach to multilateral activities by the two major parties would be to have each join the civic educational and democracy-promoting efforts of the transnational parties. The immediately available agencies for such a contribution are the two major party national committees and the NED.

As is noted elsewhere in this volume, the establishment of the NED in 1983 was accompanied by the creation of four statutory recipients of its funds: the Free Trade Union Institute (associated with the AFL-CIO), the Center for International Private Enterprise (of the U.S. Chamber of Commerce), the NDI and the NRI. The party institutes are auxiliaries of their respective party national committees.

The Free Trade Union Institute represents the U.S. trade union movement's longstanding experience in the struggle against totalitarian repression. The Center for International Private Enterprise is designed to bring the business sector into the Democracy Initiative. The two party institutes are supposed to relate to the endowment in a fashion similar to that of the West German *Stiftungen* to their respective parties.

Unfortunately, there is a fundamental difference between the West German arrangements and those of the United States. The *Stiftungen* were the offspring of the West German parties, with relatively well-defined goals of domestic civic education and overseas political aid. In the United States, the party institutes were, for all practical purposes, the offspring of a nonpartisan body, the NED, whose goals are relatively ambiguous and whose support comes form a skeptical Congress. Neither the endowment nor the party institutes have been supported by constituencies as potent as those of the *Stiftungen*.

The party institutes have had other handicaps, several of which have been noted earlier in this chapter: a long antiparty tradition in the United States; a dearth of national party experience with foreign or transnational party affairs; an approach to foreign aid that emphasizes military and economic aid and ignores political aid; a national policy of nonintervention in the politics (read: party politics) of other nations; a recent history of Central Intelligence Agency covert efforts to provide financial and other aid to pro-Western parties overseas; and a recent decline in popular confidence in party and other institutional leaderships. In such an environment of constraining policies and negative attitudes, little wonder that the U.S. parties are considered by many to be unlikely promoters of democracy abroad.

All this notwithstanding, there continues to be a significant role for the Democratic and Republican parties in U.S. politics. More than two-thirds of the voters still identify themselves, to one degree or another, with the major parties. Candidates campaign hard for the nomination of their party and for election by their party's constituencies, in a political environment that is increasingly competitive. The business of political consultation thrives. And in no other country has the scholarly study of political parties been more actively pursued by social scientists.

There has also been a place for parties in the conduct of U.S. foreign affairs. This experience should bear significantly upon guidelines for involving the two parties in the promotion of democracy abroad.

The first such guideline would be based upon the parties' sustained awareness of and commitment to the democratic mission described in an earlier chapter. The United States has always been a self-aware and assertive democracy. Both major parties have had a hand in advancing the democratic mission. The party system has been the principal domestic institutional means of bringing together disparate constituencies to make local government work, uniting scattered communities to make state governments function, integrating state and national governments to give coherence to a federal system, and coordinating officials in the different branches of government to prevent chaos in a system of divided powers. It would be a mere extension of those bridging accomplishments if agencies of the national parties were to become an important means of traversing the political space between the United States and the global community.

A second guideline would be derived from the tradition of bipartisanship in foreign policy. The tradition calls upon (party) politics to end at the water's edge in the interest of national unity. The tradition has been strong, although at times inhibiting of domestic debate on controversial foreign policy issues. In keeping with the tradition of bipartisanship, most projects for the promotion of democracy should be bipartisan, that is, jointly sponsored by the NDI and the NRI.

The statute governing the NED does in fact encourage projects jointly sponsored by the two parties. Joint projects benefit from the symbolic unity of bipartisanship. Joint NDI-NRI projects are less likely to have partisan content and more likely to address general issues of global civic education for democracy. Joint projects assure Congress and the public that the parties are monitoring each other with respect to financial responsibility and ideological balance.

Joint projects need not be a long-term requirement. In time, each party will surely choose its individual path into the transnational party system and pursue its own strategy of multilateral civic educaiton for democracy through its particular transnational party affiliation. By then, the legitimacy of NDI and NRI participation in the promotion of democracy will undoubtedly have been well established and their affiliation with one or another transnational party more widely accepted.

A third guideline addresses the issues of content and expertise for a multilateral promotion of democracy. A model that seems particularly appropriate is the Truman administration's Point Four program, which was widely applauded for the technical knowledge it disseminated. This model should be imitated in any program for promoting democracy. Proponents of democracy all too often become bogged down in antitotalitarian rhetoric and strategies. Probably the best antitotalitarian strategy is to build more democracies. What is urgently needed is specific technical knowledge about the building and preserving of democratic institutions.

This need relates to technical knowledge pertinent to the effective administration of secret-ballot elections, the conduct of open election campaigns, the measurement of public opinion, the design of truly representative and responsive legislative and political party bodies, the building of a professional military establishment that is subordinate to civilian authorities, the maintenance of a free and responsible press, the protection and implementation of bills of rights, and so on.

As for expertise, while many Americans know something about the technicalities of democratic political institutions, few are sufficiently expert to apply the U.S. experience with predictable results in a foreign setting. The need for the technical knowledge and for experts is clearly evident from the increase in the number of U.S. public relations and campaign consultants engaging in overseas work under contract to foreign candidates eager to win elections or otherwise influence their domestic politics. The training of such experts is perhaps one of the joint activities most appropriate for the two party institutes.

The United States is hardly the sole repository of technical knowledge on democracy questions. The British, the French, the Dutch, and other imperial powers of earlier centuries have accumulated much experience regarding the practicalities of transferring political institutions. As with the West-German *Stiftungen*, these nations continue to have a lively interest in the promotion of democracy. Their interest and expertise should somehow be incorporated into a multilateral approach, most readily through such organizational channels as the transnational parties, NGOs, an association of democracies, a caucus of democracies at the U.N., and other forms of cooperation.

A fourth guideline pertains to the problems raised by covert political aid. The various communist internationals have specialized in techniques of political subversion, and, as was noted earlier, this has cast a pall over all transnational party movements. In an attempt to reconcile its nonintervention policy with its policy of containment of communism, the United States has itself resorted to covert political aid to friendly foreign parties, usually through the CIA. This has always been an awkward enterprise. The media and Congressional investigating committees have conducted numerous "exposés" of this type of covert aid, which is usually condemned as crass interventionism. This criticism has already carried over into charges that the NED is merely a public adjunct of these longstanding CIA covert operations. There can be only one response to such intimations: full disclosure of all NED, NDI, and NRI activities, competently presented to the public, the press, and Congress, and receptive to feedback, criticism, and open debate.

In this area of U.S. foreign policy, a shift from covert to overt political activity is itself significant and nothing less than an acknowledgment that secrecy and democracy do not go well together. Democracy is in the business of promoting public debate, disseminating valid information, and conducting open processes in the operation of all its institutions. Political parties perform eminently well in these activities and may be the best mechanisms for similar foreign policy activities.

These guidelines suggest ways of supporting a multilateral civic educational approach to the promotion of democracy abroad. The available instrumentalities for implementing this approach are the NED, the NDI, the NRI, and the democratic transnational parties. Sound strategies and strong institutional relationships among these instrumentalities would add a major resource to the campaign to promote democracy worldwide. It would in effect become a political aid program complementing programs of military and economic aid. Cooperation with transnational parties enables U.S. parties to join world movements already dedicated to the dissemination of democratic civic knowledge, and this would significantly complement the United States policy of promoting democracy worldwide.

REFERENCES

1. Ralph M. Goldman. *Transnational Parties: Organizing the World's Precincts.* Lanham, Md.: University Press of America, 1983.

2. Christopher Madison. "Selling Democracy." *National Journal*, June 28, 1986, pp. 1663ff.

3. Alan Watson. *The Political Foundations in West Germany*. London: Anglo-German Foundation for the Study of Industrial Society [1977].

4. See chapter 11 by Ira Strauss.

6 LABOR'S ROLE IN BUILDING DEMOCRACY
Roy Godson

The task of building, maintaining, and improving a democratic polity can be greatly aided by organized labor. Free trade unions can provide a significant base to support the democratic edifice, an important bulwark to defend democracy against its enemies, and a means of improving the quality of life in democratic societies. In incipient democracies, or anywhere democracy is threatened, the U.S. labor movement can play an important role in assisting its counterpart unions and thus helping to build and defend the global democratic system.

This chapter first describes the bases of labor's domestic political power and shows how labor has been and can be used to affect the stability of a polity and influence the forces within it. Second, it focuses on the reasons why labor has both ideological and practical affinities for democratic rather than dictatorial polities. The goals of trade union political action will be analyzed: the forces that labor prefers in power, and the policy decisions in both domestic and foreign policy that labor tries to affect. Finally, there is a descripton of U.S. labor's efforts to help its counterparts abroad to pursue these goals, including a brief survey of some of U.S. labor's major recent initiatives and several specific training programs that foreign labor may find useful in defending and building democracy.

It should be noted at the outset that not all trade unions are democratic. Some are in the hands of prodictatorial forces. Authoritarian and totalitarian regimes sponsor "official" unions. In democratic systems, communists or gangsters seek to control unions, either by winning union elections or by building up a political machine in the union that can manipulate elections. In Nicaragua under the Somoza regime in the 1970s, for example, there were four sectors in the labor movement: one group of official unions, a communist group, and two democratic confederations, one Christian Democratic and the other basically social democratic. It is those democratic unions whose leaders are elected freely by the workers and who are not controlled financially or politically by external forces that contribute to the growth of democratic polities, not least by competing with the prodictatorial unions.

THE BASES OF LABOR'S POLITICAL POWER

The very nature and structure of labor movements provide them with the capacity to be important elements in shaping national polities and influencing the course of history. What are the bases for this capacity?

The answer: (1) organization and (2) access to millions of people. The very nature of a trade union is that of a hierarchically structured organization with procedures designed to achieve specified objectives. Organizations have staffs, budgets, and symbols that utilize these procedures to achieve their objectives. Unions have a large staff of part-time shop stewards and full-time elected and appointed officials on the local, regional, and national levels. Also, they usually have significant sums at their disposal, particularly when workers pay dues regularly. For example, in the United States, in 1984, 17 million workers belonged to unions (about 18 percent of the work force).[1] The average union member paid $100 to the union each year in dues, and some gave additional amounts for political action. Thus the unions received over $1.7 billion each year plus returns on the investment of pension funds and other earnings.

In addition to staffs and money, organizations utilize symbols. In this case, the symbols are workers' rights, democracy on the job, and better wages and working conditions. These are potent symbols in an age when everyone claims to be a democrat and concerned with everyone else's welfare.

Finally, the organization is located in strategic sectors of the economy. It is organized usually among workers in transportation, communications, energy, and government. If the functioning of any one of these sectors is jeopardized, the entire society grinds to a halt.

Though few human institutions run as efficiently as their organizational charts indicate, the leaders of a labor movement can mobilize and coordinate hundreds, if not thousands, of full- and part-time officials, millions, if not billions, of dollars, and potent symbols to promote the objectives they seek. In the United States these objectives have been, and for now remain, collective bargaining with employers over the terms of employment first and politics and social action second. In Western Europe and Japan traditionally most union leaders have been concerned with politics first and collective bargaining second. In both, though, the strength of labor lies in the ability of the leadership to mobilize the organization, particularly in strategic sectors.[2]

Access to millions of people on a daily basis is the second major characteristic of organized labor. There are few organizations that reach one-quarter to one-half of the population of their countries on a regular basis. There are two major ways in which this is done: the labor press and personal contact through full- and part-time officials.

Trade union publications are little known outside the labor movement but are an important communications link, reaching literally millions of workers in both the developed and developing worlds. In the United States alone well over 550 publications are put out by national unions, city central labor bodies, state federations, and major local unions, publications that reach approximately 17 million workers each year. The largest publications are the monthy papers and magazines that are mailed by national unions to each individual member of their union, that is, 17 million monthly in the United States. These are supplemented by weekly or monthly local union publications as well as by special publications designed for the 2 or 3 million workers who are particularly active in union as well as in local and national politics. The papers cover a wide range of human concerns in addition to parochial union issues and range from health care and recreation to domestic and international politics.

In Europe and elsewhere in the developed world, a similar pattern can be observed. As in the United States, union leaders only rarely have the opportunity to use radio and television, and so they also rely on the labor press to reach their members. In Britain in the early 1980s, for example, there were over 65 monthly publications reaching over 6 million unionized workers and an additional number of local and special publications. In France, Italy, Spain, and Portugal, the communist and noncommunist unions also put out monthly and special publications, which reach approximately 25 percent of the work force or approximately 15 million workers monthly. In Latin America the majority of sector federations and many large locals publish weekly or monthly newsletters for their members. Though more simple in format, these publications are important as the only communications network in the area produced by members of lower income groups and reaching other workers and peasants on a mass basis.

In addition to the labor press, unions also reach their members through the personal contact their officials have with the membership. While some unions have many more officials than others, of necessity they all are in contact with their members regularly, and frequently daily. In conversations on docks, ships, planes, loading platforms, factories, schools, and offices throughout the world, they reinforce and augment the message in the labor and regular press. They explain the bad times and the good times; they identify the workers' "friends" and they point to the workers' "enemies." Perhaps only the Church has as much and as persistent contact with people as does organized labor.

THE USES OF LABOR'S POLITICAL POWER

Trade unions usually seek to use their political capacity, unless blocked by government repression. Although the approaches vary from country to country, very few free trade unions forgo using their political potential and limiting themselves to collective bargaining with employers. There are a number of ways in which labor's political action affects a polity.

First, labor can, on occasion, affect the stability of the political system as a whole. Political systems, be they democratic, military dominated, or totalitarian, are affected by mass organizations, which can serve as a bridge between the populace and the government. Where no mass organization serves this function, the government often finds itself out of contact with the masses and will find large sectors of the population unresponsive to governmental direction. If unchanneled, anomic movements among the people mobilize in protest against the government, instability may result. Organized labor and other mass movements can help avoid this by channeling grievances to the government and helping to explain and assist in the administration and maintenance of the political system. The history of Venezuela illustrates how the democratic political system there, which has flourished since 1958, probably could not have been born or have survived had not the labor movement assisted the democratic polity.

After the fall of the military dictatorship of General Marcos Perez Jimenez in 1958, the fledgling democratic political system faced three threats to its stability: overthrow by the military, disruption by extremist terrorism, and internal collapse if it were unable to obtain sufficient popular support to govern effectively. The system overcame all three threats, and labor was crucial in all three victories.

Between 1958 and 1962 there were four attempted military coups against the democratic government of President Romulo Betancourt. On all four occasions the organized workers rallied to the government's side, three times through general strikes in protest against the military revolts.[3] When the Communists, under Cuban influence, called for insurrections and general strikes against the government in 1960, 1962, and 1963, the unions, led by supporters of Betancourt's Acción Democratica (AD) party, paid little heed to the Communists' appeals and helped government forces repel the insurrections.[4] The AD and its allies won the 1958 and 1963 elections mainly through their dominance of the labor vote in a country where 43 percent of the voters belonged to families that consisted of organized workers and peasants. Without its labor base the AD, and the democratic system it led, would have had neither the support needed to pass its program nor the communication with the people needed to implement it. Labor remains crucial in maintaining the stability of Venezuelan democracy.

Just as labor can be a stabilizing factor, it can also be destabilizing. Even in communist political systems, let alone less totalitarian dictatorships, worker instability and revolt have been one, if not *the*, major cause of internal instability. The clearest cases have been found in postwar Eastern Europe. In East Berlin in 1953, in Hungary and Poland in 1956, in Romania in 1977, and in Poland throughout the 1970s and into the early 1980s, workers have been in the vanguard of revolts against Communist regimes. Indeed, if the Soviet regime is ever to be overthrown from within, it is unlikely that the overthrow will result from the activities of the intellectual dissidents outside the Communist party; more likely, it will come from ethnic/nationality tensions coupled with worker unrest and revolt.

Another example of the way in which unions have been successful in challenging ruling authorities was in the decolonization process, particularly in Africa. In the Belgian Congo, Kenya, Morocco, and Tunisia, for example, the unions were in the vanguard of efforts to remove European rule.[5] While the colonial powers were able to contain the relatively small violence-prone anticolonial elements in those societies, they were unable to prevent the unions from mobilizing thousands of people to support the independence struggle, which ultimately was successful.

The second common political effect of labor is on major national political forces. In most societies, serious political movements must build a coalition of interest groups that support them and that constitute their political base. Labor is one of the interest groups that are available to be recruited into political coalitions, democratic or otherwise. Often labor is a building block of such importance that its desertion from a coalition calls into serious question the status of the political movement involved as a major political force. Examples of this phenomenon abound. In almost every one of the industrialized democracies, there is a major party that would be crippled as a serious contender for power if it lost labor's support. The French Communist party, the Social Democratic party in West Germany, the Labour party in Great Britain, and the Japanese Socialist party are all cases in point.

This same pattern can also be found in developing countries, especially in Latin America. The Venezuelan AD's labor base is matched by the

importance of labor to the viability of the Alianza Popular Revolu-
cionaria Americana party in Peru, the Peronist party in Argentina, and
the Partido Revolucionario Institucional's (PRI) political machine in
Mexico. In the developing world outside Latin America, the phenomenon of labor-based parties is much less frequent. In these cases incumbent regimes have recognized the dependence of opposition parties on
labor support and have moved to deprive them of it. In Singapore the
power of Prime Minister Lee Kuan Yew's regime has depended largely
on keeping labor co-opted into his People's Action party's political
machine because "it was a rule of the political system that the interests
which control the trade unions are vital to the control of Singapore."[6] In
Morocco, to cite another example, the power of the opposition Union
National des Forces Populaires (UNFP) party in the 1960s and early
1970s fluctuated in direct correlation with the success of the monarchy
from year to year in wooing the Union Marocaine du Travail labor
movement away from the UNFP.[7]

Besides playing a role in the generation of political movements, labor
also can influence which of those contending movements comes to
power. This is not to say that labor support is a necessary condition for
gaining power, for obviously many governing movements lack organized
labor's support. In the United States, for example, the Republican party
won the White House in 1972, 1980, and 1984 with little labor support.
In Latin America's southern cone (Argentina, Chile, and Uruguay), military dictatorships came to power in the early 1970s despite opposition
from the trade unions, which were subjected to severe repression. Totalitarian governments in Eurasia have no support from autonomous labor
groups, but most of them show little sign of crumbling. (The Polish
regime's near collapse in 1980-81 resulted not from loss of labor support,
but from the workers' massive opposition.)

Neither is labor support sufficient to gain power. At any given time
political movements with enthusiastic labor backing are in the opposition, some with little immediate prospect of forming governments. For
example, the Japanese Socialist party, though labor based, has been in
opposition for decades. The Italian and French Communist parties have
dominated the labor movements in those countries since 1945 but have
not been able to control the government. In 1982, Argentina's labor-
backed Peronist party lost the presidential election.

Although labor support is not the sole determining factor in who comes
to power, it is an important contributing factor because of its effects on
political movements and on the stability of the polity. The political
history of many countries cannot be explained without reference to the
labor factor, even if labor is not the most important force affecting the
flow of political events. But labor, by virtue of its numbers and its organization, is a force whose support most political movements will seek.

LABOR'S INTEREST IN DEMOCRATIC POLITICS

Trade unions seeking to function as autonomous organizations representing their members have a strong interest in promoting democracy in the polity. Most obviously, genuine trade unionists require freedom of association. As the AFL-CIO executive council has stated many times, and reiterated in August, 1981: "Without organizations through which to assert their rights and protect themselves from the state or other strongholds of power, citizens are deprived of the means to secure either their political liberty or a wider measure of economic and social justice." Dictatorships usually deny freedom of association, especially to workers. As George Meany put it on separate occasions: "We have learned from bitter experience that workers are the number-one victims of dictatorships of every type—right, left, Fascist, or Communist."[8] "[W]here there are free trade unions, there must be some semblance of democracy. Because when democracy goes out, there just can't be a free trade union."[9]

In addition to the freedom to organize, authentic trade unions require a pluralistic society. The free interplay among many autonomous interest groups provides a propitious environment for labor, both in its economic role of collective bargaining and in its political action. A trade union can best speak for the interests of its workers when it is controlled by them, unrestricted by government in making its voice heard. Like freedom of association, the pluralism of an open society usually is part of political democracy. Free labor's promotion of democracy stems not only from ideological commitment but also from practical political necessity.

The most ubiquitous form of dictatorship among the developing nations is military rule. Here labor has a particular interest in opposing dictatorship because free trade unions and military rulers tend to be natural political adversaries.[10] Whereas the unions need pluralism and independence, military officers believe in centralization, hierarchy, and control. Moreover, labor usually represents the lower-income groups whereas armies in developing nations often defend the interests of the upper-income groups and of the military caste itself. Even where "egalitarian" military regimes follow "progressive" social policies, it is rare to find workers' rights respected, much less labor support for the regime.

Unions usually are schools for democracy. They are modern organizations created to carry out a functional role of representation and thus tend to be programmatic rather than personalistic in nature. Their officers are elected by the members and are to be responsible to the members. As a consequence of union election campaigning, workers learn democratic procedures and the political skills of rhetoric, organization, and public relations. Through the democratic rough-and-tumble of internal trade union politics, labor leaders develop an outlook that finds pluralism and democracy congenial, and centralization and dictatorship constrictive and threatening. By necessity, conviction, and experience, free trade unions provide one of the strongest and most determined forces for democracy.[11]

LABOR'S GOALS IN DEMOCRATIC POLITICAL ACTION

Free trade unions in a democratic polity first will want to influence national and local elections. The outcomes affect the interests of the workers.

Once the electorate chooses and a government is formed, the trade unions will seek to influence policy decisions of that government. Most importantly, labor wants a voice in any legislation affecting the labor code, which constitutes the "rules of the game" for collective bargaining. If the rules are not fair, the game will not be fair. Government makes the rules and is their final arbiter.

Labor also wants to influence the government's decisions on national economic policy. In every country the government must decide periodically whether to stimulate the economy, so that production and employment expand, or slow down the economy for a period of time. This basic decision affects jobs, prices, and wages, and naturally the unions seek a voice in such decisions.

In developing countries it is also the government that selects economic development strategies. The government must choose between capital-intensive and labor-intensive industries; between emphasizing exports or substituting domestic products for ones previously imported. The government must also choose whether to try to attract investment by multinational corporations by suppressing trade unions or to protect workers by regulating the actions of the foreign firms. All these, and many other choices in the selection of economic development strategies, have important effects on the workers' interests. Therefore, the trade unions will try to influence these decisions.

Every government also makes decisions that affect the distribution of income in the country. How much higher a percentage of their income should rich people pay in income taxes than poor people? How large a fortune will the law allow heirs of the rich to inherit? What limits will be placed on the amount of farmland one family can own? How much of the government budget will be allocated to social services, and how much to the military? How much of the education budget will go to universities in urban areas and how much will be allocated to primary schools in rural peasant areas? The trade unions want a voice in these government decisions.

It is not only in regard to domestic policy that labor will seek a voice. Foreign policy decisions also affect the workers in immediate ways.

Employment in both the industrialized and the developing nations is affected by trade flows. Some workers will be employed by foreign-owned multinational corporations (MNCs). Workers pay taxes to support military expenditures, and they and their relatives fight and die in wars. Given labor's power and its ability to stabilize or destabilize domestic political systems as well as support or destroy ruling coalitions, labor's foreign policy decisions can influence a nation's alignment in foreign affairs and even affect the global power balance.

The Soviet leadership and their communist allies have understood this for decades. This is why they have placed great stress on winning and maintaining control of the labor sector abroad. Given its superpower status, Moscow now could, if it wished, rely on state-to-state relations and on the traditional diplomatic, military, and economic instruments of statecraft to influence internal developments in other countries. But the Soviet leadership has not chosen to do so. Instead, they are stepping up their efforts to acquire control of this strategic sector in many countries and to use it to shift what they call "the correlation of forces" in their favor. They are continuing to assign thousands of full-time officials in the Soviet Union, Eastern Europe, and Cuba to this work, and they are investing millions of dollars each year in these efforts.[12]

Fortunately, however, Soviet efforts so far have not enabled them to acquire complete control of the trade union movement in the noncommunist world. In the highly developed areas, they have had only mixed success at best. They have little direct influence in the labor movement in the United States, in most of Scandinavia, West Germany, Britain, and the Benelux countries. However, they have been able to use very active Communist labor minorities in these countries to promote neutralism and the Soviet concept of detente, and to reduce European interest in NATO defense expenditures and modernization. In Southern or Latin Europe, they have been the beneficiaries of post–World War II Communist control of major sections of the labor movement. In recent years, Communist strength has been decreased. Most of the Southern European Communist parties are not as responsive to Soviet direction as Moscow would wish. If, however, the democratic unions falter and Communist parties dominate the entire labor movement, the entire political orientation of the area might very well shift. Labor would become an effective part of a major effort to detach Europe from the Western Alliance as well as enable the Communist parties to compete much more effectively to seek a monopoly of political power.

In the developing areas, where increasingly they see targets of opportunity, the Soviet Union and its local allies have not, with rare exceptions, obtained significant results. Usually where the labor movement has been almost completely trained and/or financed by the Soviet labor complex, this has come as a result of the local government's close relationship with the Soviet bloc. When this relationship deteriorates, usually the close Soviet relationship with the local labor movement does so too. But as the years pass, the Soviet Union is training and financing many thousands of non-Western union officials in Southern Africa, the Persian Gulf, and the South Pacific. In Latin America the Communist confederations are among the principal labor bodies in a number of countries. By the mid-1980s, Colombia, the Dominican Republic, and Ecuador were cases in point.

Labor also plays a role in the North-South dialogue between the developing and the industrialized nations. The stands a government takes on issues in debates on the New International Economic Order or on the Third World debt problem are influenced by labor. For example, investment by MNCs in developing nations is a highly controversial issue in North-South relations today, and the workers of a developing country are directly affected by their government's decisions on the matter. When governments place major emphasis on investment by MNCs in their development strategies, and consequently go all out to attract such investment by promising low wages or tax holidays, unions are very concerned. Often unions believe it is the workers who pay the price for such a development strategy, for it is predicated on the workers receiving less per unit-man-hour than the going rate elsewhere in the world. Examples of national efforts to attract MNCs on this basis can be seen in Chile under the Pinochet regime, in South Korea under Park Chung Hee, in the Dominican Republic under the first Balaguer administrations, and in white-ruled South Africa.

Governments in developing countries that include the labor movement in their political base usually (but not always) are less blatant about advertising the attractions of "low cost labor" and generally follow policies of much greater restriction on foreign private investment. In Venezuela, for example, when the AD has controlled the Congress, and often the presidency, foreign investment has been encouraged. This has been on terms that AD leaders felt to be compatible with a development strategy that puts great emphasis on state investment, national control over natural resources, and diversification of foreign capital sources in order to avoid dependency on the United States.[13] In the late 1970s, Venezuela increased its corporate tax rates to the point where large-scale businesses have had to pay up to 50 percent of their incomes to the Venezuelan government. Venezuela is also a member of the Andean Pact and has subscribed to its strict rules regarding foreign investment. These rules are applied in Venezuela so as to require that new foreign investments be shifted to at least 51 percent Venezuelan control within 15 years. These policies are supported by the Confederacion de Trabajadores de Venezuela (CTV), which provides much of the AD's political base.

Mexico provides another example of a government that has labor support and welcomes foreign investment, but under strict regulation in an effort to assure that it advances the nation's own development strategy. In some sectors only joint ventures by foreign and Mexican capital together are permitted, with 51 percent Mexican control usually required.[14] In Mexico the labor movement comprises one of the three sectors within the governing PRI political party. In general, where labor is a supporter of the government, regulation of MNCs is tougher than where labor-opposed governments are in power in the developing areas.

U.S. LABOR'S INTERNATIONAL INVOLVEMENT

U.S. labor was active in international affairs even before the turn of the century, both in relations with labor movements in other industrialized nations and in fraternal assistance to trade unions in the developing countries. Samuel Gompers of the American Federation of Labor (AFL) played a key role in the creation of the International Labor Organization (ILO) at the end of World War I. In the 1920s the AFL helped found and sustain the Pan-American Federation of Labor and, on several occasions, was able to influence U.S. foreign policy on behalf of labor movements in Mexico, the Caribbean, and Central America. During the 1930s U.S. labor helped rescue European labor leaders persecuted by the Italian Fascists and the Nazis and, during World War II, played a part in the war effort that benefited from contact with the anti-Nazi underground.

Much of the AFL-CIO's contemporary international effort has its origins in the work of the AFL in the wartime and immediate postwar periods. Even before the end of the war, U.S. labor leaders, at the urging of their European colleagues, made plans to help restore democracy to the war-ravaged continent. These European and U.S. labor leaders realized that, once the Nazis and fascists were beaten, there would be a major threat from the Soviet Union and the communist allies in Western Europe. Beginning in 1944, AFL policy and material assistance helped to establish an international organizational framework for free labor that continues to this day.

Within a few years after the war, the United States and other Western governments put their official weight behind this policy. In 1947, Secretary of State George Marshall first proposed an aid plan for European recovery. By 1948 the plan was being translated into the Economic Cooperation Act, which set up the European Recovery Program.

The AFL, and, after the Communist faction was expelled, the Congress of Industrial Organizations (CIO) endorsed the Marshall Plan and worked actively to insure its success. The World Federation of Trade Unions, controlled by the Soviet Union, branded the Marshall Plan as an effort at "imperialist penetration" and sought to destroy the plan through worldwide strikes. The United States then helped create the Trade Union Advisory Committee (TUAC), composed of all the trade unions of the countries involved in the Marshall Plan, for the purpose of assisting in the implementation of the plan. The AFL, and then the CIO, also endorsed the creation of NATO, which pledged the United States to defend Western Europe against any attack as if it were an attack on the United States.[15]

U.S. labor cooperated closely with the TUAC to implement the Marshall Plan and, in addition, worked in the international field in a variety of other ways. Among these were:

- The initiative in 1949 to create the International Confederation of Free Trade Unions (ICFTU) to promote cooperation between free unions, first in the developed and later in the developing world.

- Participation in the ILO to maintain the principle of tripartitism in addressing worker interests, developing international labor laws (such as those pertaining to the right to freedom of association), and insisting on government compliance with these laws.

- Participation by AFL-CIO affiliates in the work of unions in the various professional international trade secretariats under the aegis of the ICFTU. It is through such trade secretariats—as those for metalworkers, transport workers, food workers, public employees, and teachers—that workers in a given industry across national boundaries can strengthen their ties and develop joint solutions to the problems of their specific industry.

- Strengthening the joint positions of free unions in the industrialized countries on issues pertaining to education, MNCs, and the economy, through the TUAC of the Organization for Economic Cooperation and Development.

- Assisting in the decolonization in the non-Western world from the 1940s through the 1970s and, at the same time, helping those unions in the non-Western world resist totalitarian or authoritarian pressures from governments and political movements.

After withdrawing (in the late 1960s) and then reaffiliating (in the late 1970s) with the ICFTU, the AFL-CIO has extended its scope in the international trade union field.

U.S. recognition of the importance of labor abroad and its pivotal roles in decolonization and democratic development led to creation of three regional labor institutes in the 1960s to provide ongoing assistance to trade unions in the developing nations. The American Institute for Free Labor Development (AIFLD) began working in Latin America in 1962, the African-American Labor Center (AALC) was founded in 1964, and the Asian-American Free Labor Institute (AAFLI) was established in 1968. The three institutes are sponsored by the AFL-CIO, which controls a majority on the board of directors of each and sets out their basic policies regarding what types of projects to undertake with which union groups in a given country. In addition to AFL-CIO funds, the institutes have received support from the U.S. foreign assistance agency, the Agency for International Development (AID).

Throughout the 1960s and 1970s, most of these projects fell into two categories.

- *Labor education*. Training courses in basic trade union concerns such as collective bargaining techniques, dues systems, accounting procedures, labor legislation, public speaking, and organizing techniques.
- *Social projects*. Credit unions, medical clinics, worker housing projects, consumer cooperatives, and other projects allowing workers to solve their problems collectively, through the leadership of the unions.

For the most part, the AFL-CIO institutes have strengthened unions abroad in their economic functions, but not in their political roles of influencing the make-up and policies of governments. In 1982, President Reagan, with bipartisan congressional support, launched a study to consider how to promote democracy throughout the world. Known as the Democracy Program, the interim report of the study group stated:

Despite the high priority given by the AFL-CIO to domestic political action in the United States, the overseas labor institutes have been far less active—in part because of government funding restrictions—in aiding unions abroad to develop similar political roles. Only since 1979 have the institutes—primarily in the Latin American region—begun to incorporate political education and political theory in their on-site education programs.[16]

The report called for labor to go "beyond the development work for which it has received helpful support from the Agency for International Development," that is, to move from only helping unions abroad in their economic roles of organizing and bargaining to helping them undertake democratic political action in defense of their members' interests.[17]

The Democracy Program's recommendations led the president to propose to Congress the creation of the National Endowment for Democracy (NED) in November 1983. The U.S. labor movement was to be the largest private-sector group to become involved in implementing NED programs. As a result, the AFL-CIO expanded its existing small general-purpose Free Trade Union Institute (FTUI), which had been providing very limited political assistance, into a major program. FTUI received $11 million of the total NED appropriation of $18 million for fiscal year 1984. With this support the AFL—CIO began to provide support to labor as a political force. Programs to strengthen trade unions abroad in their economic roles were now supplemented by new efforts to help those unions build their capacities for democratic political action.

In Asia, Africa, and Latin America, U.S. labor's political development projects in the mid-1980s have, in the main, been carried out by the three regional institutes—the AAFLI, AALC, and AIFLD; these now receive NED funds through the FTUI. The regional institutes have also continued their traditional assistance to trade unions' economic roles, with AID contract funds. In other parts of the world, such as Southern Europe, where democratic labor faces major communist competition, the FTUI administers labor political development projects directly.

Labor's new political aid projects in all geographic regions are keyed to the six purposes that Congress wrote into the NED's founding legislation.

1. *Institution-building* (including individual rights and freedoms): Aid to national trade union centers and international trade secretariats for infrastructure development; organizational support for regional trade union groups and for international labor organizations; efforts to counter antidemocratic subversion; funds for emergency organizational support; funds for trade union exiles.

An example of an institution-building project during 1985 was AIFLD assistance to Chile's Democratic Workers Center (CDT) to help it maintain nine regional offices. These offices provide legal services to affiliated trade unions. The assistance also helped the center continue an extensive information program involving publications, conferences and rallies. The CDT is part of a broad coalition of democratic groups in Chile, which, with the backing of the Catholic Church, is pressuring the Pinochet regime to allow a transition to democracy.

2. *Exchanges*: Travel that is specifically tied to other types of effort, especially comprehensive training conferences, study, and so on, in contrast to conventional exchanges, which are often isolated events.

Illustrative of labor's work in this category is a three-week trip to the United States sponsored by the AAFLI in 1985 for 12 trade union editors from 11 Asian and Middle Eastern nations. The editors received briefings and attended seminars with U.S. labor editors, journalists, professors of journalism, and AFL-CIO department heads, covering both editorial techniques and democratic concepts and practices.

3. *Training and Civic Education*: Education in parliamentary procedure, combating antidemocratic forces, and factional organizing; education in organizing, demonstrating, and servicing members; publication and dissemination of materials, and similar subjects.

A good example of labor training programs with long-range political development implications is the AAFLI-supported effort of the Malaysian Trades Union Congress (MTUC) to bring the message of trade unionism to 70,000 young unorganized electronics assembly workers in the Penang Free Trade Zone. The MTUC is setting up a workers' center in the zone. The center offers basic labor courses to the workers there, with the eventual goal of organizing them, an achievement that would greatly increase labor's influence within the Malaysian polity.

4. *Electoral Processes*: Training that deals with electoral processes, get-out-the-vote efforts, and building organizational capability to engage in electoral participation.

In Africa during 1985 the AALC helped the Liberian Free Labor Union (LFLU) conduct numerous grass-roots seminars in rural areas of Liberia prior to the national elections. These courses explained the nature and importance of the election process to rural workers so that they would be motivated to vote in an informed manner on election day. The heavy turnout in the Liberian elections, especially where the LFLU's civic seminars were concentrated, indicated that the courses may have affected the rural workers' attitudes toward elections and voting. Though the election results were voided by irregularities, a coup attempt, and widespread violence, the civic education of the workers may, in the long run, lay a basis for a more stable and democratic polity in Liberia.

5. *Democratic Pluralism*: Research and publications promoting democratic values or exposing those who oppose them; efforts to counter anti-democratic subversion; assistance to democratic efforts in totalitarian or dictatorial countries; the international promotion of U.S. labor's positions; support for trade union publications.

Illustrative of the work done to support democratic pluralism is AIFLD's project with the trade union elements in the Council for the Liberation of Surinam, formed in the Netherlands by Surinamese refugees after the massacre of many democratic leaders in late 1982 by the Bouterse dictatorship. The council is composed of labor, business, and political leaders. With U.S. labor's help, it has been publishing a monthly news bulletin in English and Dutch on conditions within Surinam and is preparing to open a radio station to broadcast tape recorded commentaries by exiled Surinamese labor leaders.

6. *Democratic Development*: Support for labor-related projects such as land reform and community development, and aid to international organizations such as the ICFTU, which sponsor similar efforts.

One of the most dramatic projects in 1985 in this category was AAFLI's support for the participation by the Trade Union Confederation of the Philippines (TUCP) in the work of the National Citizens Movement for Free Elections (NAMFREL). The labor confederation endorsed the call to convene elections and sponsored newspaper advertisements urging citizens to vote. The TUCP also organized poll-watching teams to help NAMFREL observe the conduct of the polling. The work of NAMFREL reportedly was a crucial factor in dramatizing the fraud in the 1986 elections and sparking the demonstrations that led to the fall of the Marcos regime.[18]

AMERICAN LABOR AS EDUCATOR FOR DEMOCRACY

The labor programs funded both by U.S. workers and taxpayers have sought to defend and to build a program of democratic political development. As the AFL-CIO and many others have pointed out, it will take sustained effort over many decades to propagate successfully basic democratic concepts in settings where democratic traditions are weak. Aside from providing political and material support to struggling democrats, the United States and its labor movement are in a position to provide much-needed educational assistance.

New and inexperienced urban and rural trade union leaders are requesting help in propagating the basic concepts of social, economic, and political democracy. They seek the means to explain these ideas cogently to their memberships and to defend them convincingly against the arguments of antidemocratic forces on both Left and Right. Many labor leaders in developing nations feel at a disadvantage when debating advocates of a totalitarian "vanguard party" or military officers advocating repressive measures to protect "national security" and "the Christian values of the West."

Another area in which U.S. labor can help is by providing unions in these areas with an understanding of how political democracy fits the particular needs of modernizing societies. Modern democracy in its Western, Lockean forms, after all, was devised to solve problems of political corruption, instability, and injustice in Britain and North America before the Industrial Revolution. Political systems born to facilitate development of polities conducive to industrialization and economic growth, as in Britain and the United States, may provide important guidance to more contemporary modernizing nations.

All too often, for example, labor leaders abroad hear about democracy as though it were a choice between rapid growth and political liberty. U.S. labor can help show that democratic liberties are themselves means to growth, not obstacles. If anything, it is precisely in the poor and unstable nations of Africa, Asia, and Latin America that democracy is needed most today, for they suffer most from the problems that democratic pluralism was created to resolve.

Would-be democrats among the unions in the developing nations need assistance in explaining that political democracy can lead to social justice and economic development in nations with vast disparities of wealth and with discrimination against the weak by the privileged. At present many democratic labor leaders hold an almost naïve faith that the introduction of electoral processes alone can produce rapid and thorough reforms in land tenure, income distribution, educational systems, and treatment of disadvantaged social groups. When elections are held and little changes for the poor majority, these leaders are often gravely disillusioned.

U.S. labor, using its own experience as a developing industrialized nation and as a result of decades of social struggles, can help foreign trade unionists with the realistic perspective that elections are just one, albeit vital, mechanism for democratic social change. The merit of elections is not that voting provides instant solutions to social problems, but that free elections, free speech, and freedom of association provide workers (and other sectors) with an opportunity to organize the interest groups and parties that are basic engines of long-term social reform in a democratic setting.

For labor to achieve its full potential as a democratizing force, internal democracy within trade unions also is vital. Unions in a developing country (or perhaps anywhere) that contain political machines controlled by political bosses can hardly serve as maximal vehicles for democratizing a national political system. Here again, U.S. labor, while far from perfect, can offer useful experience and an outside perspective to trade unionists in societies traditionally accustomed to authoritarian and clientelistic organizational structures.

Two dangers in particular arise when unions—or any other democratic group—are subject to bossism. First, the democratic movement, of which labor is a part, will become prone to complacency and corruption. If few leaders in the middle levels of the union have autonomous power, if they are all clients serving at the pleasure of the organization's boss, then no one can blow the whistle when corruption appears in the organization.

Second, if a labor movement with weak internal democracy allies itself with a corrupt political party that comes to power, and should the government move in the direction of dictatorship, there would be few internal checks in the party or in the labor movement to prevent this. More likely, the machine in the party and trade unions would welcome authoritarian power passing into their hands. For these reasons building democracy abroad is as much a task of promoting democracy within major organizations as it is of building a competitive, pluralistic democracy among interest groups and political parties.

Another part of U.S. labor's educational program should concern the role of the United States, its government, and its people in world affairs. Many politically active workers in other nations receive a great deal of false and malicious propaganda designed to discredit the United States and its leading role in the democratic world. Some of this propaganda will have been disseminated in the Third World by antiunion conservatives and even terrorists seeking to discredit what they see as a weak, decadent U.S. society bent on corrupting their own traditional values. Literature and radio programs that fit this description can be found from Central America to the Middle East and beyond.

A great deal of anti-American propaganda and intentional falsification (disinformation) is generated by the Soviet Union and its allies. Moscow has more than 15,000 full-time professionals and spends more than $3-4 billion each year to discredit the United States, claiming that it (and its labor leaders) is responsible for the poverty and misery that exist in the world. Sometimes Moscow's claims are even more ridiculous, for example, that the United States developed and spread the AIDS virus intentionally. Unless foreign union leaders and workers have an opportunity to learn the truth about U.S. and other democratic societies, the huge Soviet propaganda and disinformation apparatus will not always fall on deaf ears.

U.S. labor's educational programs can take on both Soviet and other forms of extreme anti-American propaganda not only to provide the truth about the United States, but also to put the United States, as one of the most powerful symbols of democratic society, in historical perspective.

Propagation of democratic ideas and attitudes alone will not make labor an effective bulwark of democracy. These ideas must be supplemented by a sophisticated knowledge of political tactics: how to run a meeting; how to organize a rally; how to deal with hecklers and obstructionist maneuvers by communists at a union convention; how to select and package an appealing set of issues for a political campaign. These are an essential ingredient of a working democracy, particularly in nations just emerging from long periods of dictatorship, where trade unionists have little experience in democratic political tactics.

Skill in political tactics is of special importance in developing countries because of the frequent challenges from antidemocratic groups there. Communist labor leaders are trained to lever minority status into dominance of an organization. Their means: dilatory tactics at meetings until only the communist faithful are left to vote; disrupting meetings that they cannot control; infiltrating democratic groups under false colors; building front organizations that use specific social issues shared with democrats to promote extremist goals, and the like. In Soviet bloc labor training schools, labor leaders from developing nations practice over and over how to draft a leaflet that will catch the reader's eye, how to write slogans that appeal to workers' immediate interests, and how to discredit democratic opponents, particularly the United States and its labor movement. Democratic trade unionists need equally intensive courses in tactics. U.S. labor's long experience is often readily transferable across borders and cultures, as it was in Europe after World War II.

In addition to providing assistance in relatively peaceful polities, U.S. labor can help protect labor leaders where physical repression is used against them. Foreign union leaders can be made aware of a variety of nonviolent tactics that can impede those who seek to jail, murder, or maim them. Tactical examples: keeping their colleagues apprised of their schedules, so that sympathetic forces can be alerted if they fail to appear; international publicity and diplomatic pressures to obtain the release of jailed activists. These tactics have been effective. While U.S. trade unionists are mercifully free from the need to be skilled in such matters, U.S. labor can support training courses where tactics against repression and terrorism can be taught by those with practical experience, that is, by experienced practitioners from non-U.S. democratic labor movements.

Another skill with which U.S. labor could help is the building of national coalitions in favor of democracy. Where such groupings cross class and occupational lines, including trade unions, business associations, community groups, and peasant leagues, they can be powerful forces. Coming from a background of pluralism, U.S. labor is familiar with such coalition building—to further civil rights, to promote education in economics, or to support trade legislation in which unions and business may have a common interest. In developing countries such coalitions can serve the broader task of nurturing the democratic system itself. In the 1980s in Nicaragua, for example, the Coordinadora Democratica has been a bulwark against the efforts of the Sandinista regime to impose a totalitarian control system on Nicaraguan society. Business, free labor, and democratic political parties all cooperate in the Coordinadora Democratica, even though they know full well that when democracy returns to Nicaragua, they will have to compete and bargain with each other. The severity of the threat they face from the Sandinistas, however, has made clear to them that all have an immediate common interest in building a democratic system so that they can continue to compete later.

Free labor has an important role to play in the development of democracy. To promote democratic systems abroad, the United States can be of help to this strategic sector with political, material, and educational assistance. While the existence of an effective democratic labor movement may be neither necessary nor sufficient for democracy to flourish, it certainly can be an important contributing factor. Where democratic labor leaders are struggling against heavy odds to develop democratic values in their societies, the United States and its labor movement are in a crucial position to provide much-needed and perhaps vital assistance.

NOTES

1. See *AFL-CIO News*, February 15, 1986, pp. 1, 4.

2. On this phenomenon in Latin America, see Gary W. Wynia, *The Politics of Latin America Development* (London: Cambridge University Press, 1978), pp. 77, 79.

3. See John D. Martz, *The Venezuelan Elections of December 1, 1983*, part 1 (Washington, D.C.: Institute for the Comparative Study of Political Systems, 1964), p. 3. See also Robert J. Alexander, *The Venezuelan Democratic Revolution* (New Brunswick, N.J.: Rutgers University Press, 1964), pp. 17, 18, 239.

4. Martz, op. cit., p. 3.

5. On the Tunisian example, see Willard E. Beling, *Modernization and African Labor—A Tunisian Case Study* (New York: Frederick A. Praeger, 1965), and Werner Plum, *Gewerkschaften im Maghreb: UGTT-UMT-UGTA* (Hanover: Verlag für Literatur und Zeitgeschehen, 1962).

6. See Thomas J. Bellows, *The People's Action Party of Singapore: Emergence of a Dominant Party System* (New Haven: Yale University Southeast Asia Studies, 1970), p. 90.

7. On the Moroccan case, see Plum, op. cit., esp. pp. 30-32, and I. William Zartman, "Political Pluralism in Morocco," in I. William Zartman, ed., *Man, State, and Society in the Contemporary Maghrib* (New York: Praeger, 1973).

8. George Meany, speech to the Commonwealth Club of California, San Francisco, April 23, 1958.

9. George Meany, quoted in Archie Robinson, *George Meany and His Times* (New York: Simon & Schuster, 1981), p. 126.

10. See Martin J. Ward, "Labor, Human Rights, and Democracy," *Freedom at Issue*, March-April 1980, p. 21.

11. For an application of these principles to South Africa, see Roy Godson, "Black Labor as a Swing Factor in South Africa's Evolution," in Richard Bissell and Chester Crocker, eds., *South Africa into the 1980s* (Boulder, Colo.: Westview Press, 1979).

12. For further analysis of Soviet efforts and an analysis of their effectiveness, see Roy Godson, *Labor in Soviet Global Strategy* (New York: Crane Russak, 1984).

13. See Wynia, op. cit., pp. 194-95, 197, and Cecilia M. Valente, *The Political, Economic, and Labor Climate in Venezuela* (Philadelphia: Industrial Research Unit, University of Pennsylvania, 1978), pp. 80-88.

14. See Wynia, op. cit., p. 294.

15. On the history and effectiveness of AFL and AFL-CIO foreign policy, see Philip Taft, *Defending Freedom* (Los Angeles: Nash, 1973), and Roy Godson, *American Labor and European Politics* (New York: Crane Russak, 1976).

16. Democracy Program, Interim Report, *The Commitment to Democracy: A Bipartisan Approach* (April 18, 1983), p. 21.

17. Ibid., p. 38.

18. Free Trade Union Institute, AFL-CIO, *Report to the National Endowment for Democracy* (October-December, 1985). Much of the section that follows is drawn from this report.

7 A MARKET-ORIENTED APPROACH TO DEMOCRATIC DEVELOPMENT: THE LINKAGES
John D. Sullivan

The United States government has long sought to accomplish the twin goals of private-enterprise-led economic growth and development of democratic institutions within the overall foreign assistance strategy. These goals have shaped U.S. foreign policy to varying degrees since the end of World War II, although the emphasis has shifted from an ''idealist'' pursuit of democracy to a ''realist'' opposition to communism on numerous occasions. Unfortunately, the current dialogue on democratic development has become polarized to a large degree along these same lines, largely because of an inability to specify the conditions necessary for accomplishment of either goal.

In many cases, polarization has resulted simply from the desire to avoid the complexity inherent in a world of 165 independent states with extremely diverse cultures and political systems. Frankly put, it has long been time to divorce policy debates from either an East-West or a North-South perspective and come to grips with a diverse and complicated world. While there has been a natural tendency to reduce foreign policy, including foreign assistance, to simple one-line approaches, this has ill served both the nation and those the United States seeks to assist.

Taken together, this chapter and the following one attempt to craft a framework for looking at complexity in the area of democratic development pursued through private enterprise approaches. This chapter is

The views expressed here are those of the author and do not necessarily reflect those of the U.S. Chamber of Commerce or the Center for International Private Enterprise.

focused on the relationship of economic to political systems and the continuing "war of ideas" about these relationships. In the process, most attention is devoted to the relationship of competitive market economic systems and democratic institutions. The following chapter offers an analysis of attempts by various U.S. government programs to foster the development of private enterprise as an element of democratic development and suggests some areas for further work.

RELATIONSHIP OF DEMOCRATIC THEORY TO MARKET SYSTEMS

In the concrete world of national systems as opposed to the realm of theory, there is an intimate relationship among politics, economics, culture, religion, and other elements of everyday life. All of these factors influence and are influenced by one another in the long and continuing process of national development. When proponents of democratic development speak of strengthening the institutions and values of democracy or pluralism, they must keep in mind that the purely political values and institutions cannot be treated separately from the larger economic and social reality in which these institutions and values are embedded. For example, the political system establishes, through law, the economic frame work of a nation within a social and cultural context. Further, the extent to which the political government attempts to control rather than to regulate economic affairs or the social and cultural life of a nation is one of the most basic distinctions between democratic forms of government and the dictatorships of the Right and Left.

Despite the fact that national systems must be treated as whole cloth in order to portray accurately the full range of political, economic, and social interactions, people commonly argue over the political or economic relationships in the abstract. Indeed, this is the determining characteristic of most of the ideological debates of our time. Such debates arise from the tendency for people to form allegiance to and be motivated by ideas and values. The war of ideas, as it is popularly known, occurs worldwide. It is not, however, simply a contest between the stark alternatives of U.S.-style democracy and the Soviet version of communism. Rather, there are numerous competing systems of ideas, some of which can be called ideologies and others of which are simply open-ended sets of values. For example, there are distinct differences between classical Marxism, Marxism-Leninism, and the various evolving streams of Chinese communism. Similarly, liberation theology and social democracy express very different visions of social order and national governmental policy. In addition, there is a well-articulated Christian Democratic movement and the emerging conservative International Democratic Union, both of which have highly developed belief systems. Many other variations of these theories are found in all regions of the world, some of which are national and indigenous in nature and others of which are transnational.

There are numerous reasons for the continuing global competition of values. The U.S.-Soviet competition obviously contributes substantially; the Chinese occasionally offer a challenge to both. Equally important, however, is the emergence of distinctly Latin American and, to a much lesser extent, African approaches to governance and economic thought. Numerous other trends could be listed as contributing factors, ranging from the spread of Islamic fundamentalism to the communications revolution that enables the rapid exchange of ideas. There is every reason to believe that the global competition of ideas will continue to accelerate and spread given the increasing restraints on war between major powers and the fundamental importance of ideas in the organization of human institutions and systems.

At the most basic level, the competition of ideas responds to a need that all of us share. People are motivated to action and guided, in large part, by a positive vision of the future that offers hope of improvement in their lives. It is in this respect that basic distinctions can be made between various ideals, values, and ideologies. Some, such as classical Marxism or contemporary Soviet thought, offer detailed strategies complete with foes who must be overcome to ensure material progress for the average person or family. Others, such as liberation theology and European social democracy, simply appeal to concepts of class solidarity and moral values specifying good and evil.

Conversely, those who advocate democracy, for the most part, have tended to do so in process-oriented terms or in reference to concepts like civil rights and freedom. However, the emphasis on institutions and law, while important, is not a sufficient counter to those who claim that these very institutions and laws are tools for the exploitation of the poor by the oligarchic rich. Similarly, the promise of freedom is no substitute, on a pragmatic level, for the promise of immediate material improvement among those living on the margins of human existence. This situation has placed democratic thought and values in a defensive and reactive posture. Many of the most articulate proponents of democracy tend to be uncomfortable talking about economics and economic systems. Rather, they tend to argue in favor of land reform, government spending for education and social services, and public works. These are important, no doubt, but they do not offer solutions to systemic flaws, nor do they offer the basis for popular mass movements.

One clear contemporary example has been the ongoing debate within the European democracies over the role of Communist parties within their respective systems. Communist parties, including the well-established French pro-Soviet party, have participated in governments at both local and national levels. While domestic politics in the United States has not experienced this debate, business, academic, foreign policy, media, and other opinion leadership groups all have had to face the question of whether a coalition government that included Communists could be considered a democratic government in an historically democratic allied nation.

The fact that such a debate could take place is symptomatic of the overly process-oriented concept of democracy held by many political and opinion leaders. It is a direct result of the notion that democratic institutions are limited to political arrangements such as elections and parties or freedoms such as freedom of speech. In such a worldview, communists or nationalist authoritarian figures and movements are to be allowed to participate as long as they claim to accept the political values of democracy; the economic and social values necessary for democratic systems to survive are simply not considered. Hence, democrats all too often allow individuals and organizations deeply opposed to democracy to participate equally in the political process.

For democracy to remain competitive in the world of competing ideas and values, advocates of democratic thought must broaden their horizons to include an alternative and compelling vision of the future that specifies the conditions for both material progress and political freedom. Such a vision must explicitly include an economic component based upon and supportive of democratic institutions and values.

Overview of the Literature

Given the compelling necessity of articulately advocating a democratic message consonant with the aspiration of people everywhere for economic growth and development, it is obvious that attention must be paid to economic factors. One point of departure of such a version of a democratic message can be found in the historically close association between democratic political systems and market-oriented economic systems. In this context, it is instructive to look at some of the literature on the subject of the relationship of democracy to competitive private enterprise or market systems as a source of guidance and inspiration.[1] This section of the chapter attempts to survey, albeit briefly, some of the classical formulations regarding the presence or absence of relationship between democratic systems and market economics.

There has been a lengthy debate among democratic theorists and analysts regarding the necessity of market systems for maintenance of democratic institutions. On one side, Samuel Huntington's recent article "Will More Countries Become Democratic?" highlights the notion that democracy is more likely to survive in a market system that allows for the dispersion of economic power. Huntington notes that, among other factors,

politically, a market economy requires a dispersion of economic power and in practice almost invariably some form of private property. The dispersion of economic power creates alternatives and counters to state power and enables those elites that control economic power to limit state power and to exploit democratic means to make it serve their interests. Economically, a market economy appears more likely to sustain economic growth than a command economy (although the latter may, as the Soviet and East European cases suggest, do so for a short period of time), and hence a market economy is more likely to give rise to the economic wealth and the resulting more equitable distribution of income that provide the infrastructure of democracy.[2]

Huntington's emphasis on the dispersion of power and its logical concomitant, the maintenance of individual freedom, has a great deal of appeal. As will be further discussed below, large concentrations of economic power tend to lead to a subversion of democratic political processes. This is the case both when economic power is concentrated in the hands of a state bureaucracy under communist or fascist forms of government or in the hands of oligarchical elites under authoritarian types of regimes. Just as democracy and civil liberties can be spoken of in terms of degrees, so too can concentration of economic power. While a democratic system may survive for a time in the face of a large concentration of power, the tendency is for those holding such power to seek to expand it and ultimately to control the political process as well.

However, Robert Dahl concludes in his classic study, *Polyarchy*, that economic power can be dispersed through other arrangements than private enterprise. In particular, Dahl feels that a form of "market socialism" could be consistent with political democracy since that too would prevent the centralization of power in the hands of a governmental elite. Dahl's view is summarized in the following:

Where the equations of classic liberalism went wrong was in supposing that any alternative to competitive capitalism necessarily required a centrally directed economy, whereas in fact competition among privately owned firms is by no means the unique method of decentralizing an economy. Indeed, in recent years some of the communist regimes of Eastern Europe have been moving away from central direction; among these, Yugoslavia has gone farthest in decentralizing controls over economic enterprises. If decentralized socialist economies prove capable of handling major economic problems with a fair degree of success, then there is no inherent reason why socialism cannot produce and sustain a highly pluralistic social order, and hence competitive politics.[3]

In part, the disagreement between Huntington and Dahl may simply revolve around the fact that Huntington bases his interpretation on empirical observations whereas Dahl addresses theoretical possibilities. However, Lindsay Wright, author of a Freedom House study, adds support to Dahl's views in the conclusion to "A Comparative Survey of Economic Freedoms":

Historically, the state in advanced socialist systems has pursued the interests of a small ruling elite to the exclusion and suppression of the interests of the people it claims to represent. Capitalist systems have a mixed record of protecting and violating the economic freedoms of individuals and groups. Under autocracy, both industrial capitalism and socialism can become as abusive of power as the political system under which each operates; without proper checks, both tend toward centralization and concentration. Ultimately, the exercise of economic freedom under either capitalism or socialism depends on the ability of the country's political system to protect and promote that freedom for all its citizens. Our best hope for advancing economic freedom lies in the strengthening of the rights of all peoples to choose their own government and through that choice to determine the relationships and arrangements that frame economic life.[4]

Resolution of these differing interpretations on the dispersion of economic and, hence, political power will require analysts to develop more sensitive measures of market structures as well as democratic institutions. Michael Novak's *Spirit of Democratic Capitalism* indicates the direction such analysis must take in its emphasis on a moral or value base essential to democratic capitalism, a system that is quite different from other forms of political economy.[5] In this, Novak is supported by Seymour Martin Lipset's classic study, *Political Man*. Lipset identified several conditions necessary for democracy, including an open class system, economic wealth, an egalitarian value system, capitalist economy, literacy, and high participation in voluntary organizations.[6]

Models of Democracy and Market Systems

As may be seen in the brief review of some democratic theorists, there is considerable disagreement on the relationship between democratic systems and market economics. Though this debate will not be resolved here, there is a need to look more deeply into the issue on the basis of the patterns found in the existing democracies and comparison of these patterns with those found in the nondemocratic systems. The first step in this process is to define both democratic government and market economics in more concrete terms than those offered in the review of theories.

There are numerous definitions of democracy, as other chapters in this book indicate. Some emphasize basic values and virtues, whereas others rely primarily on legal definitions of institutional structure. An excellent approach has been offered by G. Bingham Powell. His definition is based on the following set of criteria:

1. The legitimacy of the government rests on a claim to represent the desires of its citizens. That is, the claim of the government to obedience to its laws is based on the government's assertion that it is doing what the people want it to do.

2. The organized arrangement that regulates this bargain of legitimacy is the competitive political election. Leaders are elected at regular intervals, and voters can choose among alternative candidates. In practice, at least two political parties that have a chance of winning are needed to make such choices meaningful.

3. Most adults can participate in the electoral process, both as voters and as candidates for important political office.

4. Citizens' votes are secret and not coerced.

5. Citizens and leaders enjoy basic freedom of speech, press, assembly, and organization. Both established parties and new ones can work to gain members and voters.[7]

These criteria are not intended to form a complete definition of a democratic society. That would entail further elaboration of, among many factors, the concept of citizenship, the value structure of the society, and notions of representative leadership through parliaments and other institutional structures. The value of Powell's criteria is that they provide a basic checklist for determining whether or not a system can be said to be democratic.

Comparable criteria by which nations can be said to have market economic systems are much more difficult to establish. The conceptual distinctions between various forms of economic organization are much less clear as a result of the ideological conflicts discussed previously. For example, the distinctions between socialism, communism, and capitalism are far more complex than simply the distinction between state and private ownership of property or even the more limited distinctions regarding ownership of the means of production. The governments of both the Soviet Union and France claim to be socialist in nature, as do various member parties comprising the Socialist international, yet very different definitions of a socialist economy and policy are advanced by these parties.

Similarly, most observers would indicate that the United States, Brazil, and the Philippines are all private enterprise systems despite very different patterns of economic activity. In recent years, the term *mixed economy* has come into widespread usage to describe economic systems that contain elements of both socialist and market systems. Yet, this does not resolve the question since the United States, Brazil, France, and the

Philippines all would fall into such a category even though the degree of mixture of public and private ownership varies widely. It is easy to see that the operation of these mixed systems differs greatly in the way the rules of the economic game actually function.

The approach advocated here is to identify the major elements of a market system and to distinguish the degree to which systems employ markets within the overall economy. This approach leads to a set of criteria similar to the ones employed by Powell to identify democratic political systems. The use of the word *market* as opposed to *capitalist* is deliberate and frankly normative in nature. It should be noted that there is little agreement on the essential elements of a market system; hence, the following criteria are exploratory in nature.

1. Economic arrangements arise out of voluntary and free exchange of value between individuals and/or firms. Values associated with exchanges of goods and services are set through the functioning of supply and demand as registered by an uncontrolled price system. The claim to legitimacy is that both parties to transactions perceive benefit from the exchange.

2. Freedom of association for economic activity is established and guaranteed by law to individuals for purposes of forming firms, cooperatives, unions, and other forms of economic activity.

3. Freedom to own and exchange property is guaranteed by law for all individuals regardless of socioeconomic background. Property includes both personal property and the means of production.

4. Freedom of movement and information is guaranteed by law.

5. Free entry into and out of markets is guaranteed by law for individuals and firms.

6. Competition is maintained in markets as a function of a legal and regulatory system that prevents monopoly and or collusion through restraint of trade, price fixing, government charters, and other barriers.

7. The role of government(s) is to regulate the creation and maintenance of the market system through establishment of objective laws (rules) that protect individuals, consumers, and firms from fraud and corrupt practices. Regulation should be objective and preventive in nature (not command oriented). Taxation must be applied through objective factors and not be confiscatory in nature. Access to government services and public goods must be open to all in an objective fashion.

One additional criterion should be offered, given the necessity of distinguishing between market economics and patronage-oriented "crony capitalism." Unlike the positive criteria designed to specify market system conditions, the following criterion is negative in the sense that it specifies how market-oriented systems all too often are subverted in the developing world.

8. In a market system, private firms account for the preponderance of production of goods and services. Their position in the economy results from the functioning of an exchange system operating under conditions of supply and demand and uncontrolled prices. Market system conditions are subverted when some groups of firms or individuals benefit from government patronage or favoritism through distribution of (often subsidized) foreign exchange, credit, licenses, purchases, and monopoly rights.[8]

Once a form of crony capitalism begins to seep into the economic system, the system itself is transformed from a market economy to a mercantile economy. Mercantilism is itself a form of economic arrangement that actually precedes the establishment of market systems in Europe. It is often thought of as a strategy of international trade used to subordinate colonies to a mother country, as was the case in British colonial practice. However, it is actually a broader phenomenon involving agreements, designed to perpetuate a system of mutual benefit, between governmental and business elites. In political terms, mercantilism equates with oligarchy.[9]

The importance of identifying mercantilism in the contemporary world is fundamental to the task of promoting democratic development. Even very sophisticated observers of contemporary international events tend to regard all systems that allow for private enterprise as being private enterprise or market systems. From the perspective of the market system checklist, a distinction is drawn at the level of the system itself. The rules of the economic game must be based on competition and regulation rather than control and cronyism for a system to be considered as a market system. The implications for democratic theory are immediate. As will be described below, the repressive authoritarian regimes do not measure up to the market system in fundamental respects. Although there is no doubt that such distinctions are a function of the degree of control, it will be seen that authoritarian political systems inevitably conceal authoritarian economic arrangements as well.

Numerous other criteria could be advanced to describe various aspects of ideal market systems in the areas of competition, legal systems, regulation, ownership, consumer health and safety, and the like. Such criteria, however, would tend to be derivative in nature. Since the purpose here is not to provide a complete explication of a market system but rather to provide essential criteria for distinguishing economic systems, the above should suffice.

The criteria described above represent an ideal model of a market system, just as Powell's criteria constitute an ideal model of democratic political systems. The intent herein is to describe the private exchange system of a market economy. It must be recalled that the market system is not the entire economic system. The latter includes the actions of government, such as income transfers (e.g., social security, welfare payments), provision of public education, defense establishments, public transportation systems, central banking services, and other functions to provide for public goods not produced through private initiative. In addition, the overall economy would also include the economic functions and actions performed by nonprofit institutions (churches, foundations, etc.), unions, business associations, cooperatives, and other nongovernmental organizations.

PATTERNS OF POLITICAL AND ECONOMIC ARRANGEMENTS

In the contemporary world, nearly all of the Western industrialized nations must be described as mixed economies in the sense that government has a significant stake in the economy through public ownership of productive assets, command-oriented regulations or policies, control or administration of some elements of the price mechanism (through tax systems or exchange controls), or other techniques of a command nature. Conversely, open or free markets can be seen to exist alongside the public sector to some degree in every country. For example, a legal market in agricultural products, some services, and some consumer goods exists within the Soviet Union despite the fact that the Soviet economy is arguably the most tightly centralized and controlled system in existence.[10] On the other hand, despite a strong orientation toward private ownership of firms and individual initiative, many nations in Southeast Asia, as well as South Korea, Taiwan, and Singapore, often impose tight controls over access to credit; decisions on plant locations and major investments often require governmental sanction; and governments tend to control decision making in export-oriented industries.[11]

Markets and the Existing Democracies

From the perspective of both democratic and market criteria, it becomes obvious that neither an ideal democracy nor an ideal market system exists. In both cases, classifying and describing real-world nations becomes a question of degree. Given the relative lack of worldwide comparative data on national market orientation, the best point of departure is to examine those nations that can be considered stable democratic polities and then examine their economic systems. The following is Powell's list of nations with democratic political systems during at least five years, according to his criteria, over the period from 1958 to 1976. Powell excluded from his study nations of fewer than 1 million in population, and hence several small democracies were excluded, as were those that gained independence after 1958.[12]

Continuous Democracies, 1958-76

Australia	Denmark	Italy	Sweden
Austria	Finland	Japan	Switzerland
Belgium	West Germany	Netherlands	United Kingdom
Canada	Ireland	New Zealand	United States
Costa Rica	Israel	Norway	Venezuela

Democratic Regime Seriously Limited or Suspended, 1958-76

France (1958)	Jamaica (1976)	Turkey (1960-61, 1971-72)
India (1975-76)	Sri Lanka (1971-76)	

With respect to these stable democracies, the most serious questions about the nature of the economic systems arise from consideration of nations such as Sweden and, to a lesser extent, other European democracies that are often put forth as examples of democratic socialist regimes. Such countries have extensive nationalized industries, thereby limiting the concept of private ownership of productive property. Sweden, in particular, follows policies of extensive redistribution of income through massive transfer payments financed by very high tax rates. Other European democracies, especially the United Kingdom, display extensive public ownership of housing as well as socialized health care systems. Although data are not available to analyze fully all of the market system criteria, comparative data are available for most of these nations about the relative degrees of public ownership, government spending, government employment, and employment in public enterprises. These data can be used as indicators of the relative size of the public sector versus the market system within the economies of these established democracies.

Although a complete analysis would entail an in-depth study of regulatory systems, the indicators presented in table 7.1 suggest that the relative size of the public sector varies considerably among the stable democracies. The United States and, to the extent data are available, Japan consistently rank lowest. Sweden and several other Western European states demonstrate an extensive degree of government involvement in mixed economic systems. However, even in Sweden, the bulk of productive employment and enterprise activity is in the private sector. Additionally, neither prices nor credit are controlled or determined, and essential economic freedoms are present.[14] The indicators in table 7.1 are consistent with the following interpretation: All of the existing stable democratic polities coexist with mixed economies that are based on market-oriented economic structures. Clearly, none of the stable democracies has established a centralized or command-oriented economic system.

Of the countries not included in the list of postwar continuous democracies, several can be considered to be relatively stable, according to Powell's criteria. Certainly, France, Iceland, and most of the English-speaking Caribbean can reasonably be considered functioning stable democratic states. France, which had a troubled history in the 1950s, is today a stable democracy. Similarly, the English-speaking Caribbean demonstrates a deep commitment to democracy despite the events in Grenada and the strength of nondemocratic groups in some of the smaller islands. Of the African nations, however, only Botswana and Mauritius can reasonably be said to have attained a similar status.[15] In Latin America the transitions to democracy are recent for most of the nations and incomplete in many cases. Although most of the continent is now governed by elected governments, only Venezuela, Costa Rica (both included in Powell's list) and, with some reservations, Colombia can be said to have demonstrated a continuous democratic regime for a reasonable length of time.

The comparative data on freedom of association, property, movement, and information available for most of the nations listed in the preceding paragraph demonstrates that they allow a great deal of market freedom.[16] Further, private sectors exist in all of the nations listed in the preceding paragraph, and government share of gross fixed capital formation is within the range illustrated in Table 7.1.[17] Colombia, Venezuela, and Botswana all have large portions of their populations in the informal economy, a phenomenon only now beginning to gain attention as a serious issue in political as distinct from economic development. The implications of informal economies will be described below.

Markets in Nondemocratic Systems

There are far more nondemocratic than democratic political systems in today's world. As was pointed out earlier, all of these systems exhibit some degree of market orientation.

First, in the communist world, even the Soviet Union, the archetype of the command economy, exhibits a residual market in some agricultural goods and services. Several of the Eastern European countries, most notably Hungary, demonstrate a considerable degree of market structure within the economic system, as does Yugoslavia. Further, China may be on the brink of becoming the first self-proclaimed communist regime to permit an uncontrolled price system to operate in portions of the economy and a small business market system to exist in most sectors.[18] Neither the Eastern European nations nor China, however, come even remotely close to allowing for a national market system to exist alongside

Table 7.1
Market Indicators[13]

	Public Enterprises as % of Gross Capital Formation (most recent year)	Total Government Expenditure as % of GDP 1982	Public Sector Enterprise Employment as % of Total	General Government Employment as % of Total
Stable Democracies				
Australia	19.2 (1980)	36.1	---	25.4
Austria	19.2 (1978-79)	52.4	12.4	19.2
Belgium	13.1 (1978-79)	61.1	5.2	19.5
Canada	21.7 (1982)	---	4.5	19.9
Costa Rica	19.6 (1977-79)	25.9 (1980)	---	---
Denmark	8.3 (1974)	61.2	3.3	31.1
Finland	13.6 (1974-75)	42.9	---	19.5
West Germany	11.8 (1978)	50.5	7.9	15.6
Ireland	---	59.7	5.7	14.4
Israel	---	64.0	---	---
Italy	15.2 (1978-80)	---	6.4	15.3
Japan	11.2 (1978-81)	---	---	6.6
Netherlands	12.6 (1978)	60.3	---	15.8
New Zealand	---	44.8 (1981)	5.6	19.3
Norway	22.2 (1978-80)	53.8	4.2	22.9
Sweden	15.3 (1978-80)	71.1	8.0	31.8
Switzerland	---	37.4	---	10.4
United Kingdom	17.1 (1982)	49.4	8.2	22.4
United States	4.4 (1978)	38.3	1.6	16.7
Venezuela	36.3 (1978-80)	23.6[a] (1979)	---	---
Suspended Democracies				
France	14.0 (1974)	50.9	4.4[b]	16.1
India	33.7 (1978)	28.3[c]	---	---
Jamaica	27.4 (1978-81)	---	---	---
Sri Lanka	28.4 (1978)	34.3 (1981)	---	---
Turkey	30.4 (1982)	---	---	---

[a]Omits state government.
[b]Data for eight large key industries
[c]Omits local government.

--- not available

the public sector. None of the existing systems allows for a free price system to operate across all economic sectors. Further, all of these nations allocate credit and control investment decisions. In addition, economic association in firms, associations, unions, cooperatives and other economic groups is tightly controlled, even in Yugoslavia.[19] Hence, it can safely be concluded that the Eastern European regimes do not allow true market systems to exist, despite the claims to some "market socialism," or the existence of residual markets in the case of the Soviet Union. It is, of course, too early to say what the current Chinese experiment may or may not produce. The fact remains that, at present, all of these regimes exercise political control over most economic activity.

One questionable area in any analysis of the relationship between markets and politics concerns those regimes that are clearly nondemocratic but profess to be market oriented. Such states include military regimes, one-party states, the remaining traditional monarchies, and nations such as the Philippines where democracy had been suspended in practice, if not in form, for several decades.

Even a cursory examination of nondemocratic regimes clearly shows that many follow market-oriented economic policies through authoritarian governmental structures. Numerous authoritarian regimes have allowed many, if not all, of the market system criteria to function. Chile under the military (1973-present) and South Korea (1948-present), in particular, are clear illustrations that authoritarian regimes often use a set of market-oriented policies and structures to promote economic growth. Although neither country approaches the ideal model of a market structure in all respects, both allow for a free price system, private ownership of the means of production, relatively free entry into markets, and competition in most economic sectors. However, both regimes are relatively lax in terms of antitrust legislation and, in fact, have encouraged or at least allowed a significant degree of cartelization of the economy.[20]

Interestingly, it is at the intersection of economic freedoms and political structures that nondemocratic regimes depart significantly from market system principles. Criterion number 5 in Powell's definition of a democratic state addressed freedom of speech, press, assembly, and organization. Criteria numbers 2, 3, and 4 in the market checklist specify the need for economic freedoms, including freedom of association (firms, trade associations, cooperatives, unions), freedom to own and exchange property, and freedom of movement and information. Although these criteria were derived independently, there is an obvious relationship. For example, the free flow of information has been considered central to the functioning of market systems since the days of classical economics, while freedom of speech has been seen as equally central to democratic governance. In part, this is due to the fact that nineteenth-century liberals were reacting to the close association of class-based authority and government-granted monopoly found in European mercantilist policy and political structures.

The relationship of political structure and degree of eocnomic freedom can be seen in Freedom House's 1982 survey of economic freedom. Freedom House constructed a five-point scale to measure economic freedom based on the combined ratings for freedom of association, movement, information, and property ownership. Table 7.2 is based on the Freedom House survey.

Table 7.2
Economic Freedom and Political Structure, 1982[21]

Economic Freedom	Democratic	Authoritarian	One-party Socialist	Communist	Traditional
High	39	0	0	0	3
Medium-high	13	10	0	0	2
Medium	2	32	4	1	12
Low-medium	0	18	13	1	0
Low	0	0	2	16	0
Total	54	60	19	18	17

As with any classification system, there are a number of borderline judgments. Countries like Zimbabwe, Malaysia, and Indonesia could easily be shifted from authoritarian status to one-party socialist without doing much damage to the classification system. In addition, the economic freedom ratings are, at best, rough approximations of the degree of market freedom actually practiced in a given country. The general patterns displayed in the table, however, are striking. A few points about these patterns can be made in summary fashion.

- Chile, South Korea, Singapore, and Taiwan, often cited as examples of authoritarian regimes employing market-oriented development strategies, all rank at only a medium level of economic freedom, a position that indicates a strong degree of governmental control.
- Colombia and India are the only two democracies that rank in the medium level. None ranks lower.
- The ten authoritarian states that ranked at the medium-high level of economic freedom are Turkish Cyprus, Gambia, Lebanon, Morocco, Thailand, Panama, Senegal, Djibouti, Kenya, and Brazil. All of these, except for Djibouti, have strong democratic traditions and have, at one time or another, been governed in a democratic fashion.
- The majority of the one-party socialist and communist regimes rank at the low-medium or low level of economic freedom.

One of the most intriguing areas for future analysis is the case of what may be called the episodic democracies. These countries experience, at irregular intervals, a resurgence of the democratic form, including free elections between competing parties, only to see the system collapse under pressure. Most Latin American countries would fall into this category, as would Nigeria, India (on a subnational level), the Philippines, and, for much of modern history, France and Germany. In many, if not all, cases the collapse of political institutions results from an inability to deal with economic factors in general, and especially inflation, unemployment, and corruption. It may well be that failure to adopt a system of economic democracy through market economics contributes to the systemic failure of political democracy and its replacement with centralized regimes.

Third World Applications

Most of what could be termed the episodic democracies are part of the developing world. Though Turkey would clearly fit this category, Spain and Portugal are admittedly borderline judgments. Still, it must be admitted, neither Spain nor Portugal is part of the industrialized world in the sense that large parts of their populations live and work in a developing context despite the very large modern sectors that coexist within the countries.

With respect to the developing world, Atul Koli's recent essay, "Democracy and Development," offers some fundamental insights on the structure of both democratic institutions and market arrangements.

In state-dominated societies, democracy is likely to be, first and foremost, an affair of the elites. Third World democratic regimes are thus better understood as proto-democratic. This does not reduce the significance of democracy in a developing country. The economic performance of democratic regimes is still broader-based than that of many harsh authoritarian ones. And the human rights record of democracies is often superior. What the proto-democratic nature of Third World democracies clarifies, however, is the significance of elite consensus for the functioning of such regimes. This paper has argued that elite fragmentation is exacerbated both by the numerous competing functions that Third World political authorities are expected to perform and by the intensity of personal political ambitions generated within low-income economies. The resulting elite divisiveness has often become the motor force behind destabilizing social mobilization—ringing the death knell of many a Third World democratic experiment.[22]

Koli's insights pertain equally to the economic systems of many of these same countries. In many cases, there is no national economic system in the sense of a unified monetary regime, national taxation system, and other governmental economic functions. Thus, the national economic life of developing countries is just as much a game of the elites as are the political arrangements.

In the previous section on democratic theory, reference was made to Michael Novak's work on the moral basis of democratic capitalism and the preconditions of democracy articulated by Seymour Martin Lipset. It should be noted that Novak's moral system and each of Lipset's conditions directly address economic structures as well as the political institutional structures and rules. In this sense, capitalism, as it was thought of in the nineteenth and early twentieth centuries, is no longer an accurate description of the contemporary economic structures in the stable democratic systems. A more accurate label might be "competitive enterprise market systems." Such systems allow and indeed encourage individual initiative, formation of numerous small enterprises (entry into the market), and a dynamic (changing) economy. This is quite different from the notion that free enterprise or capitalism simply equates to private ownership of firms rather than the entire system of legal structures that govern the functioning of market systems.

The implications of a market-oriented, as distinct from capitalist, analysis are seen most clearly in a Third World context. The Institute for Liberty and Democracy (ILD) of Peru is leading the way by applying a methodology based on microeconomic analysis of formal, legal structures and the impact of these structures on market behavior and incentives. According to Hernando de Soto, the ILD president, it takes 289 working days to incorporate a new enterprise in Peru because of the complex web of regulatory decrees, licensing requirements, forms, and other impediments. This compares to an estimated three to five hours to set up an equivalent firm in the United States. The systemic impact of these structural barriers to market access is that an estimated 48.1 percent of the Peruvian work force is engaged primarily in an informal (extralegal) economy.[23]

A variety of other studies conducted for the United Nations Industrial Development Organization (UNIDO) have estimated the size of informal economies in a large nunber of Third World countries as follows:

- Bangladesh: over 85 percent of manufacturing employment in the 1970s was in small-scale cottage industries.
- India: 78 percent of manufacturing employment was in the informal sector (1979).
- Kenya: 61 percent of manufacturing employment was in enterprises of fewer than 20 workers or below a specified level of capital investment.
- Mexico: 75 percent of total manufacturing employment "could have" been in enterprises of fewer than five employees.[24]

Though these studies did not address the question of barriers to market entry, the findings suggest the need to extend the de Soto methodology to other countries. This is now happening in Latin America as projects have been or are being started in the Dominican Republic, El Salvador,

Venezuela, Argentina, Brazil, and Colombia. In all likelihood the results will show some repetition of the ILD findings, although a variety of other causes are likely to surface as well. One simple method of restricting entry, as de Soto has found in Peru, is to levy high licensing fees. This can be seen as a parallel to a poll tax, which, though legal for many years in the United States, was designed to exclude a given group of potential voters.

CONCLUSION

This chapter has provided an overview of theory, a brief analysis of markets in democratic and nondemocratic countries, and a review of some studies on that subject. In general, the material supports those who argue in favor of the view that market systems are an economic precondition of democracy. This is not to argue, however, that private enterprise development will lead to democracy according to some general law of political development. As chapter 8 will demonstrate, this quite clearly has not happened in the Third World. The argument does support, however, a general conclusion that market systems are closely related to democratic government, especially through the close relationship of economic and political freedoms.

While some authoritarian governments may use market-oriented policies, they do not permit all individuals to exercise the essential economic freedoms of information, association, and movement and, in many cases, restrict freedom to own and exchange property. For democracy to exist and remain stable, governments must allow a market system to exist within a mixed economy. This assertion cannot be demonstrated in a scientific sense; it is theoretically possible to establish some alternative system. Nonetheless, the close correlation of market systems and democratic governance found within existing democracies yields strong support for those who must deal with the challenge of promoting democratic development.

In a general sense, the most immediate relationship between democracy and market systems revolves around the role of government. Governments' actions, laws, regulations, institutions are key factors in distinguishing the degree to which a market system exists within a national economy. This remains true even in cases of oligarchy or, to use the equivalent economic term, oligopoly. Although economic and political power is concentrated in such systems in private hands, it is the governmental apparatus and legal framework that is employed to preserve the concentration of power. The issue, therefore, is not government intervention in the economy versus a completely laissez-faire policy. Rather, the issue is the degree to which government acts to create and strengthen market mechanisms versus government as a controller or director of economic outcomes.

The nature of the linkage between a democratic political system and the market-oriented economic system, therefore, is to be found in the first instance in the nature of the legal structure and, especially, the regulatory structure. U.S. Ambassador Harry Barnes recently made this point eloquently but simply in a speech to the Chamber of Commerce of Concepcion, Chile.

Democracy is not simply a system of government or a set of political processes. If the government determines who may open what business, who they may hire, where they may buy their supplies, and what prices they may charge for products or services, then there is no economic freedom, whether the government calls itself democratic or not. If the government determines the number and kind of private businesses that are permitted, then the consumer has only as much freedom of choice as the government allows. If that fundamental freedom is limited, of where we work and what we do and how we spend what we earn (sic), of how much value is freedom in the political area? And indeed, how likely is it that political freedom can endure, if every area of economic activity is rigidly controlled? I am not questioning certain essential roles for government, but I submit to you that private enterprise needs democracy, and that democracy, just as much, needs private enterprise.[25]

Another essential linkage between democratic government and market principles is found in the key freedom of association. It is this freedom of association outside governmental control that allows for the existence of a private voluntary sector and the dispersion of both political and economic power. Further, a close relationship exists between the health and vitality of business associations and other associations or private voluntary organizations. In this sense, the business associations have common cause with labor unions, media associations, academic groups, cooperatives, and other voluntary groups. It is in the interest of all to preserve and enhance the freedom of association where it exists or to fight for it where it is controlled either by dictatorial regimes of the Right or Left or by self-perpetuating oligarchies.

From this perspective, the role of business groups as advocates of democratic development is straightforward, as is the relationship between business and democracy. Business associations representing both small businesses and larger firms need to recognize that their freedom of economic activity, over the long run, is dependent upon their ability to speak out as participants in a fully functioning democratic, pluralist regime. That this is not yet the case in many parts of the world does not negate the principles involved.

In many countries, democratically oriented unions exist alongside and in fundamental opposition to communist or authoritarian unions. The same is true of cooperatives and other private groups, including academia. The basic values of pluralist democracy are found in a commitment to the freedom of association and expression that leads to full participation in the policy process. No one group can bargain away the freedom of any other without placing its own freedom in jeopardy.

An important component of the effort to promote democratic development can be stated in the following terms. Democracy and private enterprise are both evolutionary systems. That is their fundamental genius. Change is a constant part of the process. In no country has perfection of form been attained, nor is it likely to be attained. However, the basic principles that allow for freedom of association, elections, private enterprise, and other freedoms and rights are closely bound together through the legal structures and rules that establish and govern both public and private institutions. Such arrangements are essential to individual initiative, enterprise, and the economic betterment of all of the people of a nation.

NOTES

1. Charles E. Lindblom, *Politics and Markets: The World's Political-Economic Systems* (New York: Basic Books, 1977), esp. chap. 12, "Markets and Democracy." Samuel Huntington, "Will More Countries Become Democratic?" *Political Science Quarterly* 99, no. 2 (1984): 198-200. Seymour Martin Lipset, *Political Man: The Social Basis of Politics*, 2d ed. (Baltimore: Johns Hopkins University Press, 1981), pp. 469-76.

2. Huntington, op. cit., p. 205.

3. Robert A. Dahl, *Polyarchy* (New Haven: Yale University Press, 1971), pp. 59-60.

4. Lindsay M. Wright, "A Comparative Study of Economic Freedom," in Raymond D. Gastil, *Freedom in the World 1982* (Westport, Conn.: Greenwood Press, 1982), p. 88.

5. Michael Novak, *The Spirit of Democratic Capitalism* (New York: Simon & Schuster, 1982).

6. Lipset, op. cit., p. 61.

7. G. Bingham Powell, Jr., *Contemporary Democracies: Participation, Stability and Violence* (Cambridge: Harvard University Press, 1982), p. 3.

8. The criteria have been drawn from several sources, as follows: Criteria 1, 5, 6, and 7 are based on commonly used economic concepts, e.g., Jaghangir Amuzegar, *Comparative Economics* (Boston: Little, Brown, 1981), chap. 5, "Decision Making through the Market," pp. 54-67. Criteria 2, 3, and 4 are drawn from Wright, op. cit., pp. 51-69. Criterion 8 was suggested by William A. Douglas.

9. For a discussion of historical mercantilism, see Robert B. Ekelund, Jr. and Robert F. Herbert, *A History of Economic Theory and Method* (New York: McGraw-Hill, 1975), pp. 28-41, esp. p. 35. For excellent descriptions of mercantilist policies and structures in the contemporary world, see Philip Revzin, "Greek Drama," *Wall Street Journal*, March 28, 1986, p. 1, and Hernando de Soto, "Legacy of Mercantilism Stymies Market Creativity in Peru," *Wall Street Journal*, January 4, 1985, p. 15.

10. Amuzegar, op. cit., pp. 278-80.

11. For an excellent review of the literature on newly industrialized nations, including those belonging to ASEAN, see Stephan Hagard, "The Newly Industrializing Countries in the International System," *World Politics* 38 (January 1986): 343-70. See also Calvin I. Bradford, Jr., "East Asian 'Models': Myths and Lessons," in John P. Lewis and Valeriana Kallab, eds., *Development Strategies Reconsidered* (New Brunswick, N.J.: Transaction Books, 1986), pp. 115-22.

12. Powell, op. cit., p. 5.

13. Sources for table 7.1 are as follows: column 1, Robert H. Floyd, Clive S. Gray, and Robert P. Short, *Public Enterprises in Mixed Economies* (Washington, D.C.: International Monetary Fund, 1984), pp. 116-22; column 2, World Bank *World Development Report* (New York: Oxford University Press, 1985), pp. 224-25; columns 3 and 4, Peter Saunders and Friedrich Klau, *The Role of the Public Sector*, OECD Economic Studies, no. 41 (Spring 1985), pp. 63, 78.

14. For an in-depth analysis of relative shares of public and market sectors in Sweden, see Ulf Jakobsson, "Economic Growth in Sweden," in Arnold C. Harberger, *World Economic Growth* (San Francisco: Institute for Contemporary Studies Press, 1984), pp. 59-74.

15. While a persuasive case can be and has been made for the existence of one-party democracy or democracy at the local level in several African nations, these factors only point to the possible evolution of democratic systems in the future. Robert H. Jackson and Carl G. Rosberg, "Democracy in Tropical Africa," *Journal of International Affairs* 38 (Winter 1985): pp. 293-305.

16. Wright, op. cit., pp. 77-83.

17. Floyd, et al., op. cit., pp. 116-22.

18. Jan S. Prybyla, "China's Economic Experiment: From Mao to Market," *Problems of Communism* 35 (January-February 1986): 21-38.

19. Wright, op. cit., pp. 77-83.

20. On South Korea, see Sim Jae Hoon, "Time Runs out for the Conglomerates," *Far East Economic Review*, December 12, 1985, pp. 70-75.

21. Gastil, op. cit., pp. 34-35, and Wright, op. cit., pp. 77-83. For those familiar with Gastil's survey and tables, the Gastil data were reclassified here as follows: "Democratic" equals multiparty centralized and decentralized except for Turkish Cyprus, El Salvador (1982), South Korea, South Africa, Lebanon, and Brazil, which were classified as authoritarian. "Authoritarian" equals the preceding plus all dominant party regimes, one-party nationalist regimes, and military nonparty regimes. "One-party socialist" here is the same as in the Gastil classification. "Traditional regimes" equals the Gastil nonparty, nonmilitary regimes, except for Nicaragua, which was reclassified as authoritarian circa 1982.

22. Atul Koli, "Democracy and Development," in John P. Lewis and Valeriana Kallab, *Development Strategies Reconsidered* (New Brunswick, N.J.: Transaction Books, 1986), p. 178.

23. Hernando de Soto, "Legacy of Mercantilism Stymies Market Creativity in Peru," unpublished manuscript available from de Soto's Institute for Liberty and Democracy, Lima, Peru.

24. Reviewed in C. H. Kirkpatrick, N. Lee, and F. I. Nixson, *Industrial Structure and Policy in Less Developed Countries* (London: Allen & Unwin, 1984), pp. 50-53.

25. Harry G. Barnes, "Democracy and the Private Sector," speech to the Chamber of Commerce of Concepcion, Chile, June 23, 1986.

8 A MARKET-ORIENTED APPROACH TO DEMOCRATIC DEVELOPMENT: PAST AND FUTURE PROGRAMS
John D. Sullivan

An overview of the theory of democratic development and its relationship to the concept of a market system was presented in chapter 7. The general conclusion was that there is a close relationship between market systems and democratic government, at least within the existing democracies. Given this finding, this chapter begins with a survey of past U.S. efforts to promote and support development of market economies in the developing world. Based on this review, some new approaches are then suggested.

SURVEY OF PRIVATE ENTERPRISE PROGRAMS

Despite the differing interpretations that may be made regarding the relationships between market structures, private enterprise, and democratic development, it is obvious that there is a close fit. Most observers would agree that efforts to foster democratic development in the Third World and the European southern flank should include a specific private enterprise component to ensure that business elites do not undermine efforts to promote democracy. If there is agreement in principle, however, there is little agreement as to specific programs. The purpose of this section is to provide a brief review of past efforts in order to put current programs in context. The survey focuses specifically on private

The views expressed here are those of the author and do not necessarily reflect those of the U.S. Chamber of Commerce or the Center for International Private Enterprise.

enterprise, market economics, and business institutions rather than the entire field of economic development. The survey first examines the policy framework, then the actual instruments, and concludes with a brief overview of the results obtained.

The Policy Framework

Democratic development through economic growth led by private enterprise was one of the principal goals of the early U.S. foreign assistance programs. In 1963, shortly after creation of the Agency for International Development (AID), an advisory committee on private enterprise in foreign aid was chaired by Arthur K. Watson of the IBM World Trade Corporation and included labor, business, and academic leaders among its membership. The report of the Watson committee, issued in 1965, offered the following general statement of goals:

In our efforts to achieve [private sector] societies of this sort abroad, therefore, we must be prepared to accept the appearance of certain seeming contradictions in our efforts. We must be prepared not only to encourage the growth of private enterprise but also to encourage other institutions with which such enterprise will sometimes cooperate, sometimes clash, for example: an effective structure of government organizations, a creative and responsible structure for the conduct of labor relations, an efficient system of cooperative organizations where such organizations are appropriate, and a series of institutions devoted to educational, philanthropic, and other non-profit activities. It is out of such a ferment that economic growth and the democratic process may be expected to appear.[1]

The policy thrust advocated in the Watson report placed substantial emphasis on private sector development and, in this respect, it reflected the prevailing mood of the period.

Dissatisfaction began to grow, however, with the results of the programs that were perceived to be benefiting the rich to the detriment of the poor majority. In 1966, Congress added a new title to the Foreign Assistance Act designed to increase the participation of the poor majority in the process of development. Title IX gave AID the following mandate:

In carrying out programs authorized in this chapter, emphasis shall be placed on assuring maximum participation in the task of economic development on the part of the people of the developing countries, through the encouragement of democratic private and local government institutions.[2]

Throughout the remainder of the 1960s and into the early 1970s, debate continued over the appropriate models of development. In large part this debate was driven by the obvious and increasing gaps evident in income distribution patterns in Third World countries. Equally important, however, was the impact of the Great Society model of economic development as practiced in the United States. Given the political tone of these years, it was not surprising that the foreign aid legislation was changed to address the problems of poverty abroad. In 1973 the Foreign Assistance Act was given a "new direction" to address "basic human needs."

United States bilateral development assistance should give the highest priority to undertakings submitted by host governments which directly improve the lives of the poorest of these people and their capacity to participate in the development of their countries.[3]

It would be misleading to assume that the new policy thrust outlined above completely replaced the earlier private enterprise thrust. What it did was to alter dramatically the allocation of funds. This shift resulted in a substantial de-emphasis of private enterprise development.

With the advent of the 1980s, the development model has once again shifted. Today the market mechanism is seen as an appropriate development model, and the emphasis on democratic development has once again surged to the fore. In 1983, for example, the Commission on Security and Economic Assistance, which was chaired by Frank C. Carlucci and included 22 members of Congress and 14 private sector leaders, issued a report entitled "Security and Economic Assistance" that addresses U.S. foreign assistance programs. Among 17 specific recommendations, the Carlucci report called for the following:

The Commission endorses the use of our bilateral and multilateral cooperation programs to promote and encourage the growth of indigenous private sectors and U.S. private sector contributions to the development process. The strengthening of free trade unions and the promotion of employment-oriented development strategies, in an environment conducive to free enterprise, are integral to sound long-term growth and security. Both bilateral and multilateral programs should be used to achieve appropriate policy reforms and to support these objectives wherever feasible.[4]

The Reagan administration, under the leadership of Peter McPherson, administrator of AID, has attempted to reinvigorate private enterprise policy as one of several key elements in the U.S. foreign assistance program. The most recent (March 1985) AID policy paper on "Private Enterprise Development" contains the following key passages:

AID assistance to an LDC should encourage social and economic development that promotes movement toward a democratic, free market society. It is AID's view that such societies are most efficient for generating broad based, sustained economic growth and social progress. AID should program its resources in support of LDC performance towards this objective.

. . . AID's promotion of free markets and the private sector should not be confused with monopoly enterprises, oligarchy or "crony capitalism," which have little to do with the free market. AID's effort to encourage competition and entrepreneurial activity is as much a challenge to the limited capitalism extant in some countries as it is in statist economies.

. . . Assistance to promote competitive market conditions and indigenous private enterprises should not be considered as a separate portfolio of activity independent of other sectors of interest to the country assistance strategy, such as agriculture, health, education, etc. The promotion of a democratic, free market economy should underpin and be incorporated in all aspects of AID's country programs.[5]

These policy statements are quite similar to those advanced in the Watson committee report issued twenty years earlier.

The Instruments

During the post–World War II period, vast amounts of funds have been transferred from the developed to the developing world. Between 1970 and 1982, for example, $185.5 billion was transferred in total governmental grants and concessionary loans from the Organization for Economic Cooperation and Development countries, and an additional $16.7 billion flowed from private voluntary agencies in these same nations.[6] Between 1946 and 1982, U.S. official foreign aid alone amounted to $157 billion, of which $106.9 billion was in the form of grants and $50.2 billion was in the form of loans at concessionary rates.[7] Unfortunately, it is not possible to segregate out of the official data the amounts related to private enterprise development. This is due to the indirect nature of these programs, some of which focused on infrastructure development, some on financing industrial development through governmental projects, and some on food assistance. Arguably, projects of these types are essential supports for development of private enterprise systems.

This section will focus on the principal U.S. agency, AID, and those of its instruments that have been directed specifically toward private enterprise development. According to a recent study conducted by Deborah Orsini for the President's Task Force on International Private Enterprise, several major private sector programs have been implemented by AID and its predecessor agencies. They can be summarized as follows:

- *Industrial Development*. During the 1950s and early 1960s, funds were loaned at concessionary rates to establish industrial centers, enterprises, and productivity centers.

- *Small Scale Enterprise Development*. During the 1960s, AID initiated a large number of financial and technical assistance projects designed to stimulate growth of small private enterprises. These projects continued on a much reduced scale during the 1970s. For example, of 240 Asian projects, 95 percent were initiated between 1952 and 1973 (half in Korea and Taiwan), and of 230 projects in Latin America and the Caribbean, 75 percent were initiated prior to 1974.

- *Technology Transfer*. Beginning in the 1960s it was recognized that technology appropriate to the industrial nations would need to be modified and explained in the developing world. Some of these technology transfer programs are directly related to the small enterprise programs described above; others were in the area of rural/agricultural development. Most continue today and have been expanded.

- *Training*. During the 1970s, AID resources were often used to establish vocational and management training centers because of increased recognition that the skills and knowledge to make use of financial assistance were in short supply in the developing world. Programs begun during this period established the Central American Institute for Management, the Panamanian Association of Business Executives, and a graduate school of business in Peru.

- *Capital Market Development*. During the 1960s and again in the 1980s, emphasis was placed on establishment of intermediary credit institutions, such as the Korean Development Bank and the Korean Medium Industry Bank, the Ivory Coast Development Bank, and widespread use of credit unions and savings and loan associations in Latin America.

- *Foreign Private Enterprise Promotion*. During the 1960s promotion of direct foreign investment was an AID priority. Programs directed to this end included investment guarantees, investment centers and groups, cofinancing agreements, and "Cooley loans" derived for sale of P.L. 480 agriculture assistance in local currency.

- *Export Promotion and Tourism*. The early foreign assistance projects run by AID and its predecessors focused heavily on import substitution. It was found, however, that developing countries also had to increase exports to generate foreign exchange and develop markets of sufficient size to support industrial development. Accordingly, AID funded several export promotion programs during the 1960s and 1970s, the most successful of which were in Korea and Taiwan.

- *Foreign Exchange Access Savings*. Over $1.7 billion has been made available through a variety of programs including P.L. 480 assistance, the economic support fund, and other instruments to generate foreign exchange or to substitute local currency.

- *Policy Dialogue*. AID has often attempted to generate change in foreign governments' economic policies that would initiate macroeconomic trends favorable to private sector development. Foreign exchange access loans and grants, including economic support funds, have often been employed in this fashion. On occasion, AID has attempted to influence government programs as well, such as manpower training.[8]

In its efforts to reinvigorate the private enterprise approach, the Reagan administration has now established a bureau for private enterprise (PRE) to conduct programs directly and to work in concert with other AID bureaus to stimulate private enterprise programs in other divisions. In 1984, PRE direct programs included the following:[9]

- investments and capital market development ($15 million)
- management and technical training ($2 million)
- technology transfer ($7.4 million)
- investment stimulus ($2.35 million)

Other recent AID private enterprise initiatives have included support for privatization of state-owned enterprises, creation of a management institute in Thailand, funding for a major study on deregulation of Peru's mercantilist economy,[10] major projects in capital market development, and establishment of trade and promotion centers in a number of African countries. In 1984, AID funded more than $200 million in direct private enterprise programs, in addition to the $30 million PRE budget. This, however, represents a very small percentage of AID's budget.

Evaluations of Foreign Assistance and Development Models

Despite the central importance attached to promotion of democratic development through programs described above, there have been very few in-depth studies of the degree to which such programs have contributed to these goals. In particular, the private enterprise model advocated in AID's early years and revitalized by the Reagan administration has not yet been the subject of independent evaluation. This is not to say that development economics has ignored the topic; exactly the opposite is true. There is a growing body of literature on models of economic growth and development. In this section, both subjects will be treated: first, the evaluations of private sector programs; second, a more general discussion of conditions for growth in the context of democratic development.

Deborah Orsini's report to the President's Task Force on International Private Enterprise reached several conclusions based on a survey of internal AID program evaluations. The technology transfer and foreign private enterprise promotion programs were seen as the most successful. The capital market development and training programs achieved satisfactory results. In contrast, the industrial development programs and policy dialogues appeared to be generally unsuccessful. Additionally, Orsini found that those programs that were demand driven (from recipient country) and involved direct linkages between U.S. business and counterparts abroad were most successful. Further, the major obstacle to capital markets and other development was found to be the lack of exposure and management skills; hence, both capital and technical assistance are necessary. Finally, subsidies and bail-outs should be avoided in favor of assistance to successful, self-sustaining firms and institutions.[11]

These program instruments were evaluated in the context of specific project goals. The larger question of the degree to which AID and other private sector programs actually succeeded in fostering democratic, market-oriented systems remains to be addressed. In this context, AID should consider funding an outside research and evaluation program to look at these and related issues.

Conversely, the extent to which foreign aid in general promotes economic growth has been addressed from several perspectives. A growing body of literature has questioned whether aid makes any contribution to growth, much less democracy. P. T. Bauer exemplifies those who have come to this conclusion, based primarily on theoretical arguments and situations (e.g., Vietnam and Angola), particularly those situations where multilateral aid has flowed from the West to countries that were neither democratic nor growing. Arguing from a macroeconomic perspective, Bauer concludes that[12]

Even though foreign aid can alleviate immediate shortages, it cannot appreciably promote the growth of the national income. It is more likely to retard this growth. Countries where government or business can use funds productively can borrow abroad. The maximum contribution of foreign aid to development in the sense of the growth of the national income cannot therefore exceed the avoided cost of borrowing. As a percentage of the national income of large Third World countries this maximum contribution is at best minute, a fraction of 1%, far too small to register the statistics.

Bauer also points out that much of foreign assistance, particularly multilateral assistance, goes to support large-scale programs channeled through Third World governments for construction of state-owned enterprises and support of projects in the public sector.

Conversely, proponents of foreign aid argue that there have been some major developmental successes. John Lewis of the Overseas Development Council, for example, points to the improvement in South Asian food production as a case where aid was a "strong, indispensable catalyst" although not the main force. Lewis also cites the building of key development institutions, lowering of birth rates, and economic expansion in South Korea and Taiwan.[13] Such efforts may not show up in macroeconomic analysis since their main efforts are felt in key sectors, especially agriculture, that create multiplier effects in the overall economy.

An alternative view has been put forth by Samuel Huntington and Joan

Nelson from a development model perspective. They argue that the liberal development model of the 1950s and 1960s (which has increased relevance today) assumes

that the causes of socio-economic inequality, political violence, and lack of demo-cratic political participation lay in the socio-economic backwardness of a society. The answer to these ills, consequently, was rapid socio-economic modernization and development, which would increase the overall level of economic well-being in the society and thus make possible a more equitable distribution of wealth, promote political stability, and provide the basis for broader political partici-pation and more democratic systems of government.[14]

In contrast, Huntington and Nelson argue that "political violence and instability have been shown to be more prevalent in societies in the midst of the process of modernization and development than in societies at the lowest level of development."[15] It is certainly true that economic growth often results in increased income gaps between rich and poor in the early and middle development stages and that such gaps, combined with increasing literacy, often lead to demands for increased political participation, which, in turn, can invite repression by elite groups deter-mined to avoid the results of such participation.

The analyses summarized above are largely unsatisfactory from the perspective of making judgments about the efficacy of foreign aid in achieving democracy-promoting objectives. Although Bauer's writings and the study by Huntington and Nelson serve to debunk much of the grand rhetoric surrounding foreign aid, they do not distinguish between individual instruments. As is seen in Orsini's study, it is certainly possible that some aid programs have succeeded in their objectives whereas others have not. What is needed is a grid against which to measure policies and programs.

The beginnings of such a grid can be found in the recent literature on economic growth. For example, Keith Marsden's recent comparative study of 17 high- and low-growth economies in Africa and Asia demon-strates that several conditions are essential for growth and effective foreign aid. While Marsden cautions that his conclusions are tentative and need to be further confirmed through inclusion of other nations, he does offer the following:

First, economic growth depends largely upon domestic policies. Second, financial flows from abroad are most likely to raise output if the policy environment is hospitable and conducive to growth. This assumes, of course, that the projects and activities being financed are well selected in the first place. Third, at least in the market economies covered in this analysis, the private sector tends to be more efficient than the public sector and flourishes best when provided ample access to credit and foreign exchange and when not burdened by heavy taxes. Fourth, countries with governments that do not resort to excessive domestic or foreign commercial borrowing to finance budgetary deficits appear to sustain more rapid growth. Fifth, to be most useful, foreign aid should either reinforce effective policies or promote the reform of defective policies.[16]

Lloyd Reynolds's comprehensive review of the record of Third World economic growth from 1850 to 1980 reaches parallel conclusions, though foreign aid is not part of the analysis.

In this era [post 1940], as in earlier eras, some countries have progressed much faster than others, while some have not progressed at all. The explanation for these differences does not seem to be mainly in the realm of factor endowments. Some countries with poor natural resources, such as Taiwan and Korea, have done well, while some resource-rich countries, such as Zaire, are still floundering. My hypothesis is that the single most important explanatory variable is political organization and the administrative competence of government.[17]

One of the most interesting findings to emerge from this review of the sparse literature on foreign aid, growth, and democratic development is the emphasis on policy, political organization, and governmental effectiveness as major determinants of growth. This is precisely the area where AID's programs, especially the policy dialogue, have been least successful. The relationship sketched out by Huntington and Nelson regarding growth and development as destabilizing factors is undoubtedly one key reason for the failure of policy dialogues. Historically, oligarchic or dictatorial elites have been unlikely to alter their domestic economic policies when they believe that foreign aid will continue for strategic reasons related to the overriding goal of containing communism. Recently in El Salvador and the Philippines, U.S. policy has an alternative effect. The debate over the need for the military bases versus the need to support democracy in the Philippines was settled not by the administration, but by the entire U.S. political process, and this may signal a change in policy from containment to democratic development.

NEW APPROACHES TO DEMOCRATIC DEVELOPMENT

Thus far the analysis suggests that the traditional aid strategy of pursuing democratic development through economic, social, and cultural development is overly simplistic in its assumptions. While there is a clear association between market economics and democratic institutions, that association is not a simple cause-and-effect relationship. Further, few AID programs are actually targeted toward private enterprise development and, of these, even fewer seek to promote the adoption of market economics. Seen from the perspective of economic growth, the key factor differentiating low- and high-growth countries is the policy environment, yet it is in this very area that some foreign assistance programs, such as the policy dialogue, have had the least success.

The United States government has long recognized the need for explicit political development programs that could complement and enhance various economic and social development programs. It was for this reason that the National Endowment for Democracy (NED) was created.[18]

Goals and Constraints

Building on the material presented above, this section articulates an approach to democratic development that specifically employs business and the market system. What is advocated here should be seen within the context of existing efforts, including those of AID, the U.S. Information Agency (USIA), and NED. The approach is a partial one; programs targeted at other sectors, including political parties, cooperatives, academia, labor, media, women's groups, and civic and social organizations are equally essential.

Within an overall strategy of democratic development, business and economic arrangements are of fundamental importance. Most societies in the developing world have yet to solve the key problem of generating economic growth at low levels of inflation in order to create jobs and improve living standards. While this problem is generally recognized, it is not always felt that democracy is the optimum system to provide a solution. In fact, it is often said by developing country leaders that "we are too poor to afford democracy." Further, in many countries, private enterprise is viewed very negatively as a result of the misperception that economic arrangements practiced by colonial regimes constituted market systems when in fact they more closely resembled mercantilist regimes. Leaders in developing countries, therefore, have often adopted some variant of an authoritarian structure, based on central planning, government investment, and wage and price controls as the preferred solution. Even in those cases where there is a genuine aspiration for democracy, there are usually alternative elites that would prefer an authoritarian structure.

The first goal, therefore, is to establish, beyond doubt, that democracy can and does provide solutions to the growth dilemma. This requires two steps. First, the relationship between market systems and democratic institutions must be further specified on a country-by-country basis. In order to gain elite acceptance for institutional reform, the analysis and the logic must be based on indigenous factors, otherwise people simply say, "That's fine for other countries, but we have special problems."

Comparisons are indeed very important, but their value is established only once the unique country problems are addressed.

The second part of the task is to gain popular acceptance of the value of democracy and market economics. Obviously, this involves a full-scale program of communications and education on a country-by-country basis. However, some economies of scale can be attained once a critical mass of Third World prodemocracy movements is reached. For example, once there are a number of regional (Latin American, African, etc.) opinion leaders who support democratic market systems, the movement will gain credibility and, hence, adherents across national borders. Indeed, several of the recent transitions to democracy in Latin America probably emerged from such regional influences, and the remaining authoritarian regimes have come under considerable pressure to liberalize as a result of regional trends and movements. Though the existence of these regional movements does not eliminate the need for individual national programs, they should generate increased local resources and spontaneous, locally initiated efforts.

As a second goal, democratic movements and governments must not only promise growth, but they must also deliver. In the short run, pressures for change in system structure may be channeled into elections and alteration of parties in office. Over the medium term, however, poor economic performance may generate pressures sufficient to overthrow a democratic regime. Historically, a large number of emerging democratic governments have been supplanted for exactly this reason.

Given these two initial goals, it is vitally important that the mix of structural elements and governmental policies be appropriate not only for the survival of democracy but also for economic growth. Further, this economic growth must provide benefits for all elements of the population, not just for an elite group.

A 1985 AID policy paper identifies a number of policy and structural constraints often found in the Third World that deter economic growth through market mechanisms. The paper notes that many of these constraints follow from development strategies adopted over the last 30 years, particularly those that pursue an import substitution (substituting domestically produced goods for imports) type of policy, in whole or in part. The following is a list of the principal constraints identified:

- Foreign exchange policies and regulations
- Import/export restrictions
- Banking restrictions
- Market entry restrictions
- Limitations on investments

- Investment promotion programs
- Governmental monopolies, state-owned enterprises, and restraint of trade
- Price fixing
- Subsidies
- Labor market regulations
- Taxation and user charges
- Government provision of services best provided by private sources[19]

Neither the AID paper nor the strategy offered here is intended to eliminate governments. Rather, policies and legal structures adopted by governments are seen to be a primary determinant of economic performance. In the area of labor market restrictions, for example, a minimum wage is appropriate, but it must be one that reflects economic costs in order to avoid uneconomic substitution of capital for labor. Similarly, labor rules must not be so restrictive as to prevent firings or layoffs justified by either individual performance or changes in economic conditions. In the same vein, taxes need to be nondiscriminatory and equitable in administration. Excessive use of "hidden" taxes distorts economic performance and makes products noncompetitive, and excessively high rates force capital to flee or to be put to nonproductive uses.

At the same time, the democratic market approach must resolve the issue of income distribution in the near term. As was noted earlier, the 1950s version of private sector development became unpalatable because of the excessive concentration of benefits among upper socioeconomic levels. The recent recognition of the claims of the informal or microenterprise sector will help alleviate this problem. If, once appropriate structural changes are made, it can be demonstrated that entrepreneurship is a viable development option, then market systems can gain vocal advocates among the majority of the people, even those living in poverty. Further, establishment of a viable small business economy does much to insulate a nation against drastic economic fluctuations and provides a source of employment for growing urban populations.

There are a variety of other societal constraints that must be overcome to accomplish the goals described above. As in the case of policy/structural constraints, these vary in nature and degree from country to country and region to region, but most exist in some form in nearly every developing country. These societal constraints on market development include, but are by no means limited to the following:

- *Fragmentation* of the business community into various groups according to size (formal versus informal), sector, geographic location, and organizational structure is frequent.

- *Organization* of businesses in associations, chambers of commerce, research groups, and other organizations ranges from weak to nonexistent, with the occasional exception of newly industrialized states. When they exist, such groups are often under governmental influence or control, and this inhibits collective action necessary for democratic development.

- *Voluntary service* in business associations and other civic organizations often is a foreign concept in many developing societies, as are the traditions of organizational democracy based on formal rules of order.

- *Attitudes* toward business, profits, and entrepreneurship are often negative as a result of prevailing oligarchic structures, colonial legacies, or some combination of both.

- *Knowledge* of market economics is often lacking even among business, academic, and governmental leaders, and this results in an inability to distinguish between market-oriented policies and mercantilist or oligarchic policies.

- *Educational levels* are often insufficient to support emergence of market behavior, particularly in the least developed societies, where illiteracy and lack of numerical skills inhibit even rudimentary entrepreneurship and consumer behaviors.

- *Pluralism* is often excessive, resulting in a lack of national cohesion due to systemwide cleavages along ethnic, social, or religious lines as distinguished from the cross-cutting functional pluralism engendered by economic groupings (e.g., unions, associations, occupations).

- *Corruption* is endemic in many Third World societies, occasionally reaching the extreme case of crony capitalism found in the Philippines.[20]

There are obviously other constraints of a regional or national character. For example, nations with majority or dominant Islamic cultures are often cited as examples of countries that will resist democracy, yet, it is also often suggested that they are quite open to private enterprise, if not a market system. The validity of these positions has not been fully established for Islamic cultures that have experienced either a colonial history or some Westernizing influence. The great degree of variation even among the Arab Islamic states may be seen in the differences in attitude toward democracy between Saudi Arabia and Egypt. Similar statements are often made about Asian societies, particularly those based on a Confucian tradition. Current developments in the ASEAN nations and South Korea will test such propositions. It may be that development of an extensive small business culture will challenge the hierarchical cultural values inherent in Confucian or Islamic societies, thus creating a basis for development of market systems and, ultimately, pluralist governmental structures. In any case, there is little doubt that culture, especially religion, has a direct effect on the potential for democratic development.

Equally significant are the constraints that arise when one nation attempts to influence, guide, or support developments in another country. Ralph Goldman's chapter "The Donor-recipient Relationship in Political Aid Programs" discusses these. Any effort by Americans or others to promote democratic development in foreign countries must take these constraints into account.

Program Elements

Specific programs designed to overcome the policy/structural and general societal constraints to establishing democratic, market systems must be designed for specific countries. Nevertheless, some general program objectives can be stated, based on knowledge of conditions in a variety of countries.

- Democratic, market-oriented policies, including structural reform, must be developed by indigenous leaders or groups on the basis of a carefully documented analysis of existing conditions. This must include explicit consideration of barriers to market entry, informal economies, income distribution effects, and other politically relevant topics.

- Governmental performance must be significantly enhanced, particularly as it relates to performance of key economic functions such as regulatory management, policy formation, issuance of licenses and permits, collection and dissemination of economic statistics, foreign exchange management, education, and vocational training.

- Governmental and business ethics conducive to competitive markets and democratic institutions must be encouraged through good government campaigns and enforced through rigorous applications of law.

- Knowledge of the benefits and structure of market economics and democratic institutions must be imparted to indigenous leaders and, through these leaders, to selected publics in the society.

- Rapid development of a viable small business economy must be stimulated through structural reforms that address the issues leading to informal economies, through educational programs designed to instill business skills, and through integration of all business sectors into a national economy.

- Values and attitudes conducive to private and individual initiative, entrepreneurship, market systems, and democratic institutions must be instilled in the population by and through indigenous leaders and organizations committed to the concept of economic growth.

Accomplishment of the above general objectives requires development of strong indigenous institutions, firmly supported by a domestic constituency. The reasons for this are fundamental to democratic development. In the first instance, attempts by foreign nationals, however benign, to affect policy structure and values in another country inevitably breed a nationalist reaction unless some indigenous leaders, though not necessarily all, are in the vanguard of the program. Leadership, however, is not the same as government or officially sanctioned leaders or organizations. Rather, leadership groups are those with domestic supporters, some form of organization, and, most importantly, legitimacy.

Business institutions play a central role in development of market-oriented reforms listed above. However, a fully elaborated network of voluntary business organization exists in few countries outside the industrial economies. At first glance, it would seem to require only a simple solution—establish a major trade association or chamber of commerce and centralize all activity within that institution. Such a solution, however, runs counter to the logic of the market system and fails to account for the very divergent functions performed by different types of organization. In market economies, business decision making on all issues, including policy, must remain in the hands of the member firms. If only one institution existed, power would inevitably become centralized and, thus, undermine the logic of the market. As a practical matter, divergent views in democratic societies will give rise to competing organizations when and if one institution were to attempt to impose policy on a membership or portion of that membership.

Two solutions have been adopted in various countries. The first is to require, by law, membership in a single institution. The result has tended to undermine both democracy and market freedoms, as is described in chapter 7. The second solution, consonant with both market freedom and democratic theory, is to establish a multiplicity of voluntary business institutions, each of which has carefully circumscribed functions.

Though it is beyond the scope of this paper to provide an in-depth description of a model business institution infrastructure, the following list sets out the general functions in summary fashion:

- *Sectoral trade associations* focus on matters of concern to their industry or industries, including policy representation to governments, lobbying (if allowed), setting industry standards, professional education, research, and advertising campaigns.

- *Small business associations* normally restrict their membership by some size standard. Their main purpose is to draw national (or local) attention to the special needs and concerns of small firms through legislative or policy initiatives, public relations, representation on governmental bodies and commissions, and the like.

- *National umbrella groups* or peak associations represent the business community as a whole on national issues that affect all firms regardless of size, industry, or geographical location. The national group usually has a number of the functions described above for associations and local organizations. However, its major distinguishing characteristic is the task of forming a business consensus among its membership, including the constituent trade associations, local chambers and other specialized business groups.

- *Public policy think tanks, business research centers, and policy forums* play a vital role in researching national economic conditions, formulating recommendations for reform, and articulating these views to the overall business community, governmental bodies, elected officials, academics, and other opinion leaders.[21]

A wide variety of business organizations exist. In many parts of the world, for example, employers' federations have the principal responsibility for labor relations issues, including labor-related legislative issues and collective bargaining. Other examples of special purpose groups include economic education foundations, regional or community development institutions (nongovernmental), and associations devoted to the special needs of women and racial, ethnic, or linguistic minority–owned firms.

As has been mentioned, the description of the model business organization is drawn from the advanced industrial nations. Few countries in the developing world display the entire range of organizations, although most have established some form of business infrastructure. The least developed nations, especially those in Africa, tend also to be the least developed in terms of organizational structure. The essential question, however, is not simply the degree to which an organizational structure exists but the degree to which it is: (1) representative of the private business community; (2) independent of governmental control; and (3) willing and able to address the policy/structural and general societal barriers to development of market economics and democratic institutions.

Applications

Although an attempt has been made to sketch out a general approach to development of market systems and democratic institutions, it must be recognized that vast differences obtain on a regional basis and, within regions, on a country basis. Indeed, the very terms *Third World* and *developing world* are misnomers to some extent. In this section a corrective is offered by suggestions about the application of the concepts and approaches outlined. It will be suggestive only for two reasons. First, the scope of analysis is far beyond the limits of a single chapter. Second, and more fundamental, much of the information needed for rigorous program development does not yet exist in many parts of the world and must, therefore, be developed with a degree of urgency.

Since attempts to construct political development programs employing business organizations are brand new, discussion of specific programs must be tentative in the extreme. However, over the last two years, the Center for International Private Enterprise (CIPE) has implemented a number of projects in a broad cross-section of nations at various levels of development. These projects were intended to serve as models for the type of projects that can be developed.

- *Institute for Liberty and Democracy (ILD) (Peru).* A model program of deregulation designed to remove the barriers to market entry resulting from the mercantilist legal system. ILD's program includes cost-benefit analysis of proposed regulations, public advocacy of deregulation in major media, redesign of municipal regulations, creation of an ombudsman's office in the national government, and public hearings on law and public policy issues.
- *Center for Studies in Economics and Education (Mexico).* An education and advocacy program that provides economic education for journalists and prepares editorials expressing a market system viewpoint on major public issues. The editorials and stories written by journalists appear in 25 leading papers.
- *Chamber of Free Enterprise (Guatemala).* A seminar to expose over 100 Guatemalan and Salvadoran business leaders to political techniques, including survey research, issue identification, direct mail, youth programs, interest group development, and media relations.
- *Philippine Chamber of Commerce and Industry.* An institution-building program designed to strengthen local chambers in the provinces, build an external communications capability within the organization, and conduct surveys on important national issues.
- *Journal of Economic Growth (Worldwide).* A quarterly journal published in English and Spanish and featuring articles by an international group of authors on the political economy of rapid economic growth.

In addition to the specific examples listed above, many of these program types are replicated in other countries. For example, work in the informal economy is also proceeding in Argentina, Central America, and Kenya. Enterprise education programs are being implemented in Mexico, Panama, and Argentina to improve understanding of market economics and popular attitudes toward business. Programs similar to the Philippine institution-building effort are ongoing in Zimbabwe and the Dominican Republic. Equally important, professional development programs are being carried out through regional centers in Costa Rica for all of Latin America and in India for South Asia.

Each of the projects described above is intended to address the constraints to development of market systems and democratic institutions described previously.

Experience gained through projects run by AID, USIA, NED, and CIPE suggests some redirection that could well be made in official U.S. government efforts. Although official U.S. government programs are precluded from involvement in direct political programs such as those the endowment can support, there is still a great deal of room for substantial program efforts.

AID's foreign assistance efforts are targeted at the least developed countries of Central and South America, Africa, and Asia. In these cases, AID's private enterprise efforts should focus heavily on development of business institutions, small business development, resolving the issues of informal economies, structural and policy reform, and economic research. Such projects should rely heavily on joint efforts between the U.S. private sector and its counterpart organizations in the target countries, primarily because the private-sector-to-private-sector approach has been found by AID's own evaluations to be the most effective instrument.

The Peace Corps can play a vital supportive role in private sector development by emphasizing its greatest success story—education. The Peace Corps should put priority emphasis on economic and business education in primary schools, adult literacy programs, high schools, and colleges. Such projects need not divert attention from traditional subjects since they can be integrated into an existing curriculum. Peace Corps education efforts, however, should not attempt to transfer business skills unless the agency is prepared to recruit experienced small business people to take on the assignments.

USIA has a key role to play since its programs are not limited to the least developed nations. In recent years, USIA exchange programs have begun to include business association staffs and business-oriented policy organizations that would form linkages between such groups internationally. These could be expanded, particularly in Africa and Asia. USDA television, radio, and print media need to focus much more heavily on business and economic topics of interest to the European nations and, especially, small business topics of interest to the developing world. In many cases information and knowledge are much more scarce than capital. USIA's ability to reach Eastern Europe and the Soviet Union is especially vital in any long-term effort in this region.

The State Department can play a major role in the development of democratic market systems, as may be seen in the Philippine case. However, the State Department should also look into the role of international business organizations as potential recipients of assistance. In contrast to labor, international business organizations are fragmented, weak, and often ineffectual. Priority attention to the International Chamber of Commerce and the International Organization of Employers could create multiplier effects in many countries where a more direct U.S. message could be counterproductive.

CONCLUSIONS

This chapter began with the observation that democratic institutions and pluralist values are embedded within a larger economic and social context. Some have suggested that both democracy and market systems, as defined herein, are uniquely institutions of the North and West. There is merit to this argument; of all the stable democracies, Japan is the only one that is non-Western, and this may be a result of the U.S. occupation. Of the emerging democracies, India, along with the few African democracies, the Philippines, and all of Latin America, could be similarly seen.

There are two fallacies in this view, however. First, it is certainly possible that democracy could be imposed, but it must be acknowledged that democracy can be quickly replaced by the peoples concerned. Second, there are today articulate and intensely nationalistic leaders in most countries in the world pressing for democratic reform in the interest of achieving systems that guarantee individual rights and liberties.

There is also considerable support for the notion that some cultures, most notably Confucian and Islamic societies, are not compatible with democracy. These two cultures, historically, have been hierarchical in nature and adherents of fairly rigid codes of conduct. It may be that neither Confucian nor Islamic society will develop or sustain democratic institutions or Western-style market economies.[22] Conversely, it is also possible that cultural change will occur as a result of the communications revolution, the worldwide demand by women for equal participation, and, most significantly, the need to sustain economic growth. It should be recalled that for most of recorded history, economies grew as a natural result of population growth; the economic base grew simply because the number of producers and consumers increased. Only in the last two centuries in the industrialized nations, and only since 1850 in most of the rest of the world, have economies grown as a result of increased productivity and industrialization. The consequences of this historical shift are only now being felt.[23] Some form of democracy and market freedom may be necessary to sustain such patterns of growth once an economy reaches full industrialization and becomes consumer-oriented and urban.

However, it is essential to reiterate the observation that political systems do not simply evolve out of social, economic, or cultural patterns according to some law of political development. Rather, democracy or any alternative form of governance must be willed by the peoples concerned. In some cases, as in Eastern Europe or Afghanistan, the will is obviously and brutally suppressed by outside forces cooperating with indigenous factions. The same, however, cannot be said of the Soviet Union, China, Cuba, and Nicaragua. In these countries, the most that can be said is that one elite group has imposed a system with the active cooperation of a dictatorial minority, despite continued opposition by a counterelite and a substantial minority that is democratically oriented. In all of the communist countries, economics is one of the primary elements in the governments' control systems.

The history of Western democracy suggests that most stable democracies have followed a path of sequential development. Europe and the United States were not market systems or democracies throughout most of the eighteenth century. Rather, they were mercantilist systems wherein close alliances were formed between the government and the owners of capital to perpetuate a system of mutual advantage. Indeed, the American Revolution was stimulated in large part by the mercantilist system of controls employed by the crown in its regulation and taxation policies in the colonial governments. Gradually, over a period of some 200 years, both democratic and market freedoms expanded, by both peaceful change and violent conflict.

Although it is quite risky to venture historical generalization, one broad pattern does seem to exist: Political democracy and competitive market economies tended to develop together in a phased progression. Each step forward in establishing a democratic political system seems to have reinforced a parallel step forward in the expansion of market freedom. The increase in economic freedom then supported demands for increased democratic freedoms, and so on. This has not been an inevitable process; indeed, it has been fragile and uncertain. Any number of outside forces, such as war, assassination, or national or international economic collapse, have halted, reversed, or altered the path of change. The contemporary developing world, however, seeks to advance both democracy and market systems all at one time. This is especially true of the least developed nations, but also, to a lesser degree, of newly industrialized nations.

The same observations could be made about the functioning of economies. The more advanced countries in the developing world have established truly national economies based on a money system of exchange subject to a system of law and regulation emanating from a national government. Many others continue to have dual economies, with a traditional economy coexistent with a modern exchange economy. In almost all cases, creation of a functioning market system would require considerable agreement among the elites and considerable change in existing patterns. National governments and elites would deliberately have to adopt rules of a market system through legal and regulatory mechanisms.

As has been repeatedly suggested in this paper, the developing world or Third World is not a homogeneous entity. The range of variation within the developing world is extreme. This fact implies that a policy of democratic development, including the market-oriented portion of the policy, must adopt very different timetables for accomplishing its goals. In countries such as the Philippines or Argentina, it is practical to talk of structural reform, elections, market systems, and the like in the near term, whereas in other countries a very long time frame is required.

Special reference must be made to Latin America, given the recent dramatic transitions to democracy made in most of the nations of the region. Within the last several years, the two giants of the southern part of the hemisphere, Brazil and Argentina, have made sudden and dramatic returns to the democratic form by casting off military-dominated regimes. Equally impressive has been the struggle waged by advocates of democracy in the Central American region. While this regional trend may represent a historic turning point, a cautionary note must be sounded. This is not the first time that many of these nations have attempted to implement democracy. Indeed, their history has been one of alternation between democracy (or more appropriately, proto-democracy) and authoritarianism. Such cyclical history need not be repeated in the Americas, even though disintegrative pressures on the transitional democracies, and even on the more established regimes, are substantial. Despite strains on political stability ensuing from the debt crisis and other economic burdens, representative political institutions are demonstrating resiliency. Nevertheless, the cumulative effect of high inflation, crime, population growth, unemployment and underemployment, capital flight, and violent Marxist movements threatens the viability of the democratic form.

While these trends and challenges are most evident in Latin America and the Philippines, Mediterranean Europe, including Spain, Portugal, Greece, Turkey, and, to a lesser extent, Italy, face many of the same issues. The transitions to democracy should not be seen as irreversible facts.

In most African societies the challenge of democratic development is at least a generation away. However, the encouraging transitions from government control of the economy to a freer private enterprise form of economic arrangement (although not yet market systems) can provide the basis for further liberalization of political systems. Countervailing trends are evident here, too. Zimbabwe's leaders, for example, talk of creating a socialist system and have adopted socialist theory as the basis of instruction in the school system. At the same time other African states are attempting to remove socialist controls.

The picture in Asia is just as mixed. It is unlikely that the Philippines will provide a role model for the ASEAN states. However, several of these nations are looking at measures designed to remove excessive government involvement in the economy and may, in time, become market systems. There is, for example, a considerable amount of pressure for increased political liberty and other freedoms in South Korea, although it is far too early to predict the direction events may take.

All these regional and country developments must be welcomed. However, it must also be frankly admitted that building democratic institutions and values, including the market system, is a long-term proposition in most of the world. Even in those nations that are currently experiencing a transition to democracy or a growing interest in market systems, it will be at least one generation and perhaps longer before stability can be attained.

The noted political observer Walter Lippmann once observed that democracies, especially the United States, have great difficulty in sustaining a long-term foreign policy. This is equally true of foreign assistance strategies. Somehow the United States must find a way to sustain the current interest in development of democratic government and market-oriented economic systems long enough to achieve these goals. This requires increased sophistication, a willingness to tolerate complexity, and a realization that successes will come only over the long term.

NOTES

1. Report of the Advisory Committee on Private Enterprise in Foreign Aid, *Foreign Aid through Private Initiative* (Washington, D.C.: U.S. Agency for International Development, 1965), p. 9.

2. U.S. Congress, Senate Committee on Foreign Relations and House Committee on Foreign Affairs, *Legislation on Foreign Relations through 1984* (Washington, D.C.: GPO, 1984), p. 76.

3. Ibid., p. 14.

4. Commission on Security and Economic Assistance. *A Report to The Secretary of State* (Washington, D.C.: Department of State, 1983), p. 4.

5. AID Policy Paper, *Private Enterprise and Development* (Washington: U.S. Agency for International Development, 1985),. pp. 10-11.

6. U.S. Department of Commerce, Bureau of the Census, *Statistical Abstract of the United States* (Washington, D.C.: GPO,. 1985), p. 890.

7. Ibid., p. 829.

8. Deborah Orsini, "AID Private Sector Initiatives: Past, Present, and Lessons Learned," in *Selected Papers, The President's Task Force on International Private Enterprise* (Washington, D.C.: U.S. Agency for International Development, unpublished, 1984), pp. 129-59.

9. Orsini, op. cit., pp. 169-72.

10. This was Hernando de Soto's work, described in chap. 7.

11. Orsini, op. cit., pp. 169-72.

12. P. T. Bauer, *Equality, the Third World, and Economic Delusion* (Cambridge: Harvard University Press, 1981), pp. 100-101.

13. John P. Lewis, "Development Assistance in the 1980's," in Overseas Development Council, *U.S. Foreign Policy and the Third World: Agenda 1982* (New Brunswick, N.J.: Transaction Books, 1982), pp. 102-8.

14. Samuel P. Huntington and Joan M. Nelson, *No Easy Choices* (Cambridge: Harvard University Press, 1976), p. 19.

15. Ibid., p. 20.

16. Keith Marsden, "Foreign Aid, the Private Sector, and Economic Growth" in *Selected Papers, The President's Task Force on International Private Enterprise* (Washington, D.C.: U.S. Agency for International Development, unpublished, 1984), p. 8. See also Keith Marsden, *Links between Taxes and Economic Growth*, World Bank Staff Working Papers, no. 605 (Washington, D.C.: 1983).

17. Lloyd G. Reynolds, "The Spread of Economic Growth to the Third World," *Journal of Economic Literature* 31 (September 1983): 976.

18. See articles by Bill Brock, Frank J. Fahrenkopf, Charles T. Manatt, Lane Kirkland, and Michael A. Samuels in *Commonsense* (Washington, Republican National Committee) 6 (December 1983). Michael A. Samuels and John D.

Sullivan, "Democratic Development: A New Role for U.S. Business," *Washington Quarterly* (Summer 1986). Michael A. Samuels and William A. Douglas, "Promoting Democracy," *Washington Quarterly* (Summer 1981).

19. AID Policy Paper, *Private Enterprise and Development*.

20. For a similar list of constraints that emerged from a survey of over 100 world businesses and government leaders, see Ruth Karen, *Toward the Year 2000* (New York: William Morrow, 1985).

21. For more complete accounts, see John P. Windmuller and Alan Gladstone, eds., *Employers Associations and Industrial Relations* (Oxford: Clarendon Press, 1984), and *Principles of Association Management* (Washington, D.C.: American Society of Association Executives and U.S. Chamber of Commerce, 1975).

22. For contrasting views, see Peter L. Berger, "Democracy for Everyone," *Commentary* 76 (September 1983): 31-36.

23. Reynolds, op. cit., pp. 958-59.

9 PEASANT ORGANIZATIONS IN DEMOCRATIC DEVELOPMENT
Richard L. Hough

This essay offers a framework for the development of democratic peasant organizations as an aspect of promoting democracy generally. The writer has relied primarily on his own cumulative experience over more than two decades working with and observing a wide array of rural politico-economic development programs in many Third World countries. The views expressed are the distillation of the experience of a practitioner more than the systematic findings of a field researcher. More than a little of this experience is drawn from Central American examples in which the writer has been recently involved.

IS THE PEASANT SECTOR AMENABLE TO DEMOCRACY?

There is considerable skepticism among respected commentators as to the wisdom and practicality of the United States seeking to support the development of democratic institutions within non-Western countries. This skepticism is particularly related to Third World countries in which the demographic and socioeconomic characteristics are predominantly rural, or at least to the peasant sector within such countries. This sector, with few exceptions, has been the least amenable to structural alteration. The tempo of change in agricultural societies is traditionally slow; the massive quality of life problems they share are the most intractable to solution.

Village inhabitants are largely preoccupied with the daily problems of sustenance and survival. The political culture tends to be passive and introverted. Traditional leadership is hierarchical and paternalistic. On issues beyond the village border, the collective reflex action essentially is one of nonparticipation. This conservatism in part relates to the unsparing and exacting conditions of life and also explains a strategy of risk minimization. The peasants—given their lack of education and political experience and their marginal economic position—are not prone to risk much, or expend their energies on national or regional questions. Though such questions may impinge on their lives, they do not feel that they can in any significant way control or affect the outcome, or that the economic and political dangers of involvement, of taking sides, generally will outweigh the potential benefits of participation.[1]

Further, the peasant sector, particularly if it is predominantly subsistence and nonmodern in character, tends to be structurally amorphous or undifferentiated. It has not as yet broken down into the unions, associations, and other interest groups that are the spin-offs of such modernization processes as agricultural diversification, specialization, and new services and markets. The disaggregation of the rural mass into economically differentiated groupings, which facilitates political organization and representation so as to protect the new interests being generated, generally lags in insular agricultural societies. In addition, in such societies, assets have only been partially monetized. Consequently, there is little of the growth in commerce and the play of broader market forces that disperse economic power and trigger political organization of intermediate nonstate entities.[2]

CHANGING PEASANT CULTURES

It would thus seem that the rural political cultures of Third World countries do not offer particularly good prospects for the development of popular peasant organizations. However, those who hold this expectation are prone to overstate the case, or to reflect but a partial view. Cultures are not static. They change as they are exposed to different life concepts and goals, learn about different values and practices, and adjust traditions to new realities that impinge on daily living.

In much of the Third World today, peasant societies and their village cultures are in the process of basic change. Driven by the penetration of modern technology—principally the methods of scientific farming and fertility control—traditional peasant attitudes of fatalism and the rejection of mediated experience, which lead to a sense of personal powerlessness, are gradually being altered. These views are giving way to a more modern mind-set that accepts the possibilities of human change—of change being generated by technological revolution in the villages themselves. The possibilities for a better quality of life based on increased production and wealth, smaller family size and improved opportunities for education, and a lifestyle based on choices and expectations removed from the cruel ambit of survival are becoming real for millions of rural small producers, principally in Asia, and loom on the horizon for millions more.[3]

Rural economic modernization and varying rates of growth, triggered by decreasing population growth rates and increasing agricultural productivity, have taken hold across a wide swath of Third World countries, first largely in Asia, where the great majority of the world's peasants live. Further, economic, social, and psychological changes cannot somehow be walled off from political change or consequences, given the indivisibility of the development process itself. Political, economic, and social traditions and structures are intertwined; changes in one will affect the others. Thus, alterations in the distribution of wealth and economic opportunity will have consequences for the distribution of political power and on social mobility.[4] The agricultural revolution galvanizing Third World villages today, narrowly conceived, is characterized by higher yielding, faster growing grains and the use of high productivity technologies, such as intensive fertilizer application, multiple cropping, and efficient irrigation systems. Broadly conceived, the revolution includes the new economic interests and demands being created and the new political forms that will evolve to represent and protect these interests. Samuel Huntington's recent words, addressed to the prospects of democracy and, inter alia, the role of economic development, seem particularly appropriate to countries with developing peasant societies. "As countries develop economically, they can be conceived of as moving into a zone of transition or choice, in which traditional forms of rule become increasingly difficult to maintain and new types of political institutions are required to aggregate the demands of an increasingly complex society and to implement public policies in such a society."[5]

No doubt some countries are more likely than others to find ways of shaping such political change into democratic molds. This depends on variables such as the extent of diffusion and penetration of democratic ideas from without and their blend with the special context or "preconditions," favorable or unfavorable to democracy, existing within.[6] However, the point here is to put into perspective the central role of peasant societies, especially the role of the new popular organizations that will inevitably emerge from these societies as they modernize, in the evolution of more open democratic structures and governments in the Third World.

The majority of the world's population, roughly 61 percent, live in rural areas or in villages. In Asia, 73 percent of the population is rural; in Africa, 75 percent; and in Latin America, 39 percent. These figures also reflect understatement in that they do not include people who now reside and are more or less employed in urban areas but maintain their village links. Moreover, the great historic migration to the cities shows signs of having played out, or indeed to be now in reverse.[7]

Looking at these numbers alone, if one cannot foresee, or reasonably postulate, the effective penetration of democratic values and practices into the woof and warp of these peasant societies, then the long-term outlook for the spread of democratic institutions in the Third World is indeed substantially diminished.

TRADITIONAL DEMOCRATIC FORMS IN PEASANT SOCIETIES

Technological, socioeconomic, and attitudinal changes in peasant societies—the modernization process itself—intrinsically do not engender the development of democratic political forms, as has been too facilely assumed by many Western commentators on the Third World. What this process does is to vent the *Weltanschauung* of the society, leaven it with new attitudes and opportunities, and, by causing substantial instability, compel new choices as to the organization of power and authority. The character of the choices made will depend in some part on the interplay between the forces of change and the indigenous customs and institutions in the given country.

It should not be assumed that the cultural bases for the existence or development of democratic forms will generally be unfavorable or unresponsive in non-Western nations. Raul Manglapus, a Filipino politician and writer, in a critique of George Kennan's view of democracy as a distinctively Western creation, points out that indigenous institutions in a number of Third World cultures whose existences predate Western colonialism have been strongly laced with democratic values. For example, he cites the customary law, the *adat*, among the Malays that sanctioned consensus building through free discussion at the village level; the genuinely democratic means used to select the leaders of local villages (*barangays*) in the Philippines; and the traditional popular governance provided by the egalitarian village assembly in Malagasy.[8]

One does not have to go back to precolonial history to find similar examples. In the postindependence period in India, "caste associations," derivatives of however rigid a traditional hierarchical social order, nevertheless played a modern role as intermediate communal groups, educating and organizing their mass memberships in the principles and practices of political democracy.[9]

In Taiwan the authoritarian character of the mainlander Kuomintang government surely was moderated by the growth of the mass-based network of Farmers' Associations—village, township, county, and province— in the post–World War II period. These Taiwanese-dominated popular organizations, particularly influential and vigorous agents at the village and township levels, were democratic in structure and practice and provided a major training ground for Taiwanese politicians and public officials. Large numbers of provincial assemblymen, magistrates, mayors, and township heads are former elected officers of the Farmers' Associations. The associations, and the leaders they have produced, have played a major role, perhaps the dominant role, in local issues in the rural politics of Taiwan. The Kuomintang, as the party of the national government, has been largely content to function as a broker between local factions rather than as a participant arrogating direct power to itself.

There are two other examples, both national peasant movements in Central America: the National Association of Honduran Peasants (ANACH) and the Salvadoran Communal Union (UCS). These organizations have played significant roles in the democratic political development of their countries, however inconstant and fragile that development has been and notwithstanding a cultural legacy and structure of authority customarily viewed as resistant to democratic institutions.

ANACH has been a major force in the development of grass-roots democracy in rural Honduras almost from its inception in 1962. Claiming a membership of 85,000 *campesinos* (peasant farmers), ANACH is organized along democratic lines into local and sectional groups, regional cooperatives, a national staff, and an annual congress. Its leadership has characteristically come from inside the movement, from competition within the *campesino* ranks. In the first two decades of its existence, ANACH was principally a pressure group dedicated to obtaining land for the landless, a mission that it has carried out with notable success. Its political influence within the national body politic has been, and continues to be, impressive. ANACH's leadership has been able, through various formal and informal arrangements with government agencies, the political parties, and the legislature, to ply its influence as a centrist democratic force and make its voice heard with considerable effectiveness over the years, particularly on issues that concern its constituency.

The UCS in El Salvador has had a roughly similar experience. Established in 1968 while one of the more moderate military juntas was in power, UCS has grown into a mass *campesino* organization of some 100,000 members. (As in the case of ANACH, if the regular payment of dues is used as the basis for defining membership, the number of affiliates would come down considerably. If, on the other hand, the definition is more liberal and includes those who are active, though intermittent, participants, occasional contributors, and other working family members, the number of members would go up quite substantially.) UCS service programs are national in scope. It has an organizational presence in all of the departments and the capability to operate at the local level, and it is active on a wide range of *campesino* issues. A substantial number of its members are organized in cooperatives, and its internal practices are markedly democratic in character. UCS has been relatively more effective than ANACH in providing various kinds of services to its local groups, a factor that has contributed to its ability to mobilize its mass following on political issues with greater facility and impact.

UCS profited greatly from its identification with the Salvadoran land reform programs in the early years of this decade. Its vigorous support brought in new members and much enhanced its political visibility, both domestically and internationally. The price exacted was the shedding of more than a little of its blood in that country's civil strife.

UCS is now a component element of a clustering of democratic forces that stand between the extremes in El Salvador, that is, the modern absolutists of the totalitarian Left and the traditional elitists of the authoritarian Right. As part of this fragile center, UCS was instrumental in the election of President Duarte in 1984.

Neither UCS nor ANACH is without its problems. They have not as yet been able to institutionalize their existence in such a way that their future as mass peasant movements devoted to democratic principles is assured. UCS continues to be threatened by the pressures of both the nondemocratic Left and Right in a civil war situation; ANACH, by the slower-working poison of loss of mission and militancy. Both suffer intermittently from divisive factional struggles that leave them vulnerable to co-optation and/or splintering. Yet, however real these dangers, they are not the point here. UCS and ANACH are cited because they have both survived and grown over a considerable period. They are authentic expressions of democratic will and values in peasant societies; they have endured in supposedly alien cultures.

The numerous examples above suggest that a nondeterministic interpretation of the role of peasant organizations in democratic development is called for. An approach grounded in cultural determinism does not square with a protean reality and carries with it unwarranted implications with respect to the future of democracy in the non-Western world.[10]

DEVELOPMENT OF DEMOCRATIC INSTITUTIONS: A FRAMEWORK

This section will lay out a general framework for developing democratic institutions in peasant societies. This framework does not follow any preconceived notions of change but rather highlights elements that appear to have wide application or reflect broadly similar experiences among countries.

The Centrality of Economic Factors

The initial motive power for the development of a popular peasant organization must contain a substantial economic component, that is, a set of activities, services, or reforms designed to improve the quality of life of its peasant constituency. It is likely that these activities will address the central problem of improving living conditions primarily through agriculture, the livelihood for the overwhelming number of rural families. The range of agricultural activities and issues that a peasant organization may embrace as its raison d'être and as attractive to members can vary greatly, from issues such as the rural-urban terms of trade, or agrarian reform, to access to services such as credit and production technologies. Given the paramount aim of organizing rural producers into a mass-based peasant movement, any particular organization must provide—on a sustained, credible basis—real incentives to participate. The incentives that will be most valued relate principally to practical services designed to increase production and income, or, more broadly, to attack the miserable economic conditions that mark the poverty of the potential membership.

The importance of economic factors for developing peasant organizations was not sufficiently appreciated in the Third World during the first two decades or so of developmental experience after World War II. Rather, much program emphasis, albeit mainly by governments and foreign donors, was placed on sophisticated concepts of community development that stressed political and social goals, largely imposed from above. In practice these programs almost inevitably denied the promise of economic growth as the animating force for popular participation and responsiveness. The core idea was to mount, through local community organizations, a set of related activities, say adult education, rural health, public administration, and economic efforts such as extension and credit, to be implemented more or less simultaneously. The rationale, or rather the mystique, of this approach was that through a synergistic interplay of these activities, modern organizations or communities would somehow emerge, committed to democratic practices and able to resist the attractions and/or subversion of communist-led movements based on more revolutionary models of change.

This community development doctrine, many of whose precepts were later incorporated into counterinsurgency programs in Third World countries, had largely spent its force by the early years of the 1970s. It failed in most countries simply because the peasant communities themselves rejected it as not being responsive to their needs as they saw them, or as not providing credible incentives for participation.

In retrospect, the premises of these community development programs, which swept Asia and parts of the Middle East and Latin America a generation ago, seem terribly naïve, particularly the faith in the emergence of democracy, or the efficacy of what were essentially short-term political impact programs to produce it. In any case, given the survival-level conditions of economic existence in most of the peasant societies of the Third World, the denial of the primacy of economic growth, that is, allowing practical means of improving material well-being to become secondary, fatally flawed these programs from the beginning. Interestingly enough, the father of the community development movement was a Third Worlder, Dr. Y. C. James Yen, who pioneered its programs in China and other Asian countries.

The basic point is that economic needs and interests are integral to the development of democratic peasant organizations. When these needs are serviced, the organization is likely to grow and the possibilities of genuine democratic evolution are enhanced. When the needs are poorly serviced or neglected, the opposite is the case: the organization's constituency tends to atrophy.

Complementarity of Economic Interests and Democratic Political Development

There is a discernible pattern in the economic and political dimensions of developing popular rural bodies. However untidy the pattern may be in particular instances, it appears central to the democratic evolution of such groups. The challenge to the groups' leaders is to create and foster a complementary, reinforcing relationship between economic and political development, between material improvements and democratic practices. Of course, this relationship can be viewed in conflictive terms as well, as reflected in the customary admonitions of developmental experts that politics and economic development do not mix, as if they were somehow in different worlds.

In any case, it is the positive, constructive relationship that we seek here in what is at best a long-term, indeterminate process. To illustrate, let us look more closely at the more recent experience of ANACH in Honduras.

During its early years, ANACH was mainly a movement of the rural landless; it functioned primarily as a political pressure group with short-term goals. However, as ANACH became increasingly successful in achieving its goals, new constituency demands were generated. In order to satisfy these demands and retain its members, ANACH got into the business of providing a range of economic and technical services, principally through the development of a cooperative movement within the organization. However, these services have not been efficiently delivered. They have been considered secondary to immediate political concerns and, in fact, have deteriorated in the face of the demands, which have grown more numerous and technically complex.

ANACH is now only marginally tendering the economic development support and assistance that provide opportunity to the *campesinos* to improve their economic station, give them a stake in the economy, and encourage their membership and payment of dues. The consequence is that the fundamental political mission of ANACH of representing the economic interests of the *campesino* sector—thereby contributing to the evolution of democratic competitive politics in Honduras—is being blunted by waning support and/or creeping nonparticipation of its constituent gorups. What is now at risk is the still impressive popular political base of ANACH. ANACH can reverse this situation. Clearly ANACH must develop greater complementarity between political purpose and economic service, or, more broadly, between political and economic development over the longer term.

To state the argument positively, the development and representation of economic and related interests create a considerable part of the popular support that ultimately is the basis of political power and influence of an agrarian union or a national peasant movement. By effectively performing these functions, and by exploiting the complementary trade-offs and possibilities that exist, the movement clearly enhances the importance of its own role within the body politic. More significantly, the movement also contributes to the broader democratization process by incorporating new constituencies into the political system; by adding to the competitiveness and pluralism of the system; and by generating new economic assets among its membership. These new assets facilitate expanded opportunities for education, literacy, upward mobility, and exposure to the mass media, all of which, on balance, are conducive to democracy.

The Role of Great Issues

One of the more striking features of peasant organizations is that the impetus for their growth has come in numerous instances from their identification with and exploitation of great issues. Land reform is the prime example of this.

As has been noted, ANACH in Honduras was little more than a national pressure group for land reform in its early years. It gained its political prominence largely through this one transcendent issue. In El Salvador, UCS, and also a second, smaller but politically vigorous *campesino* organization, Asociacion de Cooperativas para la Produccion Agropecuaria Integral, emerged as powerful forces on the national scene as advocates of democratic politico-economic change almost wholly through their identification with the Salvadoran land reform programs of the early 1980s. In both the Honduran and Salvadoran cases, land reform became a means for the mobilization of mass popular support and the development of an organized constituency among the peasantry that was not there before. The land issue generated a militancy within the peasant organizations themselves that sustained momentum and resolve in the face of adversity.

In Venezuela a similar pattern unfolded after World War II, concurrent with the struggle to establish and maintain a democratic constitutional government. Today, a national peasant movement is integrated into the

Venezuelan body politic and is one of the mainstays of support for what
has become a stable democratic system. The Federacion Campesino de
Venezuela (FECAVE) is a genuine mass-based popular body of approximately 700,000 members, organized at the local level into *ligas* (leagues)
and *sindicatos campesinos* (farm unions) and linked into the national
political scene principally through its 'affiliation with the powerful
Confederación de Trabajadores de Venezuela (CTV).

However, the origins of FECAVE in the 1940s, as well as the well-
springs of its growth and later troubles and divisions, are embedded
almost solely in one continuing issue: the structural redistribution of
land assets in Venezuela. It was indeed the severe maldistribution of
land ownership—the system of *latifundia*—that provided the focal point
for the initial political organizing efforts of the peasant leagues and the
first national congress of FECAVE in 1947. Further, it was principally the
leaders of the national political party, Acción Democratica (AD), who
vigorously exploited, directly and through FECAVE and CTV, the great
potential of the land issue in galvanizing peasant participation in and
support of their party and the new democracy.

Further, it was the promulgation of a new agrarian reform law in 1960
by the Betancourt government that precipitated a major split in the peasant movement and the ensuing struggle over the next few years between
the government-supported AD/CTV faction and the faction led by the
Venezuelan populist, Ramón Quijada, for control of FECAVE and its
state and local organizations. This struggle mirrored well the growth in
the political role of the Venezuelan peasantry over the previous two
decades and the centrality of land reform in generating this growth.[11]

One does not have to limit examples of the role of major issues in
providing the dynamic for the development of peasant organizations
either to one region, Latin America, or to one issue, land reform. Japan
provides an excellent example of the impact of long overdue reforms in
the rural-urban terms of trade, particularly for rice, as well as land
reform, on the burgeoning of a new, more democratic and nonpaternal-
istic structure of farmer organizations in rural Japan in the post–World
War II period. Long struggles to raise real wages among farm workers in
a number of the states of India, such as Kerala and West Bengal, have
gone hand-in-hand with the development of vigorous democratic representation and political activism by increasingly strong rural unions.[12]

In turn, there is manifest future potential in all the regions of the Third
World for popular peasant organizations to emerge and spread as spin-
offs of the momentous issues being generated today by the large and
growing mass of unemployed and underemployed, landless and impoverished farm laborers in rural societies who have been marginal to, or
untouched by, the programs of agricultural development and modernization in their countries.[13]

Issues of this kind also become particularly potent and capable of effective exploitation if they contain a confluence of interests that facilitates a national focus transcending local interests and jurisdictions— for example, those issues that can bind together in common cause the rural and urban elements of organized labor. When industrial workers or employees in public sector unions embrace the cause of the peasants to obtain land or more social services because these goals also are of benefit to themselves—for example, by helping to stem the flow of unemployed farm workers into the cities—then the political staying power of the peasant organization is substantially enhanced. In Venezuela, the longstanding, close ties the FECAVE enjoyed with the CTV reflected for the most part common social and economic interests and positions on issues and concomitantly gave the former national visibility as representative of a large-scale peasant movement.

Building Political Competence and Cohesion

A fundamental challenge for peasant organizations, particularly in largely subsistence and traditionally passive rural societies, is that of developing effective political participation, that is, the progressive building of competence and cohesion among the leadership and members. Instituting the practical means of political participation, or, more broadly, of democratic institution building, is not only inoperative for instilling the foundational democratic values and practices themselves—giving them viability and vitality within the organization—but also for the success of the outreach mission of the organization. Without effective institutional development strategies, broadly wrought to include political education in ideals and doctrine, organization and promotion programs, and training in the multifaceted aspects of political activism, the peasant organization will not be able to defend and extend the interests that are the very reason for its being.

Charles Beitz has noted that "owing to lack of education, literacy, and political competence, some groups are systematically unable to defend their interests through democratic processes" and that "electoral mechanisms among peasants are especially prone to manipulation by traditional elites, who mobilize uninformed and frequently illiterate peasant constituencies by offering selective incentives in return for electoral support."[14]

If the peasant organization is to strengthen the fabric of democratic politics, be able to compete effectively and protect its interests, and be something more than an easy source of support and votes in return for material favors, then the organization has to develop its own internal political cohesion and competence as well as a sense of mission and confidence in dealing with the outside forces that impinge on its vital interests.

In Ecuador recently an able official of a democratic *campesino* federation candidly noted to the writer his care and hesitancy in involving his organization too soon and too much in provincial and national politics. His fear was that at this point in the early development of the federation and its component agrarian unions, involvement could "prostitute" or "cheapen" his groups, given their vulnerability to the politicians, who inevitably solicit support and votes from *campesinos* with "cigarettes, tee shirts and other *regalos pequeños*" (small gifts) that make a mockery of democratic participation. His meaning was clear. He elaborated the things that had to be done, or begun, on the political and economic sides, such as vigorous programs of political education and the development of agricultural services to provide more economic strength so that his *campesino* groups could compete and bargain as democratic equals, not as supplicants.

The key to practical and effective programs of internal education and training in peasant organizations is not only their quality but also their sequence and interrelation. The programs should mirror the complementary relations that exist between economic interests and services on the one hand and democratic political development on the other. This complementarity at the training level should reflect the real-life situation, or the broader reality and goals that the organization is specifically seeking to achieve with its various outreach and service programs.

Thus, an ideal training program, tailored to the needs of the different cadres, whether leaders, paratechnicians, promoters, or rank and file, would include technical subjects, such as financial management and the design and implementation of development projects in, for example, credit, marketing or production inputs, *interrelated* systematically with nontechnical, essentially political subjects such as democratic trade unionism, political ideologies, trade union organization and promotion, and methods of political activism. The Agrarian Union Services program of the National Confederation of Workers (CNT) in Costa Rica for its constituent farm unions illustrates a conscious effort to blend these technical and political elements in a mutually reinforcing pattern of training.[15] Although it is too early to evaluate in depth the project experience with this thoroughly integrated training approach, it seems clear from informal field observations that at least the officials of the *sindicatos agrarios* being supported by the project have a greater appreciation than is usual in *campesino* efforts of this kind of (1) the central requirement of providing the building blocks of genuine democratic political participation, and (2) how the different parts of the project should converge and feed this requirement. No doubt this has been facilitated in Costa Rica by the country's democratic traditions, indeed the thriving open society, that exists there but cannot be found elsewhere in Central America.

The Centro de Estudios Laborales del Peru earlier conducted a similar experiment in urban and rural trade union education with the support of the American Institute for Free Labor Development (AIFLD). The workers were taught "that economic, social and political democracy must form an integral system, . . . that only social reform and economic development can provide long-term prospects of improvement in the life of the organized workers, and that the labor movement must therefore spearhead reform."[16] Here again the emphasis was on the fusing of subjects within a more holistic conception of the role of labor in a democratic society.

Building genuine political competence and cohesion in peasant organizations is a long-term, essentially bottom-up process, a process that is learned collectively and is cumulative. Well-conceived training programs certainly help, as do the charisma and commitment of outstanding peasant leaders. There are also the opportunities for political visibility and drama offered by great national issues that the organization is able to exploit. However, there are no political quick fixes, no short-term magic that creates a peasant organization whole cloth, particularly in a society that resists heightened political consciousness and assertive expression by a traditional underclass.

To make the same point from a somewhat different vantage point, there has to be a set of reasonably distinct economic and social interests that provide the bedrock raison d'être of the peasant movement. These interests do not emerge overnight. Without them, all the political activity and all the organization and promotion will progressively lose credibility for lack of sustained response from the organization's local constituency.

Pluralistic politics in significant measure is the representation of economic interests, almost starkly so in many of the underdeveloped nations of the Third World. If these interests remain amorphous, or if they are neglected by the leaders of peasant groups in favor of the more attractive games of short-term, manipulative politics, or if they are treated narrowly as technical issues bereft of their political content (as developmental advisers and experts are so apt to do), then the building of political cohesion and competence within the peasant organization itself will inevitably lag or become a rather futile exercise honored in rhetoric but without enduring substance.

Similarly, the leaders of the peasant movement should hold to as simple a model of internal development as possible, one that integrates the principal functions of its agrarian unions under one roof. For example, the movement should probably avoid the establishment of cooperatives to meet the demands for economic and technical services by its local memberships. Rather, it is feasible in most instances to mount and implement such services under the management of the agrarian unions themselves. This avoids setting up another layer of special-purpose organs such as cooperatives.

There is also a real question whether the cooperative is an appropriate model in any case for farm unions to use in dispensing their constituent services. Rather than linking the services to the special political mission of the union, the cooperative tends to separate the two. At the very least, one can argue that, in the early years of a peasant organization, the cooperative route should be avoided. The reasons seem clear. First, there is the usual lack of trained manpower at the local level. What there is becomes spread too thin between the union and the cooperative. Second, in many cases there is not sufficient wealth in the rural communities to support cooperatives. Operations become highly subsidized, generally by resource transfers from an outside source. An unhealthy top-down financial dependency soon sets in that probably could have been avoided in the first place with a more modest structure of operations within the union itself.

Last, an inherent tendency toward separatism is built into the cooperative approach. Cooperatives develop their own style, their own leaders, their own institutional contacts and relations, and, in some cases, their own sources of support outside the agrarian movement that created them. The divisive tendencies built into cooperativism for farm union organizations are readily apparent, for example, in Honduras today, where the ANACH regional cooperatives are only more or less under central ANACH control. Conflicts and the possibility of breakaways are never far removed from the surface.

The External Environment

The character of the external environment most conducive to the development of democratic peasant organizations is a far-ranging subject that can be addressed here only on a limited basis. Our interest is not only with respect to the impact of the external environment on peasant movements—the extent to which the former constrains or facilitiates the growth of the latter—but also the reverse, the impact that these movements may have on the democratization of the broader body politic itself.

The prospects for the development of democratic peasant organizations would appear to be best within a political system or culture that is itself democratic. This appears self-evidently true. Peasant groups, like other interest groups, need political space in which to operate and grow. The experience, for example, of the national *campesino* movement in Venezuela suggests this. Similarly, in a negative way, the present dearth of popular peasant organizations in the countryside of Haiti after almost three decades of the oppressive Duvalier dictatorship suggests much the same.

However, some qualification is in order. A cardinal ingredient of effective peasant groupings is their militancy. It has been this writer's observation in many Third World countries that the cutting edge of effectiveness and strength of organized labor, both urban and rural, has been militance of spirit and commitment to a set of goals, engendered at least in part by strong outside forces of resistance or opposition. How else may we explain the fact that the most politically influential and relatively advanced *campesino* movement in Central America is the one in El Salvador, whereas one of the least advanced is in democratic Costa Rica? The movement in El Salvador developed over the past decade within the interstices of a culture of repression and violence; in Costa Rica, where a divided movement is still struggling for identity and the trust of its constituency, democracy was bestowed, not fought for. Indeed, in El Salvador, the democratic *campesino* organizations have made a major contribution in securing the present fragile democracy.

A second ingredient is resourcefulness. Peasant organizations must have the resourcefulness and vigor to exploit an external environment that almost inevitably will provide, through the public and private sectors and through foreign assistance donors, the resource transfer programs—-most importantly of technology and modern expertise—crucial to opening up the vistas of education, social mobility, and economic advance for their deprived constituencies.

The challenge for peasant organizations is to tap strategically into these institutional channels of resources and to serve as the vital intermediate link between grantors and recipient members. They must do this without sacrificing their autonomy and self reliance. The trap, of course, is that the flow of largess will create dependent groups that progressively lose their collective will and sense of mission. This hazard is a ubiquitous one for farm unions in resource-scarce, poverty-ridden rural communities in Third World countries.

However, this is not an argument for nonparticipation. It is best viewed as a caveat, not a reason for opting out. Emergent peasant organizations simply cannot afford to remain marginal to the historic modernization and development problems that impinge on their constituencies. Only by confronting these problems, or engaging them by exploiting the external resources available, will the organizations establish their political legitimacy as representatives of the interests of their people. Idealistically, peasant movements should take the long view of participation in the economic and social development process. They should assiduously pursue the purpose of transforming that participation, and the cumulative successes achieved, into democratic outreach activities and not fall prey to the shorter-term games of spoils distribution and the exploitation of dependency relations with client agencies. Realistically, however, the world is much grayer. The choices available to farm union leaders are inevitably limited by the politics of the moment but are still capable, one should insist, of being illumined by visions of longer-term change—by the unfolding of the democratic revolution itself.

And third, it is often noted that peasant movements have fared better when they have been able to have support bestowed upon them by national power holders of various kinds, for example, heads of state, government agencies, or political parties. This view assumes that the authoritative political commands and actions necessary to facilitate the reforms or programs sought by the peasant groups can be engineered or mandated only from above by these power holders. In effect, modern peasant mobilization presumably relies less on grass roots than on national politics, as well as more on the dispensation of those who wield decisive power.

The prime example of this view of the indispensable role of top-down power in enhancing peasant movements is post–World War II Japan. The countryside was indeed democratized in the decade after Japan's surrender. A sweeping land reform program was carried out, the urban-rural terms of trade were adjusted to become more favorable to the small producers on the land, and new farmer organizations emerged representing the interests of the new property owners. These organizations were largely stripped of the old paternalistic influence of the traditional landlord class. Much of this was accomplished, of course, under the aegis of a foreign occupation force, General MacArthur's SCAP (Supreme Commander of the Allied Powers) command in Tokyo. The small farmer associations that progressively evolved appeared to have been creatures of top-down intervention by a dominant outside authority.

However, it has been too easily forgotten that the animus of these sweeping changes came from the militancy of the Japanese small tenant farmers themselves, who were demanding reforms, particularly with regard to the existing land tenure system. Militancy generated fear of serious social disturbances if changes were not forthcoming.[17] The beneficiaries of the changes were far from passive players. Indeed, for a good part of the first half of this century, the Japanese countryside and its peasant farmers were a major source of political radicalism in Japan. In other words, if the Japanese agrarian time frame is extended somewhat, it becomes clear that the structural changes of the post–World War II period involved considerably more than top-down fiat. The reforms were essentially a culmination of a long process of activism, organization, and tenacious advocacy by the peasants themselves.

In an opposite vein, one of the reasons for the failure of the land reform efforts in the Philippines over roughly the last three decades has been a pattern of central government attempts to impose laws and programs without recognition of the indispensability of having an organized peasantry participate in and tailor the programs to local needs and popular acceptance.[18] President Marcos further distorted this top-down predisposition by using land reform and numerous other rural development programs, as well as ostensible peasant groups, to extend the authority of his government and buttress the political position of local rural leaders who found it prudent to support him. The commitment to common cause and drives to organize among the Filipino peasantry have manifested themselves twice since World War II, but in the form of radical, communist-dominated peasant movements: the Hukbalahaps and the New People's Army.

The point to emphasize is that, regardless of how significant factors in the external environment may prove to be in furthering the growth and effectiveness of peasant movements, there is no substitute for the mix of internal militance, political will, and competence in competitive politics for exploiting the external factors. The contribution that peasant organizations can make to the development of the democratic system as a whole depends on a key antecedent: the strength and vitality of democracy within the organizations themselves.

THE ROLE OF U.S. POLICIES

It remains to address the development of democratic peasant organizations from the perspective of the role of outside agents, specifically that of U.S. programs and their attendant problems. The discussion will be confined to U.S. support provided through public and private means to peasant organizations per se. Broader questions of U.S. policy supporting democratic institution building, regimes, or oppositions generally are left for other contributors to this volume.

In democratic change, there is a fine line between constructive engagement by external actors and counterproductive intervention. Specifically, direct visible involvement by U.S. government agencies in the promotion of various kinds of peasant groups carries a risk of crossing that line in the wrong direction, and surely it is to be avoided. Proconsul proclivities inevitably are deeply resented in Third World nations regardless of place on the local political spectrum. As a consequence, U.S. private groups have a comparative advantage over public sector agencies in supporting the programs of agrarian unions and similar types of farm worker associations. An organization such as AIFLD, for example, can reach and involve union beneficiary groups through different programs, such as courses in democratic ideology and techniques of political activism, that are ordinarily beyond the pale of U.S. government agencies overseas for many reasons, including the latter's official relations with the host government. AIFLD has greater operational freedom in the host country than, say, the Agency for International Development (AID). The former's field of action is farther removed from host government authority and oversight. AIFLD has to cope to a considerably lesser extent with the constraints and uncertainties of working directly with foreign government officials and agencies, and it has the strategic advantage of greater latitude and flexibility in cooperating with other unions in the implementation of economic and politico-social change (reform) projects.

The potential for constructive engagement in democratic change in the agrarian field is thus greater through U.S. private organizations and less likely to leave the United States open to charges of undue intervention. Further, reliance on organizations like AIFLD, U.S. cooperative groups, and a host of other private U.S. agencies dedicated to working in the rural sector has the added advantage of bringing to bear the full vitality and diversity of our pluralistic society on the complex problems of long-term democratic institution building in the developing world.[19]

This private sector emphasis is not to minimize the role of the U.S. Foreign Service in helping to strengthen democratic trade unionism, urban as well as rural, in Third World countries. Through its instruments of diplomacy, economic assistance, information, and trade, the overseas U.S. mission has a significant role to play, especially in influencing the broader political and economic environment within which democratic peasant movements survive and grow. For example, if the U.S. mission is able to negotiate a package of reform measures with the host government, including price changes in the urban-rural terms of trade on major crops, as a quid pro quo for greater U.S. financial and technical assistance to the rural agricultural sector, the positive impact on the life of the agrarian unions would likely be of major consequence, particularly if the unions had been strong advocates of the reforms in the first place.

Indeed, the AID, with its programs of economic assistance in agriculture and rural development, its support of delivery systems of economic and social services, and its traditional emphasis on the technical requirements of economic development, always influences the viability and prospects of peasant organizations simply as a consequence of the indivisibility of the economic and political dimensions of development.

The area in which this observer feels that U.S. private organizations have been most effective, and where there is still great potential for inculcating the precepts and practices of democratic trade unionism, is that of support for political and technical education programs for rural union leaders. The AIFLD experience in Latin America reflects this. Few campesino leaders who are upwardly mobile within their organizations have had the opportunity for much formal education through the public education systems of their countries, much less for advanced professional training relative to their offices and responsibilities. What AIFLD and a number of other international labor organizations do is help to fill this vacuum, to satisfy unmet leadership and skill needs in fledgling peasant groups.

The surface has just been scratched with regard to the training of *campesino* union officials by outside organizations. AIFLD for the past 20 years has tended to concentrate on education programs of various kinds for urban trade union officials. Only in the past few years has it turned more systematically to the training challenges in the diverse *campesino* sector with its mass of non-wage-earning small producers, tenants, and sharecroppers, as well as seasonally employed farm laborers and the landless.

The political consciousness of this sector is manifestly increasing in most of the countries of this hemisphere. The massive political potential for organizing its major popular components is all too apparent to the different parties, democratic and otherwise, that compete for power and favor. The stakes will indeed be high for the balance of this century with respect to how Latin countries solve their *"campesino* problem": specifically, how an awakening, traditionally deprived rural mass is to be disaggregated and absorbed within the economy and body politic, and under the aegis of what political persuasion.

This process can be significantly influenced in cumulative ways by outside actors. Organizations such as AIFLD have had, and can have considerably more, impact on the course of change, moving it in democratic directions through the access provided by their education and training programs. However, much depends on the type and quality of the education offered to the leaders and members of the farmer unions and associations of different kinds that are now surfacing in large number in the Latin American countryside. The ideal training approach, which thoroughly integrates the technical and political elements of the union's mission, has been discussed above. The central point, worth repeating, is the need to conceive a practical curriculum that links in overlapping ways the requisite economic and technical skills and services on the one hand to the achievement of goals through institutional political competence and dedication to democratic values and practices on the other hand.[20]

An education program of this kind, to be effective, should involve agrarian union officials and potential leaders at the local, regional, and national levels in a progression of courses, seminars, and field training. In addition, international training of rural union leaders, as is the case with AIFLD's *campesino* education program given yearly in the United States and Latin American countries, can be instrumental in exposing the participants to a broader professional and democratic environment. If perceptively drawn upon and adapted by the course organizers and teachers, these programs can indeed be relevant to the local conditions and problems facing the union officials in their own countries.

Last, the involvement of outside agents in the democratic development of peasant movements through the education route has one major advantage over other alternatives. It allows the outsider to get in and out quickly, financially and technically. Advisers can limit their presence to short, frequent stays, avoiding the encumbrances that surface during longer-range commitments of external support. Given the importance of avoiding dependency on these subsidies by the recipient unions, this advantage has much to recommend it.

This leads to another key subject, that of mounting other programs of external support that, however necessary, run the risk of drawing both parties, donors and recipients, into a subsidy/dependency relation. The core of this problem is economic. Peasant organizations typically are root and branch reflections of rural agricultural sectors that are poor and deprived, perhaps just beginning to emerge from the backwash of under-development. Poverty militates against even marginal investments by the small peasant farmers beyond the farm. At a minimum, such invest-ments or contributions are resisted initially.

Peasant organizations characteristically must build from a very shal-low economic base. Resources are scarce, income is very limited, and dues collections difficult at best, even among active members. External financial assistance in one form or another is often imperative in order to get the organization off the ground and to sustain it for some period of time. If the foreign agent provides budget support, picks up the salaries of the agrarian union officials, and takes care of other recurrent costs of operation, it may be meeting genuine requirements, perhaps of survival, but at what costs? There is no one answer to what is a ubiquitous problem for peasant organizations and their external supporters. So much depends upon mutual cooperation and understanding at the point of implementation. Relevant questions, such as how much budget sup-port, over what period of time, and in exchange for what self-help measures, are best worked out in the individual situation.

Generally, this observer has found that the problem of dependency is best dealt with in the context of specific projects rather than through general budget support. The project approach is more amenable to the setting of finite time limits and goals and the design of an agreed-upon plan of disengagement by the external donor. I would also subscribe in large part to the imaginative proposals addressed to this same set of issues in chapter 3 of this volume, "The Donor-recipient Relationship in Political Aid Programs."

However, the ideal or normative only provides guides for the practi-tioner, who must deal with an ever changing reality marked by exigen-cies and crises, large and small, where the relationship of strategy to tactics, or the ideal to the practical, is easily lost in the blur of events. In dealing effectively with the challenges of democratic institution building of and through peasant movements from the perspective of U.S. organi-zations, there is no substitute for the tested skills and judgment that come with the "hands on" experience of day-to-day implementation and decisions in the local situation. This is perhaps a truism. However, many sound and hopeful programs of both private and public U.S. agencies have failed precisely because of the lack of this experience.

For example, today in the Dominican Republic, a new national *campesino* movement has emerged, the Consejo Nacional de Juntas y Federaciones Campesinas Dominicanos (CONOCAD), which shows great promise. From its beginning in 1983, CONOCAD expanded to 18,000 members by the end of 1985, organized into 35 federations and 450 associations. This growth has taken place with little outside financial support. Apparently, the generative forces are largely coming from within and flowing from the local areas to the center. The question is how to sustain this healthy growth.

On the one hand, we know that CONOCAD, after the first flush of success, is going to have to provide an array of services to its constituents and that it will have to seek outside funds to do it. On the other hand, we know equally well that front-loaded, overly generous support by the outside donor, particularly if it is not tied firmly to performance, will soon change the character of the movement, and for the worse, progressively dulling its inner vitality and sense of independence. In this case, as in so many others, there are no pat formulas that can be quantified in a firm budget or a long-range projection of mutual costs. The donor agency, if it is smart, feels its way carefully, relying on the judgment and experience of its local representative who, if he or she is also smart, should know the right turns to take at the right time.

NOTES

1. See Charles R. Beitz, "Democracy in Developing Societies," in Raymond D. Gastil, ed., *Freedom in the World: Political Rights and Civil Liberties, 1982* (Westport, Conn.: Greenwood Press, 1982), pp. 154-55.

2. See Samuel P. Huntington, "Will More Countries Become Democratic?" in Raymond D. Gastil, ed., *Freedom in the World: Political Rights and Civil Liberties, 1984-1985* (Westport, Conn.: Greenwood Press, 1985), pp. 199-206.

3. See Richard Critchfield, *Villages* (New York: Anchor Press/Doubleday, 1981), pp. 321-39.

4. See Robert L. Heilbroner, *The Great Ascent* (New York: Harper & Row, 1963); Mancur Olson, Jr., "Rapid Growth as a Destabilizing Force," *Journal of Economic History*, December 1963; Richard L. Hough, *Economic Assistance and Security: Rethinking U.S. Policy* (Washington, D.C.: National Defense University Press, 1982).

5. Huntington, op. cit., p. 201.

6. See Gastil, *Freedom in the World, 1984-1985*, p. 264.

7. Critchfield, op. cit., p. 322.

8. "Human Rights Are Not a Western Discovery," *Worldview*, October 1978.

9. See Lloyd and Susanne H. Rudolph, *The Modernity of Tradition: Political*

Development in India (Chicago: University of Chicago Press, 1967), pp. 29-36.

10. See also, Beitz, op. cit., pp. 150-55.

11. See John D. Martz, *Acción Democratica, Evolution of a Modern Political Party in Venezuela* (Princeton: Princeton University Press, 1966), pp. 273-87.

12. See Ajit Kumar Ghose, ed., *Path of Rural Transformation: Agrarian Reform in Contemporary Developing Countries* (London: Croom Helm, 1983), pp. 31-141.

13. See Erik Eckholm, "The Growing Legion of the Landless,"; *People,* November 1983.

14. Beitz, op. cit., pp. 161-62.

15. This program is supported by the AIFLD through a technical and financial assistance project with the CNT. The USAID Mission in Costa Rica provides financial support to the joint effort.

16. William A. Douglas, "U.S. Labor Policy in Peru—Past and Future," in Daniel A. Sharp, ed., *U.S. Foreign Policy in Peru* (Austin: University of Texas Press, 1972), pp. 223-24.

17. Takekazu Agura, "Economic Impact of Post-war Land Reform," in James R. Brown and Sein Lin, eds., *Land Reform in Developing Countries* (Hartford, Conn.: University of Hartford, 1968), pp. 223-77; Gary L. Olson, *U.S. Foreign Policy and the Third World Peasant: Land Reform in Asia and Latin America* (New York: Praeger, 1974), pp. 24-33.

18. See Jeremias U. Montemajor, "Progress and Problems of Land Reform in the Philippines," in James Brown and Sein Lin, eds., *Land Reform in Developing Countries* (Hartford, Conn.: University of Hartford, 1968), pp. 199-223.

19. Michael A. Samuels and William A. Douglas, "Promoting Democracy," *Washington Quarterly* (Summer 1981), p. 54.

20. See Neale J. Pierson, "Peasant and Worker Sindicatos and Democracy in Latin America," in Howard J. Wiarda, ed., *The Continuing Struggle for Democracy in Latin America* (Boulder, Colo.: Westview Press, 1980), pp. 86-87.

10 COOPERATIVES AS AGENTS OF DEMOCRACY
Ted Weihe

Land O' Lakes, Watergate Apartments, CARE, Nationwide Insurance, Sunkist, Associated Press, Blue Ridge Electric Membership Corporation, Recreational Equipment Incorporated (REI) and Group Health Association are familiar names to many Americans. Yet, when you mention that they are cooperatives, most will reflectively think of only a baby-sitting, handicraft, or small natural food coop.

America's cooperatives are big business. They provide a majority of agricultural supplies to the farm and are large marketers of products with household names, such as Welch's, Ocean Spray or Blue Diamond. Nearly 25 million Americans receive electricity from rural electric cooperatives. Many others live in cooperative housing or shop at a coop store. One in five Americans is a member of a credit union, but few know that credit unions are cooperatives. Today, 89 million Americans are members of cooperatives.

Cooperatives exist in virtually every country and fit into the ideology of the West and centrally planned economies of Eastern Europe, Soviet Union, and China. It is estimated that there are a half billion members of organized cooperatives worldwide who are represented through the International Cooperative Alliance, the largest nongovernmental organization in the world. See table 10.1.

WHAT ARE COOPERATIVES?

Cooperatives are people's movements, concerned with the economic, social, and cultural well-being of their members. They are private sector

Table 10.1
Cooperatives Represented by the International
Cooperative Alliance, 1985

	Number of Societies		Individual Members	
Agricultural	256,392	(34.6%)	66,612,740	(13.0%)
Consumer	69,296	(9.4%)	129,581,131	(26.0%)
Credit	204,461	(27.6%)	127,895,439	(25.5%)
Fishery	15,467	(2.0%)	2,162,641	(0.5%)
Housing	69,278	(9.4%)	17,394,554	(3.5%)
Industrial	53,938	(7.3%)	6,292,708	(1.5%)
Miscellaneous	71,825	(9.7%)	150,025,422	(30.0%)
Total	740,656	100.0%	499,964,185	100.0%

Source: International Co-operative Alliance, Summary of Statistics for 1985.

businesses providing goods and services to members and the public.
Also, they advocate practical, mutual assistance for members to resolve
common needs often unsatisfied by government or other private sector organizations. Cooperatives are nonprofit. As respecters of their members,
regardless of race, religion, or sex, they are member owned and controlled
organizations practicing and advocating democratic principles.

Cooperatives are capable of doing many things. They can give people
access to financial systems, such as credit unions or the Federal Farm
Credit System for agricultural loans. As nonprofit businesses designed
for their members' benefit, they counterbalance market imperfections
often created by local monopolies. Rural electric cooperatives provide
services that governments or private utilities fail to provide and make
modern technology available to members who would not otherwise have
access to it. Cooperatives raise member incomes, mobilize their savings
and human resources for productive activities, and provide goods and
services to members often at lower cost or of better quality.

Cooperatives are an alternative to violent change. They are a way to
achieve positive social and economic change in the face of high foreign
debt, low investment, and high underemployment or unemployment, all
of which are undermining many political systems and economies in the
developing world.

DEMOCRACY IN U.S. COOPERATIVES

Membership control is fundamental to U.S. cooperatives ideologically,
practically, and legally. It represents the major reason for treating co-

operatives as unique business institutions. The Capper-Volstead Act of 1922, which has been called the Magna Carta of cooperation, provides that farmers "may act together in associations . . . in collectively processing, preparing for market, handling and marketing in interstate and foreign commerce." Such organizations may not, however, "monopolize or restrain trade" to the "extent that the price of any agricultural product is unduly enhanced." The act requires democratic control in that "no member of the association is allowed more than one vote because of the amount of stock or membership capital he may own."

This legislation stands as the guardian of farmers' right to organize and operate strong cooperatives for marketing. It resulted in an explosion of cooperative activity, with a doubling of cooperative businesses in the ealry 1920s. Subsequent legislation, such as the Marketing Act of 1929 and the Rural Electrification Act of 1934, continued to promote member-owned farmer associations. Similarly, the Federal Credit Union Act of 1934 paved the way for the growth of cooperative thrift and credit institutions, which grew rapidly during the Great Depression.

The U.S. government has given financial support to cooperatives by establishing the Farm Credit System, the Credit Union Administration, the Rural Electric Administration, and, most recently, the National Cooperative Bank for the development of consumer cooperatives.

In the United States, cooperative members elect their boards of directors, who represent member interests and make the major decisions in the cooperative organization. The directors have the responsibility to make sure that management decisions fulfill the needs and objectives of the membership. Members may also be consulted to amend by-laws, pass resolutions, and set long-range objectives and plans.

Directors may seek feedback on major expansion of facilities and capital expenditures, expansion into new products, and purchase of major assets of another firm or cooperative. Directors may ask members to approve policies pertaining to credit, pricing, sharing net margins, and other issues. In all of these areas, federal and state statutes do not usually require member participation. However, under most state laws, members are required to vote for the initial approval and subsequent changes in the articles of incorporation, and for mergers, consolidations, and sale of all assets.

The pressure to achieve business efficiencies places stress on a cooperative's democratic functioning. Increasing size and consolidations through mergers have threatening implications for member control. In a recent study of forty English retail cooperative societies between 1933 and 1954, researchers found that the larger the cooperative society, the smaller the proportion of members attending and voting at annual meetings. The increase in size and decline in member participation can also intensify special interest group struggles in the internal workings of the cooperative.

As cooperatives gain in size and market strength, they have been forced to defend their existence. Identification by larger cooperatives with a corporate model of organization can lead to a reduction in the role of members. Members may place a higher value on the cooperative's economic performance than its internal democracy. So long as members feel that management and their directors are sensitive to the needs of members and the cooperative's performance is good, members may remain loyal without caring about personally influencing decision making. However, during times of cooperative hardship, such as is now occurring in rural parts of the United States, members find it necessary to become more active in order to maintain their cooperative.

Studies more recent than the one of English societies have indicated that factors other than business growth and membership size may help explain the erosion of memberhsip use of the democratic mechanisms in U.S. cooperatives. Though members of small cooperatives generally express a higher level of perceived control, there has been little difference in member satisfaction with decisions and operations between large and small cooperatives. Previous studies of cooperatives have focused on smaller cooperatives of 10 to 1,000 members. When a cooperative reaches a certain point, increased size may not influence membership participation. Members may want to participate more in a large cooperative because they want to associate with a thriving organization.

Throughout the history of the U.S. cooperative movement, there has existed a conflict between those who want their cooperatives directly involved in politics and others who strenuously oppose political action. In the 1880s and 1890s, the Farmers Alliance created hundreds of cooperatives for bulk sales and purchases as a means of getting free from the merchant-controlled credit system, which held most farmers in economic bondage. The organizational impulse generated by the farmer cooperatives led to the formation of the People's party. This party was the political expression of rural radicalism and came to be known as "populist." The politicization of farmers occurred as their cooperatives found it impossible to compete against the monopolistic merchants, railroads, supply and marketing companies, and the establishment in general, including the two major political parties. Then as now, cooperative leaderships were split between those who advocate nonpolitical, economic self-improvement and those who urge direct political action. Even though the People's party had a brief existence, it is significant that its leadership was able to bridge these contending forces in the cooperative movement.

The role of cooperatives in U.S. democratic politics continues to be complex. In general, U.S. cooperatives concentrate almost exclusively on their business goals. These cooperatives, however, must maintain a social purpose lest they lose member loyalty and, often, fail as businesses. U.S. cooperatives have created state and national federations with the principal purpose of protecting the cooperative way of doing business through nonpartisan politics. Yet, U.S. cooperatives are heavily involved in politics. They have large political action committees that help finance the election campaigns of friendly state and federal legislators. They have numerous lobbyists who spend much time at state capitols and in the halls of Congress. Clearly, for U.S. cooperatives, nonpartisanship does not mean political inaction.

THE COOPERATIVES' ROLE IN DEVELOPMENT

Cooperative development attempts to bring people together in democratically governed businesses to meet mutual needs. As a development tool, the cooperative structure permits participatory decision making and a self-help approach to shared problems and goals.

The involvement of U.S. cooperative organizations in overseas activities grew out of the conviction that U.S. cooperative techniques, many of which were perfected during the Great Depression, could be transferred to help poor and low-income people in developing countries to a better way of life.

With U.S. cooperative assistance, thousands of cooperatives overseas—agricultural, marketing, purchasing, thrift and credit, electric power, housing, handicraft, consumer, and insurance—have been organized; thousands more have been strengthened. Men, women, and children have learned to participate in and benefit from cooperative membership.

The U.S. government's development policy places an emphasis on programs that will meet basic human needs and help the poor to participate in the development process. For these objectives to become a reality, indigenous institutions that outlive temporary outside assistance must be developed and strengthened. Cooperative development requires a long-term commitment in building institutions that belong to the people themselves. Cooperatives thus are an important tool for developing the human resources and self-sustaining institutions for economic and social progress.

U.S. cooperatives have worked to promote cooperative development overseas for more than three decades. Begun modestly with funds contributed by each organization's members, U.S. cooperative activities abroad have greatly expanded in number, magnitude, and geographic distribution. The impetus for this expansion was an amendment to the Foreign Assistance Act in 1961 that provided legislative authority for the U.S. Agency for International Development (AID) to use funds "to encourage the development and use of cooperatives" in developing countries.

U.S. cooperative development organizations include the Agricultural Cooperative Development International, the Cooperative Housing Foundation, the Credit Union National Association (affiliated with the World Council of Credit Unions), the National Rural Electric Cooperative Association, the National Cooperative Business Association, Volunteers in Overseas Cooperative Assistance, and Cooperative for American Relief Everywhere, better known simply as CARE. Individual U.S. cooperatives such as League Insurance of Michigan and Land O'Lakes are also directly involved in overseas development activities.

BUILDING DEMOCRATIC COOPERATIVES

U.S. cooperatives are proud of the cooperatives they have helped and of the fact that millions of people have been assisted economically. But it is the broader concerns—economic self-determination and dignity, human rights, and democracy—that are the most significant achievements. However, the linkages between cooperatives and political processes have been ignored. At best, political involvement has been seen as a link into bureaucracy. A new focus on democratic institution building opens up important issues.

In responding to the initiative of President Reagan, announced before the British Parliament in June 1982, Congress created the National Endowment for Democracy (NED) in 1983. From its inception, NED has recognized cooperatives as a significant component of nongovernmental programs to promote political and economic democracy. The initial study of the Democracy Program acknowledged the role U.S. cooperatives have played in assisting democratic cooperatives through technical assistance. The study also points out that "no mechanism (is) available for the political corollaries of development" by such nongovernmental organizations. In a statement of principles and objectives for *Strengthening Democracy Abroad* (1984), NED notes:

Another significant private-sector economic organization is the cooperative. Groups of people uniting in cooperatives to carry out economic enterprises can acquire an invaluable grass-roots experience in democratic decisionmaking. The Endowment will consider funding programs that reinforce the democratic character of cooperatives and enhance their contribution to the democratization of developing countries.

The legislative history of U.S. cooperatives' involvement in overseas cooperative development as part of U.S. foreign assistance is replete with references to their role in promoting democratic institutions: self-help, participation, broad membership, and economic democracy within society. However, cooperative development programs, often funded by

AID, have concentrated principally on economic technical assistance, not on democracy within cooperatives or the relationship of cooperatives to political democracy. NED's goals provide an opportunity to take advantage of those democratic qualities of cooperatives that build political democracy.

CHILE AND OTHER EXAMPLES

In Chile, U.S. cooperatives have undertaken a project to examine the role cooperatives play in maintaining grass-roots democratic institutions and their relationship to political forces working for a transition to democratic rule.

Cooperatives there were found to be functioning well as democratic self-help organizations committed to assisting low- and moderate-income people. Adversely affected by Chilean politics and economics, they suffered for 15 years under the current and previous administrations. As a result, many cooperatives failed. But the situation has stabilized in recent years, and cooperatives are growing again. They remain a force for economic and political democracy.

Table 10.2 shows the number of active Chilean cooperatives by sector over the last 35 years. The government-instigated precipitous decline in all but housing cooperatives between 1970 and 1985 is revealed, as is the decline in housing cooperatives that occurred btween 1975 and 1985. The statistics show a 43.7 percent decrease in the number of active cooperatives over the last ten years.

Table 10.2
Development of Cooperatives in Chile

Year	Agrarian	Consumer	Credit	Housing	Other	Total
1950	25	80	20	20	15	160
1963	160	109	159	334	68	830
1966	825	119	190	569	142	1,305
1968	404	171	227	743	213	1,758
1970	456	137	201	944	337	2,075
1975	600	100	100	1,500	300	2,600
1985	112	44	118	875	316	1,465

Source: ICECOOP, *Las Cooperativas en Chile*, 1985.

As member-owned businesses governed under the principle of "one person, one vote," cooperatives are often the most direct experience of low- and moderate-income people in democratic practice. Cooperative elections are usually honest. Divergent viewpoints on issues important to members are openly expressed, debated, and voted on. Leadership is developed through elections to voluntary boards of directors. Annual meetings are often well attended, and support from members is demonstrated through the use of cooperative services in areas such as credit, agricultural supplies and marketing, electricity, and housing.

Chilean cooperatives encompass a variety of political viewpoints ranging from support of the current military government to active opposition. They have extraordinary access to diverse elements of society: the Catholic Church, the business and civic communities, the press, and labor unions. Chilean cooperatives are divided between smaller, peasant cooperatives, which usually grew out of the land reform era during the Alliance for Progress years in the 1960s, and more conservative, businesslike cooperatives, such as rural electric and larger agricultural cooperatives. Though the latter have excellent access to the current military government, they do support, for the most part, an early return to democratic rule. They tend to speak to the government officials only about commercial concerns. Largely cut off from government influence, the smaller cooperatives are closely tied to the political opposition pushing for an immediate democracy.

This pattern of cooperative development is typical of Latin America. In contrast, U.S. cooperatives have kept their political feet firmly planted in all ideological camps—Democratic and Republican, conservative and liberal. In observing the U.S. cooperative approach to politics, a delegation of Chilean cooperative leaders recently came to realize what strength lies in a united front on cooperative issues. They saw the need to build a base for democratic support across the full political spectrum of their membership.

In the Allende period, with its Marxist slant, and the early Pinochet years, with its Milton Friedman–type free enterprise philosophy, cooperatives in Chile diminished and suffered economic decline. In both cases, the incumbent administration was hostile to true democratic and independent grass-roots institutions that political leaders in power could not control and use to serve the prevailing economic and political philosophy.

Chile is a dramatic example of a cooperative movement that faced adversity consecutively from the political extremes of both Left and Right. National experiences in other countries attest to the ability of cooperatives to survive such trying circumstances. For example, during Idi Amin's rule in Uganda, credit unions grew as the national banks were plundered and Ugandans moved savings into institutions they themselves controlled. After Amin's rule, coffee and cotton cooperatives, despite having had all their facilities destroyed, became the major vehicles for providing relief supplies to rural areas. As human institutions, the cooperatives endured; the leadership and the base of members survived despite a loss of physical assets.

In Guatemala the highland Indians have clung to their small agricultural cooperatives in the face of right-wing attacks by National Guardsmen, who killed an estimated 10 percent of their population and intimidated their cooperative leaders. Cooperatives have been one of the few "imported" organizations from outside that the Indians consider their own and that brought unity to their people.

In Nicaragua coffee and small merchants' cooperatives have been among the grass-roots organizations most resistant to the Marxist Sandinistas. The latter's drive to control the means of production is often implemented by setting up parallel state-run and state-controlled "cooperatives" to undercut the genuinely democratic and independent cooperative.

On the West Bank, Palestinian cooperatives became stronger after the 1974 Arab-Israeli war as neither an Arab war nor peace appeared likely to liberate them from Israeli military occupation. As significant membership institutions with a clear Palestinian identity, cooperatives provide village-based economic and political unity. Unlike some Palestinian organizations, such as youth clubs or student organizations, cooperatives have remained neutral and clear of the fractious disputes between various Palestinian political groupings.

Why are cooperatives, then, so important to their members, especially when confronted with political and economic challenges? The answer lies in their democratic nature.

DEMOCRACY IN COOPERATIVES

There are two ways to look at the relationship between democracy and cooperatives: the extent of democracy in cooperatives themselves, and cooperatives as they affect political democracy. The basic cooperative principles, as adopted at the 1966 Congress of the International Cooperative Alliance, provide for open and voluntary membership; democratic procedures, including "one member, one vote"; education of cooperative members and the public on cooperative economic and democratic principles; and cooperation among cooperatives at local, national, and international levels.

It is important not to look only at "one member, one vote" or attendance at the annual meeting as the test of democracy in cooperatives. Members' equity in their cooperatives is also a measure of involvement. Leadership training, member education, rotation of directors, free flow of information to the membership and broad-based decision making are democratic elements as well. A true cooperative is democratic in structure and in its operation.

The specific purposes of democracy in cooperatives are to achieve a positive attitude on the part of members toward the organization they own and to establish open channels of communication enabling members to exert their influence on decision making. The need to upgrade the processes of democracy in cooperative organizations is one of the most urgent challenges confronting the worldwide cooperative movement today.

The democratic nature of cooperatives is as relevant to cooperatives in developed countries as in the developing world. In developed countries, democracy addresses issues such as declining participation of members in the affairs of their often large cooperatives. In developing countries, democratic procedure is the essential feature that provides for the full participation of members in their own development.

Cooperatives advance political democracy because they provide a basis for the involvement of individuals in their larger society. Democracy cannot be transferred whole and intact as a Western ideal, but institutions such as cooperatives can shape peoples' identities and the manner in which they relate to larger structures of a modern society. In India a large regional dairy cooperative in Anand collects buffalo milk twice a day from small producers, often women. The cooperative weighs the milk on a first-come basis. Indians of different castes, men and women, queue up together in the same location to deliver their milk despite a cultural history of a socially segmented society based on sex and family background.

NOT ALWAYS DEMOCRATIC

All cooperatives do not meet democratic standards. A cooperative may be controlled by a charismatic leader, such as a village priest, and may disintegrate when the leader withdraws. While strong leadership is essential to cooperative development, it may also produce a cooperative that is democratic in form only. It is incumbent upon cooperative founders and leaders to broaden participation and bring members into leadership positions; otherwise, the cooperative will not only be undemocratic but will fail over time.

Cooperatives are often chameleons of the society in which they operate and may assume the same power structure. However, if there is wide participation, cooperative benefits do change societal attitudes through constructively bringing together disparate elements of society and narrowing the gap, for example, between the better-off and the poor farmers.

In the case of agricultural cooperatives, spin-off effects to small farmers can occur in opening up new markets for their products or providing lower-cost farm supplies because cooperative operations pool resources for enhancing the members' economic interests. Thus, an agricultural cooperative dominated by large farmers may still benefit small farmers. For democratic institution building, it is essential that the cooperative provide a mechanism to draw the small farmer into full participation in its governance and operations; otherwise, the cooperative can become discriminatory.

In general, large farm owners are not interested in cooperatives and do not need volume discounts on supplies or marketing power. They are often hostile to agricultural cooperatives—just as village moneylenders will oppose credit unions. They want to prevent competition in the marketplace. On the other hand, better-off cooperative members may hold the view that their participation in and support for cooperatives is an expression of their concern for helping low- and moderate-income people in their society. These richer members may be motivated to serve on cooperative boards to repay society for the benefits they themselves have received.

Over time, a cooperative can be the bootstrap that elevates its members to economic strength, leaving others behind and outside the cooperative's direct benefits. Cooperative development strategies, which are primarily concerned with member equity and the democratic participation of those in the cooperative's service area, may need to be designed to withdraw financial and technical support as members gain economic strength. Limited outside cooperative resources should be focused on the poor in society and should support mechanisms either for bringing them into the cooperative or for creating separate cooperative institutions. While a cooperative can be exclusive, even monopolistic, such a cooperative does not live up to the cooperative principles and ideals on which it is founded.

COOPERATIVES AS MEDIATING STRUCTURES

Cooperatives are mediating structures. Peter Berger of Boston University noted that "mediating structures are the sociological soil from which political democracy, if absent today, may grow tomorrow." As such, they may prevent an individual from falling into apathy or alienation. They can ensure that government and society remain connected to the values of ordinary people. Thus cooperatives, if allowed to function relatively freely, form part of the "potential matrix for a future democracy."

In Guatemala the desperately poor and distinct ethnic population of Indian farmers of the Western Highlands possess, each, from one-half to one or two acres of steeply sloping land. Most are unable to subsist on these micro farms and must do part-time labor on big plantations along the coast to eke out a living. Over a number of years, outside technicians were able to build six regional cooperatives serving 2,000 or 3,000 farmers each in these highlands. The cooperatives provide credit, know-how on fertilizer and improved seed, and a simple, one-page combination farm plan and credit application. They also provide portable threshers to work members' wheat, which is then sold by the cooperative.

These regionals are built on a two-tiered system of market-town offices and village groups. The latter serve as a preliminary credit screening committee and, frequently, as a fertilizer and seed distribution point. The leader of each village group comes to the central office each month as a member of an advisory committee that is the major channel of communication between the members and the central cooperative office. This provides effective feedback from the Indians to the Guatemalan management.

The board of directors elected by the members is all-Indian and is, in fact, in control. Most of the management is not Indian because it is hard to find Indians with sufficient background to become managers and accountants. For the last six years, these cooperatives have been operating entirely under Guatemalan control. They were established as completely neutral economic enterprises outside the political realm. But they have been, in effect, the only institutions controlled by the Indians that have provided a bridge into the Spanish-speaking world.

Previously, the Indians had their own leadership, their own culture, and self-government. However, they were a community apart and viewed institutions of the "white man's world" with great suspicion. Because their cooperatives hewed to the economic nonpartisan line, the cooperatives have survived the violence in Guatemala. Two or three of these cooperatives lost more than one-third of their members. However, the cooperatives as institutions were not attacked by the right-wing death squads, the army, or the guerrillas.

COOPERATIVES AND NATIONAL GOVERNMENTS

Democracy in cooperatives may have special significance in the developing world because of weak national governments and traditional exploitative structures, as in the case of large landowners who control the economic and political life of peasants. The distance from those in power—economically and politically—may be greater; thus, the impact of people controlling their own destiny can be greater.

Does the increased participation of people in cooperatives, which in turn make demands on the state, threaten governments? Government officials may indeed see cooperatives as a political or economic threat or potential irritant, but they may also look at citizen participation in cooperatives as a means of expanding political involvement and economic resources. Cooperatives provide an opportunity for the exercise of political rights. Each member has one vote. Meetings may be well attended and not confined to business trivia. Important issues may be discussed, such as the proper role of management and directors, their relation to members and the structuring of the cooperative for member control of its business. There are significant opportunities for debate and for the resolution of important issues. These political opportunities and lessons are not lost on members when their attitudes and behavior become more inclined to joint political action. From these evolve positive attitudes toward political unity and group action.

In the absence of a middle class, the cooperative has a greater appeal to the needs of the lower strata of society. The rich can fend for themselves; the less fortunate need cooperatives and the services they provide. Leadership in cooperatives need not be, as is often the case where there are no cooperatives, bestowed by "a patron" or other individuals of high economic status. Membership of the boards of directors may rotate, giving more cooperative members an opportunity to develop leadership skills. Elections to boards of cooperatives are virtually always honest, a phenomenon that is not as common in the political field. There are important economic incentives for lower-income members to exert themselves for their own benefit. The practical experience with grass-roots democracy is positive and tangible.

There is also a changed attitude toward fellow cooperative members. The traditional elite can no longer divide members of cooperatives through favoritism. Members become more willing to exchange political views. Concepts of trust and solidarity are built into the cooperative. Social activities may become more frequent. New thought patterns emerge, such as a feeling of equality among differing ethnic groups.

However, this local solidarity may not be readily transferred to national and regional organizations. Cooperatives can become inward-looking islands of democracy. They may look to government for needed services—registration, finance, and the like, but often these demands are not transformed into strong federations for advocacy of more general cooperative concerns. In some cases, governments will resist national cooperative organizations, preferring to retain control of marketing, processing, pricing, and other economic functions. The government may also want to resist more specifically political demands from a large cooperative membership represented by a strong national federation.

In turn, cooperative members may grow mistrustful of government officials who send mixed signals about helping or hurting the cooperatives. The government may control the hiring or firing of managers, place various limitations on the cooperative and, in general, try to maintain control through its bureaucracy. To the extent that a government wishes to make changes, cooperatives may provide a means for doing so.

Weak governments in the developing world are often unable to achieve positive changes for their citizens. In such circumstances, they may collaborate with cooperatives—rather than see them as competitors for allegiance—in order to achieve economic development.

THE ROLE OF GOVERNMENT

The relationship of cooperatives to government is one of the most difficult subjects in cooperative theory and practice. The history of cooperative development in the West is generally one in which governments have been neutral and have considered cooperatives as one part of the economic system, to stand or fall on their own. Official endorsement and enabling legislation usually followed the spontaneous growth of cooperatives. In contrast, cooperatives in the developing world are often part of a colonial legacy, though pre-cooperative structures may have existed in some cultures. These governments frequently adopted cooperative development as an integral part of their national development plan and therefore became directly involved in the creation and management of cooperatives.

Democratic cooperatives need a climate that allows them to be autonomous and self-governing, including suitable legislation, recognition of their legitimacy, and assistance when meeting the special needs of the less fortunate. However, excessive government control and involvement have been major constraints to genuine democratic cooperative growth. In such cases, national cooperative development plans have needed to focus on the "weaning procedures" by which cooperatives, started through government initiative, can become more self-reliant.

A troubling issue in Latin America, for example, is that, as the cooperative systems grow, they become more prone to government interference. With rapid turnovers in governments, the chances increase that a government hostile to the cooperative movement will hold office from time to time. It may be unwilling to tolerate strong and independent grass-roots organizations that it cannot control. The government may try to impose its political viewpoint through its party structure. The government may try to co-opt the cooperative system. And, if government changes again, a close identity with the previous government can be disastrous. In Chile, for example, cooperatives were closely associated with the Christian Democratic government of Eduardo Frei. Later, both the Marxist-led government of Allende and the Pinochet military rule have restricted cooperatives because of this previous association.

As the cooperative movement grows, it begins to have a significant impact on the economy; for example, credit unions may absorb a high percentage of the country's savings. The regime of a developing country often will not tolerate strong financial centers, cooperative or not, that it cannot directly control. Similarly, the government may want to control processing of commodities for export and not allow independent cooperative control of key economic sectors. Also, as the cooperative movement grows, there is increasing resistance from vested interests. For example, an effort to build vegetable oil cooperatives in India came face to face with the entrenched power of several families that had a monopoly on this huge market. These families tried to stop the cooperative efforts by resorting to violence against cooperative leaders and facilities, but the cooperative was eventually successful in breaking the monopoly.

GOVERNMENT PATERNALISM

In many countries cooperatives have functioned under governments that have been friendly to them. The principal problem that the cooperatives have faced has not been governmental hostility, but governmental paternalism. Cooperatives have suffered from government efforts to foster them, which, in fact, have tended to weaken them. This results from the inclination of many government leaders to view cooperatives as instruments of social improvement and ignore the fact that they must first be economically viable institutions.

Governments have fostered cooperatives with subsidies that have undercut financial discipline. In some cases they have used coooperatives for price control—keeping food prices down for urban consumers. In a few cases, cooperatives have been assigned duties such as financing and operating health clinics, schools, and roads. These services should be functions of local governments, which, in many cases, have not been capable of providing them.

In a number of Latin American countries, plantations have been nationalized and production cooperatives have been formed among the previous plantation workers to take over and run the farms. This approach has been a social movement, a political movement, a self-consciously reformist, even revolutionary, effort led by government. For example, young military officers in Peru undertook such a land reform, creating thousands of small agricultural cooperatives. The results in many cases have been chaotic because of mistaken ideas about what democratic operation means. Workers, now cooperative members, have tried to make operating decisions by collective vote, meeting once or twice a week. They voted to pay themselves wages in advance of harvest, which the cooperatives could not afford. In some cases the managers of these cooperatives were former foremen or government extension agents. In other cases they were members of the elected committees of the collectives who took turns being manager for a month at a time. None of these people, even the previous foremen, have ever had experience in the business of running a large farm. This lack of training has had a disastrous impact on production in many cases, particularly in Peru and El Salvador. Too much democracy in cooperatives can become self-destructive.

Cooperative movements usually resist excessive government intrusion. Members will fight to maintain their cooperative, which, in many cases, is the only structure in society that they really control. Although they can successfully defend their cooperative from direct physical attack, it is the more subtle governmental intrusions that tend to be most destructive— usually through financial leverage. For example, in Chile the Pinochet government called in government loans to Unicoop, a large cooperative food chain in Santiago, even though the cooperative was financially solvent. Earlier, Unicoop had successfully resisted the physical occupation of its stores by Marxist elements of the previous Allende government. But there was no effective way for the cooperative members to prevent dissolution by government edict.

PROMOTING DEMOCRATIC COOPERATIVES

Outside experts must be careful how they approach democratic institution building in other countries. In the memory of current leaders is their colonial past. It is their present government the outsiders are "reforming." These governments are newer, and democracies, if they exist among them, are more fragile. Developing country leaders remember when it was a point of honor to oppose the colonial power. Now, they see their governments—good or bad—as their own. In dealing with this nationalist predisposition, outside cooperative experts should guard against linking up with those cooperative leaders who may be more interested in exploiting this predisposition in order to become antigovernment heroes than in helping the people meet their own immediate needs.

Cooperative leaders—whether outside technicians or those in the country—should avoid using potentially inflammatory terms such as *human rights* and *social justice*. Cooperative development may be related, but these terms should be left to the politicians. If one talks about the "exploitation of the poor," one will be labeled a partisan and will not be effective in the practical ways of helping people. Instead, a humble approach is more effective. "You, the government leaders, are concerned about the people; we, as cooperative leaders, have the same concern. Let's work together." This is the way a famous Korean credit union leader put it.

With this approach in mind, there are various techniques for influencing government to create or maintain a conducive climate for the growth of independent cooperatives. For example, a cooperative should ask government leaders to address its members. These leaders will usually say "nice things." The cooperative may want to follow up by inviting the official to say the same kind words before another membership audience. In general, the approach should be personal and one-on-one: get to know government and political leaders, gain their confidence, and stress mutual aspirations for the people.

Another approach is to use the cooperatives' organizing ability. In considering the relationship of cooperatives to a country's politics and government, it is a good strategy to organize cooperatives, such as credit unions or consumer stores, to serve influence centers, such as the police, the military, or the ministry of finance. If government and political leaders experience and understand cooperatives as nonthreatening democratic institutions of which they themselves are members, they will be more tolerant of the independence of cooperatives generally.

There is much evidence that cooperatives are a good training ground for future country leadership and hence a way of assuring that friends of the cooperatives are in the government. For example, a former president of Costa Rica grew up in the cooperative movement. Cooperative leaders were the only group welcomed to dinner regularly in the president's palace. The current president of Honduras was an employee of a technical service organization that built housing cooperatives. In Korea, 25 members of parliament came out of the credit union movement—one of the most successful in Asia.

Cooperatives may want to encourage their leaders to move into the political arena, but it is important that they leave official cooperative trappings and functions behind. Furthermore, a particular cooperative ought not to become too closely identified with a few political leaders or a single political party.

Cooperatives are appealing to the Right as free-enterprise businesses and to the Left as socially and economically valuable ways to help the less fortunate. This appeal enables cooperatives to relate to a broad political spectrum. It is important that cooperatives do the co-opting and not allow political parties or political leaders to co-opt cooperatives. Unfortunately, the latter appears more prevalent than the former.

THE RELATIONSHIP OF COOPERATIVES AND POLITICAL PARTIES

Cooperatives have a role with respect to political parties. The Christian Democratic and Socialist internationals include endorsement of cooperatives in their political planks. They also view cooperatives as an acceptable form of private enterprise. Often, however, party leaders look to cooperatives for a political rather than an economic purpose, especially in government-led land reform efforts.

Cooperatives in developed countries have a mixed record with regard to following the original Rochdale principle of nonpartisanship. Even followers of the Rochdale pioneers formed a political party that, later, was absorbed into the Labour party in Britain. In the U.S. two-party system, cooperatives have support in both parties. Cooperative organizations are nonpartisan with respect to endorsing candidates, but political on cooperative issues. This stance may be harder to maintain in a developing country.

In Argentina the housing cooperatives had not been encouraged during the recent military rule. As elections approached, they joined together through a federation to undertake a campaign to influence federal legislation. They approached the Peronista, Radical Civic Union, and the Christian Democratic parties and hosted a three-day conference for their top political leaders. The ban on political activity for half a decade under the military regime had smothered grass-roots participation. Party leaders felt the lack of dialogue with a broad constituency. They welcomed discussion with self-help housing cooperatives, even though these cooperatives represented a small portion of the population. In this way the federation of housing cooperatives was successful in having its blueprint for housing policies adopted by both political parties. This is the same political model used by cooperatives in the United States. It may also have application to Chile and Uruguay as those countries move toward a transition to democracy.

CONCLUSION

Ample evidence exists regarding the role cooperatives can perform in building democratic structures and understanding among large numbers of people. However, there is a notable lack of information and analytic experience on the precise relationships of cooperatives to democratic political systems. Certainly in a country like India, with over 300,000 cooperatives, they are consequential for maintaining democratic governance. Yet a full understanding of the value of democratic cooperatives is not known, nor has it been a subject of extensive examination.

In the early 1960s, when cooperative development was more in vogue and many programs were started, there was a strong focus on developing model cooperative laws and policies and encouraging cooperative education. This interest has slackened although the need has not diminished.

National cooperative federations in developing countries remain weak without a strong economic base of member financial support in dues or through services. This results in overdependence on governments by

national cooperative leaders and lack of ability to undertake independent political actions. Because cooperative federations are financially
weak, the traditional three-tier cooperative structure—primary cooperative, federations by sectors (housing, agriculture, credit unions, and so
on) and a confederation or apex organization—needs to be reexamined. A
two-tier system consisting of a single national organization and primary
cooperatives could reduce the need for government subsidies to maintain the human infrastructure needed by cooperatives. A strong national
organization with organic links—ideological and economic—to primary
cooperatives could also result in more political clout for cooperatives
within developing countries.

Questioning cooperative structures should be undertaken with the
purpose of developing an explicit theory of political corollaries for
cooperative development. There may not be a single model, but various
relationships of cooperatives to political systems should be analyzed for
insights about promoting democratic change.

Unfortunately, the predominant view of cooperative leaders is that
they should try to stay completely out of politics. This is simply not
possible. Any ideological movement premised on democratic rules has a
political viewpoint. With large numbers of supporters, cooperatives will
be called upon to take political positions. Too often, a void is filled by
opportunistic politicians who set the cooperative political agenda.

If cooperatives are truly "laboratories for democracy," as the literature suggests, then cooperative leaders should use their national experiments to test various political postures aimed at advancing national
democratic governance. Cooperatives must face the need to translate
democratic rhetoric and practice into political corollaries and tangible
political programs for building democratic societies.

REFERENCES

Berger, Peter L. "Some Observations on Democracy and Cultural Relativity."
    Address, Conference on Project Democracy, USIA, Washington, D.C., May
    9, 1983.
_____. "Democracy for Everyone." Commentary 76 (September 1983): 31-6.
Cooperatives in Chile's Transition to Democracy: Findings from a Study Tour by U.S.
    Cooperative Representatives. Washington, D.C.: U.S. Overseas Cooperative
    Development Committee, March 1985.
Cooperatives, Small Farmers and Rural Development. A report on a Wingspread
    Conference (April 1978). The report sponsors were the Agricultural Council
    of America and the Overseas Cooperative Development Committee.
Democracy Program. Final Report. The American Commitment to Democracy:
    A Bipartisan Approach. Washington, D.C.: American Political Foundation,
    November 30, 1983.
Douglas, William A. Developing Democracy. Washington, D.C.: Heldref, 1972.

Hadkarni, R. V. "Democratic Character in Cooperative Housing Societies." *NCHF News Bulletin* 2 (October 1983): 1-3.

Harvey, Bartlett. "The Role of Cooperatives in Latin American Democracy." *American Cooperation 1985*, Mary K. Bidlack, ed. (Washington, D.C.: American Institute of Cooperation, 1985).

Hirschman, Albert O. *Getting Ahead Collectively: Grassroots Experiences in Latin America*. New York: Pergamon Press, 1984.

Finding Co-ops: A Resource Guide and Directory. Washington, D.C.: Cooperative Information Consortium, 1984.

Laidlaw, A. F. *Cooperatives in the Year 2000*. London: International Cooperative Alliance, 1980.

Massachusetts Institute of Technology. *The Role of Popular Participation in Development* (report of a conference on the implementations of Title IX), MIT Report no. 17 (Cambridge: MIT Press, November 1968).

McClintock, Cynthia. *Peasant Cooperatives and Political Change in Peru*. Princeton: Princeton University Press, 1981.

McGrath, Mary Jean, ed. *Guidelines for Cooperatives in Developing Economies*. Madison, Wis.: International Training Center, 1969.

Page, Diana. "Community Democracy: Housing Groups in Argentina's Getting in on the Ground Floor." *Grassroots Development: Journal of the Inter-American Foundation* 8, no. 1 (1984): 38-43.

Palestinian Cooperatives on the West Bank and Gaza: Findings from a Study Tour by U.S. Cooperative Representatives. November 30, 1983. (Available from U.S. Overseas Cooperative Development Committee, 1800 Massachusetts Avenue, N.W., Washington ,D.C., 20036).

Samuels, Michael A., and William A. Douglas. "Promoting Democracy." *Washington Quarterly* (Center for International Studies, Georgetown University) 4 (Summer 1981).

Tendler, Judith. *What to Think about Cooperatives: A Guide from Bolivia*. Washington, D.C.: Inter-American Foundation, 1983.

Trevena, J. E. "Democratic Control of Co-operatives." *Cooperative Future Directions Project*. Working Papers, no. 5 (Saskatoon, Saskatchewan: Co-operative College of Canada, May 1980).

———. "Purposeful Democracy for Co-operatives." *Cooperative Future Directions Project*. Working Papers, Vol. 1, no. 4 (Saskatoon, Saskatchewan: Co-operative College of Canada, August 1983).

Weihe, Ted. "Promotion of Democracy: Political Corollaries to Cooperative Development." *American Cooperation 1985*, Mary K. Bidlack, ed. (Washington, D.C.: American Institute of Cooperation, 1985).

Why Cooperative Development: Views of Some of the World's Leading Practitioners. Washington, D.C.: Cooperative Resources Committee, 1985.

11 ORGANIZING THE DEMOCRACIES TO PROMOTE DEMOCRACY
Ira Straus

As the United States undertakes to promote democracy and considers the conditions of democratic success, we as a nation are entitled to some pride in the fact that it was the United States that for the first time in history made a real success of democracy. It was the United States that vindicated the reputation of democracy and overcame its negative connotations.

Tribal democracy has roots going back beyond recorded history. City-state democracy goes back more than 2,000 years, and for most of this period democracy has been equated with its city-state version—and consequently with turbulence, crudity, popular passions, and intolerance of culture.

Democracy on a broad geographical scale was a modern innovation. It began with British representative self-government and culminated in U.S. federalism. Its success gave democracy the new connotations of pluralism, tolerance, and stability. It made possible the phenomenal spread of democracy not only across the North American continent, but in the Old World as well.

In the late nineteenth and early twentieth centuries a small number of people, surveying the instability of democracy in continental Europe, began to consider the broader implications of U.S. federalism for the spread and stabilization of democracy. Their work grew in two phases.

In the first phase, the British Imperial Federalists proposed the spreading of democracy throughout the British Empire and the closer uniting of the empire in a common democratic structure in order to stabilize the world-historical leadership of Britannic democracy in the face of the supposed unreliability of all continentals. Their efforts came too late to achieve their highest goals, but they did have a positive impact on the development of democratic practices in India and in the emigrant dominions, and in the development of dominion status itself as a reform of the old imperial system.

The second phase, which still continues, was precipitated by the two world wars and by both the existence and the failures of the League of Nations. In 1939 Federal Union movements emerged in Britain and the United States, advocating the uniting of historically distinct nations on democratic federal principles. The movement had three strands: European Federalist, Atlantic Federalist, and World Federalist.

The World Federalist strand aimed to build a democratic world by first federating all countries. It has concentrated since 1945 on strengthening and reforming the U.N. system.

The European and Atlantic strands aimed to build a democratic world by first federating existing democracies. Their supporters inside and outside governments played vital roles in developing the European Communities and Atlantic and Trilateral Alliance systems—systems that have enabled democracy to spread and stabilize throughout free Europe for the first time in history. They have concentrated ever since on strengthening, enlarging and deepening these systems.

ORIGINS OF THE CCD PROGRAM

In the beginning of the 1980s, people with long experience in the efforts to unite European and Atlantic democracies formed Committees for a Community of Democracies (CCDs) in London, Brussels, Washington, D.C., and Seattle. Their initial aim was to develop plans for gradually linking the developed democracies (or member nations of the Organization for Economic Cooperation and Development) more closely. After an initial "circle-group" phase, during which various proposals were floated in the several groups, an international CCD conference was held in London in 1982 to establish a common foundation for further work.

A new emphasis emerged in the London conference. Whereas CCDs had previously concentrated exclusively on uniting the industrial democracies, several participants now stressed the need to supplement this program by trying to bring all of the democracies of the world together in a loose association. This view was approved in the closing declaration in London. CCD-USA proceeded to develop the new idea of the London conference into two proposals: (1) for an intergovernmental association of the democracies of the world; and (2) for an international institute for democracy.

That same year, President Reagan addressed the British Parliament at Westminster and called for a campaign to "foster the infrastructure of democracy" around the world. He thereby launched what came to be known as the Democracy Initiative, which was soon crystallized in the form of the National Endowment for Democracy (NED). As will be seen, NED has come to play a major (and entirely legitimate and constructive) role in the effort described in this chapter.

The idea of organizing democratic solidarity was genuinely bipartisan and, indeed, international. During the 1984 presidential campaign, Walter Mondale proposed the establishment of an assembly of democracies, thereby raising CCD proposals high in the public domain. European ideas and experience of promoting democracy also provided important background for the president's speech at Westminster, for NED, and for the CCD proposals.

Unfortunately, NED was plagued from the start with funding troubles in Congress. It has managed only with difficulty to stay funded on a level of about $18 million a year, and this is widely recognized as being far less than what is needed for its mission. We shall see how the constraints and uncertainties placed on its funding have been disruptive to those who have planned together with NED for the promotion of democracy.

CCD offered a way to fulfill the promise of the Democracy Initiative. Indeed, a presidential letter specifically praised CCD for having "taken up the challenge" of his Westminster speech, adding, "I hope that the international meeting you are about to convene will develop practical measures to help build meaningful cooperation at the inter-governmental level."

In July 1984, NED granted CCD-USA $75,000 to fund the main portion of the first year's costs of preparing for a global association of democracies. The funding was earmarked specifically for organizing and conducting an international meeting in 1985 (Preparation for a Conference, PREFACE).

Preparing for PREFACE

In the initial stage a private meeting was preferred to a governmental initiative, because it would be freer from diplomatic commitments and from habitual national suspicions. The meeting had to be limited in size and yet include broad geographical representation, as well as expertise on international affairs, area and cultural matters, and democracy. To get broad participation, CCD-USA sought the cooperation of other associations in the field, such as Freedom House, the Center for the Study of Democratic Institutions, the Atlantic Council, and CCD groups abroad.

PREFACE was to lay plans for a further nongovernmental conference of all democracies (the "main conference") to complete the proposals for organizing democratic cooperation and to present them to governments for action. In particular, PREFACE would

1. propose agenda for the subsequent main conference, which would consider establishing an association of democracies and an institute for democracy;
2. make recommendations on the participation at the main conference, and
3. consider ways to develop further private support in as many countries as possible for closer cooperation among practicing democracies.

The subsequent main conference would still be primarily nongovernmental. The participants would be carefully selected from mainstream groups in the more than 50 practicing democracies. It would consider various areas for improved cooperation among democracies, ranging from trade and investment to journalism and terrorism, and would recommend permanent institutional means for such cooperation as it would deem advisable.

Gearing Up

CCD's first task in carrying through its program was to organize its volunteers and enlist capable personnel who understood its task. It engaged Charles R. Tanguy, a retired U.S. Foreign Service officer, as program director. It opened an office in downtown Washington, D.C. It established a newsletter—*CCD Courier*—to disseminate the substance of draft proposals and of reactions to them, so the process of discussion and consensus formation could be sufficiently advanced by the time PREFACE began that it would have a chance to get through its business in the few days its participants would be able to stay together in one place.

Samuel DePalma, an expert on international organizational affairs in the Department of State from 1947 to 1973, became CCD-USA president, while James Huntley, CCD's founding chairman, went on to other duties. DePalma had served in U.N., NATO, and Arms Control and Disarmament Agency posts until 1969, and had been assistant secretary of state from 1969 to 1973. Bringing with him considerable experience in international conferences and multilateral diplomacy, he assumed active leadership of the CCD project.

A working group of volunteers, which came to be dubbed the Gang of Six—Samuel DePalma, Robert Foulon (CCD-USA secretary), James Martin (CCD-DC secretary), Thomas Stern (treasurer), Ira Straus (editor) and Charles Tanguy—put together the plans for PREFACE in regular weekly meetings. The six were eventually augmented to seven with Eugene Rosenfeld (media relations) and continued as staff at the PREFACE meeting proper.

SUBSTANCE OF THE PROPOSALS

The proposal for an association of democracies had originated in the observation that there was no global forum of democracies. An association of democracies could enhance the prestige of democratic ideals and practices globally, much as the Council of Europe had done within Europe. It could also enhance solidarity and cooperation across North-South lines, both in economic matters and in the support of the development and stabilization of domestic democratic institutions.

An association could also be the sponsoring or governing body for a second organization: an international institute for democracy This institute, independent of any particular national identity, could support needed academic studies on democracy, provide training and technical assistance, and help in finding the way through obstacles to democratic practices and to cooperation among democracies.

These two proposals were developed in some detail in the course of the preparatory discussions.

Association of Democracies

A draft for the proposal for an association of democracies was prepared, in consultation with the Gang of Six, by Raymond D. Gastil of Freedom House. It took as its point of departure the consideration that the democracies need to focus on their common values as a major concern in their international relations, above and beyond special economic and geopolitical interests. In fact, the solidarity achieved by working together to preserve and promote democratic practices could undoubtedly assist in harmonizing more concrete interests and encouraging cooperation in economic and other fields and could thereby enhance international peace and security.

The proposed association would therefore concentrate on promoting democratic political practices and human rights both among its members and in countries aspiring to democracy. It would not be a direct source of economic assistance but would help countries to perceive common interests and problems and thus facilitate economic cooperation in other forums. It might also take up such matters as common approaches to refugees from authoritarian countries and a concerted approach to terrorism.

In conjunction with an institute for democracy, the associaton would provide a forum for assessing the needs of new and fragile democracies and would foster mutual support for the protection and promotion of democracy.

Merely by providing visible solidarity for democratic practices and a feeling of identity with the democratic world, an association could help stabilize new and fragile democracies. By further showing that political and other benefits would accrue from democratic practices and membership, it could draw additional countries toward democracy.

An association of democracies could eventually have a charter and an institutional structure, but the first step toward this structure might be an informal forum, with periodic meetings of representatives of democracies. Once formalized, the association might still be modest in size, with a secretariat staffed largely by seconded officials and a site placed at its disposal by a member government.

A preliminary listing, based on the work of Freedom House, showed the existence of 54 democracies then eligible for membership in an association. Once established by deposit of the requisite number of instruments of ratification, membership in the association would be open to any state that accepted the charter's principles and undertook to make its practices conform to them, subject to acceptance of the application by the existing membership. Default on these obligations could lead to suspension of membership.

Regional groupings of democracies, such as already existed in Europe, could be promoted under the aegis of the association as a way of overcoming the sense of powerlessness of small democracies. Such groupings, along with "coalitions of the willing" and functional affiliates, would be ways for the association to develop cooperation. A prime functional affiliate would be an international institute for democracy.

Institute for Democracy

The draft proposal for an international institute for democracy was prepared, again in consultation with the Gang of Six, by Ralph M. Goldman of San Francisco State University. It took as its point of departure the consideration that democracy is consistent with common human needs and involves forms and methods that are basically replicable and transferable, even though historical and cultural conditions may require adaptations.

The institute would assist in the establishment and improvement of democratic institutions and serve as a center for the development and promotion of democratic ideas. It would study conditions in which democracies thrive, provide information and training in democratic studies, and offer expert consultation in techniques and procedures of democracy—the administration of elections, the conduct of campaigns, the drafting of constitutions, the adjudication of human rights, and so forth.

The institute could produce studies on prospects and procedures for peaceful transition from authoritarian and totalitarian regimes to pluralistic democracy. Consultation teams visiting a country could study conditions relevant to democratic development and conduct seminars for leadership groups. An educational services division could assist in developing democratic curricula and instructional programs.

Research would come under five headings: democratic assessment data, democratic institutional development, democratic theory, relations among democracies, and program evaluation procedures. Publications could include scholarly monographs, popular multilingual magazines, and materials to encourage prodemocracy productions in the private media.

The proposed institute would have an international governing board, chosen from distinguished democratic statesmen and political experts, to oversee operations, finances, and formal policy statements. The Association of Democracies might appoint this board, which in turn could select a small executive committee and appoint an executive director. The institute could in turn help the Association of Democracies in assessing a country's democratic qualifications or intentions and in identifying indigenous democratic groups.

The institute might establish small regional centers, probably linked with existing academic institutions. Funding would come from governments, private sources, and international organizations, in the form of endowment and project grants.

The institute could be launched with a core program that would inspire further development and funding. It was intended that, after PREFACE, a multinational group of experts would estimate prospective costs for launching the institute in this manner and survey potential sponsors, participants, and users of institute services.

The Democracies and the U.N.

A third proposal was prepared for PREFACE by CCD. Having spent most of his career in dealing with the U.N. system, De Palma found the continuing erosion of U.N. effectiveness a matter of deep concern. He had seen the division into North and South blocs grow and bring destructive confrontations. He proposed a caucus of democracies in the U.N. and UNESCO to ameliorate this situation.

The caucus would enable democracies to harmonize views on U.N. questions where common values and interests were at stake. It could meet at the beginning of each U.N. and UNESCO session, and as necessary thereafter, to review the U.N. agenda and try to concert approaches to particular items or to add its own items to the agenda.

Such a caucus would not constitute a bloc with uniform interests, nor could it seek to establish monolithic voting patterns. The caucus was later rechristened the Consultative Group of Democracies in order to emphasize this caveat. Like the association, it was not aimed against any existing international organizations, nor at duplicating their work, but rather at supplementing them, filling a major gap in international cooperation: cooperation among all democracies. This, DePalma was convinced, would help the other organizations function more effectively.

A caucus of democracies would strengthen the U.N. and UNESCO by drawing them back toward the democratic tenets that inspired their charters. It would advance human rights by encouraging an authentic and balanced approach to human rights questions in the U.N. system. Also, through coalitions of the willing, perhaps working in turn through the association, it could implement projects consistent with the U.N. and UNESCO charters that those organizations might be unable to undertake. The caucus could be formed on the initiative of democratic delegations in the U.N.

PRE-PREFACE DISCUSSION OF PROPOSALS

CCD's initial dissemination of the draft proposals led to a wide-ranging discussion. Several matters received special attention, namely:

- Should the association begin informally, as an intergovernmental or even private forum, or formally, as a chartered intergovernmental organization? Or would it be best not to prejudge this, but simply to encourage the governments to go as far as they might prove willing?
- With what functions should the association begin? What functions should it eventually take up? What functions should it avoid?
- How could room for growth and development best be built into the charters of the association and the institute?
- Who should fund the institute—governments or private sources?
- What were the pros and cons for various countries of participation in these organizations? In particular, how could the program be made attractive to democracies in both the First and Third worlds, in view of the confrontational rhetoric that has tended to divide them in recent years?

Following are some of the highlights of this pre-PREFACE discussion.

Economic Aspects

It was generally agreed that the association should not be a source of economic aid. One respondent added that it must "skirt the issue of economic assistance initially" if it was to have any chance of getting off the ground in the United States, but this need not prevent it from *discussing* economic issues.

There were differing opinions on the idea of preferential trade arrangements for democracies. Most respondents found this attractive in general, but one warned that "U.S. experience with selective preferences and embargos has been bad. MFN [Most-favored Nation] and GSP [Generalized System of Preferences] for less developed countries have been the best principle; the GATT [General Agreement on Tariffs and Trade] and U.S. trade laws provide adequate protection against foreign dumping, subsidies, etc.; and it would be dangerous to depart from these agreements and principles which have developed on the basis of experience."

Two respondents were of the view that, despite the fact that it is so rarely mentioned—or perhaps for this very reason—there was a need for "explicit discussion of the economic aspects of democracy: the role of free enterprise, free trade, property rights, and a strong middle class in promoting stable democracy."

Passive or Active?

One respondent drew attention to the different needs of an organization designed to agitate and press for democracy as distinct from one designed to gather and provide knowledge about democracy: "A *propaganda organization* would want a small, executive style leadership with highly centralized authority and access to media and operational communications links. A *passive organization* would want a wide membership with an emphasis on respected academicians/educational institutions and would invite prospective clients to come to its fountains of knowledge at their initiative, being careful to avoid any suggestion of funding or otherwise actively engaging itself on behalf of factious elements in potential democracies." This distinction corresponded to some extent to the distinction between the proposals for an association and for an institute. There were differing opinions as to the costs and benefits of combining both functions at times within a single organization.

It was generally felt that the institute should begin with one centralized location, where multinational contact would provide useful cross-fertilization.

One respondent questioned whether the institute could be competent to determine "the best methods of assisting democracy in emerging democratic states," since "this kind of decision is not an academic problem; it is a critical political decision." Others felt that this political decision would on the whole benefit by being informed by the work of an institute, and also by the moral background of solidarity provided by an association.

Informal or Intergovernmental?

Some respondents preferred an informal or even nongovernmental forum to a formal intergovernmental association, since the latter would cost the governments money and diplomatic time, which were already in short supply. Others suggested that the association should begin as an informal forum—perhaps as a meeting place for transnational political parties and other nongovernmental organizations—with the hope of later developing into an intergovernmental institution.

Most, however, held that the term *Association of Democracies* should be reserved for a formal intergovernmental institution, and that governments should be encouraged to go as far as possible. They anticipated considerable symbolic value in a formal proclamation of an intergovernmental association and regarded an informal forum as having far less value and staying power than a formal association. They argued that the costs of staff and facilities of international organizations are practically marginal in view of the importance of their functions, noting that there has been gross overreaction on this point. They maintained that inter-democratic institutions in particular, because they have a meaningful basis in political solidarity, have been well worth their costs, and govern-ments still regard them quite favorably.

The "informalists" and the "intergovernmentalists" shared some immediate tactics. Intergovernmentalists anticipated a few years' more work on the private level as preparation for official action. They also hoped that the transnational parties would come to give vigorous support to the establishment of an association as a means of enhancing their own significance. And they agreed that, if the governments were not willing to start out on a formal intergovernmental plane, an informal forum would be a positive interim step.

However, intergovernmentalists suggested that it would only harm the prospects of establishing an association if preparatory meetings and informal forums were already to be named an association or to be expected to get on with the substantive work of building solidarity among democracies. They anticipated that this would interfere with the preparatory work the informal meetings should be doing; and by giving them goals far beyond their capabilities, it would set them up to have their shortcomings cited as evidence against the value and feasibility of forming an intergovernmental association.

Leaving Room For Institutional Growth

There was also preliminary discussion of the future development of an association. All agreed that it would need room to grow, since there was not at present sufficient solidarity among all democracies for it to be given much initial authority.

Many tacitly assumed that, by beginning small, an association would have room to grow. Others maintained that room for growth must be consciously built into its charter. They cited the examples of the U.N. and the Council of Europe as institutions that began with many countries but few powers and, because they were dependent on unanimous consent for major changes, lacked the room they needed for growth.

Gastil's draft anticipated that the association would stimulate member countries to come together in other organizations. Examples would be a caucus within the U.N.; new functional organizations (the institute); new regional structures (on models like the Council of Europe, the European Communities, and the Association of Southeast Asian Nations); and coalitions of the willing to act during crisis situations (such as the transition of a particular country to democracy).

One respondent suggested that stimulus to other organizations or coalitions would be the main means for association growth, since it would not be easy for the association itself to gain new areas of authority. He suggested that the charter of the association include provisions for giving coalitions and functional organizations an affiliate status and for collaborating actively with them, so that people would come to see and speak of them as a common "world democratic system." The preamble to the charter could be worded to establish this as an integral part of the aims and outlook of the association. Groundwork could be laid by encouraging existing interdemocratic institutions to give expressions of support for the establishment of an association.

This concern was reflected in the warning by one delegate at PREFACE that, if the Council of Europe was to be used as a model for the association, it should be recalled that the council had proved an obstacle as well as an aid to initiatives for real integration among some of the European countries.

Ways of Promoting Democracy

Questions were also raised about how far the association should go in promoting democracy. Should it, for example, limit its membership to fully certifiable pluralistic democracies, or should it establish a category of associate or candidate membership for countries with elements of democracy and with an apparently sincere desire and intention to develop toward democracy? Should it work mainly by setting an example, improving the internal practices of existing democracies, and certifying elections as free and new democracies as members, or should it play an active role in transitions to democracy? Should it emphasize condemnation of nondemocratic governments and support of democratically oriented oppositions, or should it try to mediate between government and opposition, to build trust between them and to encourage a peaceful transition from repression to free election? Should it limit itself to moral support of democratic oppositions and condemn military intervention as an undemocratic practice, or should it overlook interventions in favor of democracy, or even expound terms and limits within which intervention would be legitimate?

The timeliness of these questions may be gauged by developments in Haiti and the Philippines. Recent strivings toward democracy remind us of how much is at stake when a struggle for democracy nears its climax—how frightening a tightrope may have to be walked if an undemocratic regime is to be eased out peacefully, and also how the tightrope may have to be abandoned and choices made rapidly and decisively if a struggle is not to end in failure and repression.

It will be important—historically important—to be ready to give a correct answer to these questions and to act on the answer in moments of crisis. The struggle for democracy is too serious a business to approach without preparation, particularly if a successful struggle brings a country to a crisis point. An association of democracies and international institute for democracy could play a valuable role in developing answers that would have the virtues of being firm, nuanced, consistent, and broadly backed.

North/South: Divergent Interests or Common Project?

A matter of special concern was whether First and Third World democracies could all agree on formulations that would enable them to join a single association.

One respondent raised with particular sharpness the political and public relations difficulties for Third World governments in joining an association. The association, he observed, could "provide a political forum for moderates to associate with other democracies and to endorse their democratic legitimacy." However, "Third World countries are weak and vulnerable to internal and to external pressures from the international world. What they typically want most of all are independence, security, and prosperity-growth-development. The G-77, the NonAligned, and other groups, e.g., OPEC and commodity cartels, are means toward these ends. Membership in the Association could give the impression of selling out to the North." The association could not add much to the existing economic and security arrangements as a way of inducing countries to join. On the other hand, the developed democracies might be leery of the whole thing "since there are more Less Developed Countries (LDCs) than developed democracies," and "the LDCs might be expected to turn the association into another General Assembly unless a system of weighted voting is used."

In response, it was pointed out that, though both First and Third worlds have grown suspicious of each other, all democratic nations have an interest in a common political orientation, and an association of democracies would serve this fundamental interest. It would also help in allaying suspicions over the long run. It would not break up any real solidarity that exists in the Third World but only the facade of solidarity that many Third World countries like to maintain against the First World. This facade serves the interests of radical regimes, but far from representing the true interest of moderate and democratic regimes, it is dangerous to their health and growth. The affirmation of the common value of democracy, bringing with it multilateral legitimation, could in the long run prove necessary for the very survival of some democratic regimes. The benefits would not be static but dynamic; democratic cooperation is a great multiplier. And by allaying suspicions, bridging the North-South gap, and developing cooperation among democracies, an association could make for mutual economic benefit and for a more stable international order.

PREFACE: THE MEETING PROPER

PREFACE convened at the Wingspread Conference Center, Racine, Wisconsin, on April 14, 1985 with 45 people present from 26 countries at all levels of economic development and representing nearly half of the world's practicing democracies: Argentina, Australia, Barbados, Belgium, Bolivia, Canada, Colombia, Costa Rica, Denmark, Fiji, France, Germany, India, Israel, Italy, Jamaica, Japan, Mauritius, the Netherlands, Papua New Guinea, Portugal, Spain, Sweden, the United Kingdom, the United States, and Venezuela.

For four days the PREFACE delegates discussed and refined the proposals for an association of democracies, an institute for democracy, and a consultative group of democracies at the U.N. and other international organizations. They concluded unanimously that such organizations not only were proper but were needed as a matter of some urgency—except for one abstention, and that on the ground that the proposed institutions did not go far enough and would fail adequately to match the demands of a deeply interdependent world.

The PREFACE delegates even went farther than was anticipated, constituting themselves into the International Committee for a Community of Democracies (ICCD) and planning to establish CCDs in their home countries. This took the CCD-USA organizers by surprise. Before PREFACE it had been proposed only that citizens' committees for democratic solidarity be formed in the various democracies in order to advance the concepts of PREFACE and strengthen links with governments.

PREFACE endorsed plans to disseminate its conclusions through publications and seminars in several regions of the world, to develop them further in expert working groups, and to hold in the very near future the main conference, at which representatives from all of the democracies of the world would prepare definitive recommendations for official action by governments to create new mechanisms for cooperation among democracies.

PREFACE considered that the proposed institutions could be established in any order. They would all be likely to work together, and whichever came first could assist in the formation of the others. However, it was anticipated that the association would be the centerpiece of the system.

Bridging the North-South Gap

Several participants from the South were especially insistent in holding that these institutions were urgently needed as a way of helping to consolidate their democratic systems. Though they were aware that some people might suspect U.S. motivations in this connection, they agreed that PREFACE had built a bridge between First and Third World participants by concentrating on working for democracy as a common value and interest.

PREFACE provided preliminary evidence against the fears expressed earlier by some First World commentators that Third World people would not want such an association; and preliminary confirmation for the major hypothesis underlying all of the proposed institutions: namely, that people from all democracies, if they meet in the context of considering action based on their shared concern for democracy, will be better able to discuss North-South differences constructively.

This did not mean that there were no contentious questions. Differing views were expounded on the amount of attention the proposed institutions should pay to economic needs and developmental studies. Also, some Europeans expressed concern that the new institutions might impinge on their existing arrangements for cooperation with developing countries. It was noted that the preoccupation with economic development in many countries would undoubtedly become a complicating factor in building solidarity around the value of democracy as a political structure. These issues were not, as a general rule, resolved, but it was agreed that they would have to be faced in the follow-through activities.

Refinement of the Institutional Proposals

After considerable discussion, almost all delegates insisted on starting with a formal intergovernmental association among such democracies as would be willing, while leaving room for the gradual or step-by-step building of the role of the association thereafter. Concerning the pace of work toward establishing the association in the first place, participants from Southern Europe and the Third World expressed a greater sense of urgency than participants from Northern Europe.

One of the most vexing questions was the structure and membership of the association bodies at the other levels—interparliamentary and private citizens—that were proposed.

There was much discussion of how the interparliamentary body should be related to the intergovernmental body, and whether it should admit democratic parliamentarians from nondemocratic countries. In the end it was agreed that the interparliamentary body should have a consultative status and be coterminous with the intergovernmental body, that is, should have the same member countries.

The purposes of the association were agreed to be the fostering of democracy and of cooperation among democracies by

• helping new and struggling democracies
• encouraging the exchange of democratic experiences

- promoting free and pluralistic communications media
- furthering human rights
- considering the impact of economic and social problems on democratic systems
- combatting terrorism
- providing a forum for the resolution of mutual problems.

Also a matter of concern was the relation between the institute and the association. On the one hand, it was considered essential to the credibility of the institute that it have full academic freedom. On the other hand, it was considered that the association would have to rely on the institute for research in order to provide background and objective validation for its own activities and assessments. It was concluded that the institute should be fully independent of the association in structure but should share the purposes of the association, respond of its own free choice to association inquiries, and operate under the association's general aegis.

FOLLOW-THROUGH PLANS

PREFACE built considerable enthusiasm for its proposals, which led, as has been mentioned, to an unanticipated move by the participants to establish the ICCD with themselves as its founding members. Several participants who had long experience with international conferences described this as one of the best they had ever attended. In an era of conferencing, it might be appropriate to consider the reasons for this.

PREFACE was oriented toward the development of proposals for action. It considered the ideas for an association and institute that had been developed over a period of six months by CCD, offered revisions and corrections, fleshed out important particulars, and boiled them down into more concrete and feasible proposals. It then passed these proposals on to expert working groups for further development, with a view to their final correction and endorsement at a conference of citizens from all democracies within the next year or two.

There have been many conferences that have sought to build solidarity simply by meeting, discussing, and socializing. PREFACE went farther. It was carefully crafted to work out ways to act together internationally for common concerns—concerns that would otherwise be left latent because of the impracticality of initiating action on them within the framework of national politics. This is what enabled it to build living solidarity.

PREFACE was further assisted by the procedure of semipublic advance preparation of the proposals and by the plans for follow-up on the results of the meeting. This enabled the participants in the short time they had together to review the proposals as they had been developed and set them on a clear future course.

Before disbanding, PREFACE considered the plans for following through on the proposals. Having constituted themselves into the ICCD, many participants gave pledges to set up CCDs back home. There were strong statements in favor of bringing the proposals immediately to the attention of heads of government and getting action initiated. However, more gradual follow-through plans were also discussed and became the main focus for implementation.

Though not in any sense excluding or discouraging the possibility that a head of government would take the initiative on a PREFACE proposal and run with it, ICCD plans looked toward a big conference with participants from all practicing democracies within a few years. ICCD called in the meantime for workshops and seminars in various regions of the world. These interim meetings would work out specifics of the proposals and publicize them.

The big conference would give the proposals their final shape and promulgate them as the official ICCD proposals. Several delegates proposed to host it in their countries. Thereafter, it would remain only to impress the recommendations on the governments with all of the political weight that ICCD could bring to bear.

It was noted that funding would be essential for this program. Several PREFACE participants remarked how much more difficult it was to raise funds for charitable causes in their own countries than in the United States. Fund-raising was far from easy in the United States as well. Follow-up was slowed during the remainder of 1985 for lack of funds. The Pew Freedom Trust did award CCD-USA a grant toward a seminar in Africa on the PREFACE proposals. The Pew Trust also offered a $100,000 matching challenge grant toward expenses of the All Democracies Conference. After several delays due to its own funding difficulties, NED awarded CCD-USA a grant toward an Asia-Pacific seminar.

THE BROADER SIGNIFICANCE OF THE PROPOSALS: THE LINK BETWEEN UNITING AND THE FOSTERING OF DEMOCRACY

Now that it has been recognized that the fostering of democracy is a central aspect of the global purpose and policy of the American people, it is necessary to develop a broad strategy that offers specific and relevant guidance and yet is flexible and prudent.

The key to a long-range strategy for the spread and stabilization of democracy is the building of institutions for solidarity and cooperation among existing democracies.

Recent developments in the Iberian peninsula underline this point. A decade ago, Western European political foundations helped to rescue democracy in the Portugese revolution, and this was one of the original inspirations for the Democracy Initiative. Today the Spanish government feels that visible solidarity with democratic Europe through the European Communities and NATO is needed to help stabilize its own democracy.

Institutions of cooperation among democracies are needed to establish a bond of solidarity between new and old democracies. They avert potential conflicts and bring out common interests among democracies. They vindicate politicians who stake their fate on democracy. They are an integral part of a new orientation toward democracy and can prove essential to the stability of new democracies.

Germany has shown how important this can be. After 1919 bad relations between Germany and older democracies pushed Germany toward Nazism. After 1945 new European institutions made for highly beneficial mutual relations and enabled West Germany to stabilize as a democracy. Support of European unification was (and thus far remains) the United States' finest hour in foreign policy, for it consolidated the peace and liberty that had been twice won at terrible cost.

Helmut Kohl reminded the Bundestag of this in February 1985. In the 1920s, he recalled, integration with the West, attempted in the Locarno Pact, had failed. Today the Federal Republic of Germany is based, in its constitution and founding treaties, on a commitment to "permanent" and "irreversible" integration with the West through the Atlantic Alliance and European unification. The choice of the West was a choice of "enlightenment . . . and the rule of law" as against any "special national courses."

Everywhere—in some countries most dramatically, in other countries more quietly—the spread and stability of democracy requires closer arrangements for solidarity among democracies. This has a direct bearing on the resurgence of democracy in Latin America.

Argentina, Brazil, and Uruguay have joined Bolivia and Peru in returning to democratic rule. Yet each is experiencing serious problems, as are several other Latin democracies. They, along with the Philippines, will need strong political and economic support to maintain democracy. Now is the time to lay groundwork that could finally enable Latin democracy to be consolidated permanently.

The central task of democracy in the present era is to build and strengthen interdemocratic institutions on all levels and in all forms—regional, functional, and global—in order to show the solidarity of democracies worldwide, to develop cooperation among them, and to display international democracy as a plan for world order. The involvement of the United States in this task offers the nation a chance to renew its historic role in the progress of freedom in the world.

Today there is a school of thought that questions the universal relevance of pluralistic democratic norms and regards it as a specimen of peculiarly U.S naïveté that the United States should try to identify its interests with democratic self-government in other lands. However, friends of the United States abroad have never doubted the universal significance of these norms.

There is especially strong perception of both the role of the United States and the universal validity of democratic norms in countries where pluralistic democracy is new or fragile. This does not mean that they deny the United States a special role; only that they recognize the place of this concrete role in the growth of the universal norm. Giovanni Spadolini, minister of defense of Italy, has repeatedly called attention to the essential U.S. role as the "point of reference" for the spread, unification, and stabilization of democracy in Europe. And the universality of the norm and the struggle could hardly be expressed better than it was by Mario Soares, formerly prime minister and now president of Portugal, in his letter of endorsement of CCD's program.

I do not believe it possible to construct progressive and free societies without complete adherence to the elementary rules of democratic pluralism . . . To defend Democracy is, therefore, to safeguard the input of each of us in the definition of the common ways leading to general welfare. When this input is tampered with one opens the door to despotism and totalitarianism.

The world has known, and still knows, governments that sacrifice the liberty and justice owed every human being in order to indulge the egoistic interests of priviledged minorities. History, however, has taught us that, sooner or later, freedom triumphs, since it has the strength of the ideals which are innate to human nature. Since to contribute to an acceleration of this inevitable process is the duty of every responsible citizen, it appears to me that the project which you intend to carry out deserves our full support.

REFERENCES

CCD Courier, nos. 1-4

Proceedings of PREFACE (printed record)

James Huntley. *Uniting the Democracies: Institutions of the Emerging Atlantic-Pacific System.* New York: New York University Press, 1980.

12 DEMOCRACY PROMOTION AND GOVERNMENT-TO-GOVERNMENT DIPLOMACY
William A. Douglas

Formal government-to-government diplomacy is insufficient for the most effective conduct of U.S. foreign relations. Official relationships of the United States are primarily with whatever regime—democratic or totalitarian—is in power in a foreign country. A U.S. program for promoting democracy abroad can provide a useful supplement to our official diplomacy. Certain problems would also accompany such an approach, although they are not as serious as some would expect. The opportunities arise from a dual-track diplomacy whose benefits for U.S. foreign relations would greatly exceed its costs.

DUAL-TRACK DIPLOMACY

By encouraging a division of diplomatic labor, the United States can maintain relations with both the incumbent governments of other countries and their political oppositions. As is normally the case, the Department of State and the U.S. Foreign Service can maintain official government-to-government contacts. A well-functioning U.S. democracy promotion program can enable private U.S. groups—political parties, trade unions, business associations, cooperatives, and the like—to relate informally to comparable private groups in other nations, including those associated with the opposition to the government in power. Thus, when a nation's government changes hands, some segment of U.S. society will already have ongoing political ties with the incoming regime. This is what is meant by a dual-track approach to diplomacy.

Though our embassy diplomats are expected to develop informational contacts with opposition forces in other countries, this is sometimes difficult if the incumbent host country regime disapproves of such contacts. In addition, informational contacts do not provide for the depth of understanding that develops when two democratic groups work together on programs. It is much easier for private U.S. groups—political parties and interest groups—to work with opposition groups than for the U.S. government to do so. In this way a democracy promotion program can facilitate effective U.S. foreign relations with other countries without having to depend upon an incumbent regime remaining in power.

This dual-track approach has been extremely useful for the conduct of West German foreign policy since the three major West German political foundations began their overseas activities. Together, the Social Democratic, Christian Democratic, and Liberal foundations have ties with a sizable majority of the world's democratic political movements.[1] These ties are ongoing regardless of which party in a country may be in power. The official West German diplomatic corps maintains government-to-government relations with whatever party or group—dictatorial or democratic—makes up the regime of the day.

Reinhard Meier, writing in the *Swiss Review of World Affairs,* noted that "the foundations themselves, and apparently the Bonn regime as well, regard this engagement abroad as a useful supplement to official channels of international cooperation. It is likely, in fact, that some connections and points of influence are established in this way that would not necessarily be open to direct representatives of the government."[2]

The division of labor between U.S. government diplomacy and private sector programs to promote democracy abroad may be especially useful in situations where the United States is allied with a particular nation but needs to distance itself from the present government in power there. These situations occur most often when harsh dictatorships are facing an immediate threat from forces also hostile to the United States, usually either from communist armies on their borders or Soviet-supported insurgencies within their territory.

In circumstances of this type, the United States may need to adopt two different postures simultaneously: (1) reaffirm U.S. commitment to the official alliance with that nation, particularly if failure to do so might encourage an invasion or increased Soviet support for the insurgency; and (2) dissociate the United States from the dictatorship so as to deprive the Soviets of the opportunity to charge the United States with collusion with yet another "right-wing dictatorship" that is suppressing its people. By making use of the dual-track division of labor, the U.S. government can dramatize the U.S. commitment to the state-to-state alliance while U.S. political parties and other private groups engage demonstratively with the democratic opposition, thereby showing that Americans are not committed to the incumbent dictatorial regime. Since identifying the United States with rightist autocracies is a key issue for Soviet political warfare, the flexibility the United States can gain is of great importance.

Example of cases in which dual-track diplomacy could have served U.S. foreign policy well were the Philippines and South Korea during the first years of the 1980s. Given the important U.S. military interests in each of these nations, it was strategically vital to make clear to the communist powers that the United States could not and would not permit a communist takeover in either country.

It was also politically vital—in the eyes of the populaces involved and the world at large—for the United States as a society to dissociate itself from the regimes of General Chun Doo Hwan in South Korea and Ferdinand Marcos in the Philippines. Both regimes, in different degrees and in different ways, were liabilities to the Western bloc, even while the countries they governed were vital to Western interests. Both regimes permitted, under varying degrees of repression, open opposition parties to exist. A U.S. private sector program of democratic development could have worked publicly with these oppositions. Private sector activities would have indicated where U.S. political sympathies lay, while the official U.S. embassies in Seoul and Manila could have reaffirmed U.S. strategic support for both nations rather than for the governments of the day.

Long-term democratic institution building would be, by far, the most important benefit for U.S. foreign policy. The private sector democracy-promoting effort would be a kind of preventive medicine—building solidly organized democratic political parties and interest groups as the infrastructure of long-term political and economic stability. Under present circumstances, official U.S. diplomacy is confined to observing passively political events in other countries before it can react to them actively. Thus, when political institutions collapse, as in Iran and Nicaragua, U.S. policymakers must deal with the problem on a crisis basis. Often it is easier, through patient effort over many years, to prevent crises than to try to resolve them in a few weeks or months by taking purely reactive measures.

The time for the United States to "do something" about Nicaragua was in the late 1960s and early 1970s when the Somoza regime appeared stable. A democratic alternative to that regime should have been built up while there was still time for such long-term organizing. The same was true for Haiti in the late 1970s and the early years of the 1980s. A democratic opposition in the Philippines, as we have noted, could have similarly been strengthened. If a democracy promotion program can help democratic oppositions prepare to succeed the Duvaliers, Marcoses, Somozas, Stroessners, and Mobutus of the world, this would be a significant positive outcome for U.S. policy.

Recent history has demonstrated the folly of relying on such strongmen to provide "stability," while regarding efforts at democratic institution building as "destabilizing." There will be instances when the U.S. government will be unhappy with the democratizing efforts of U.S. private groups, viewing them as merely complicating an already difficult situation in a given country. However, the disadvantages that such cases will inflict on U.S. official policy will be vastly outweighed by cases in which U.S. private action supplements and strengthens official policy. Democratic governments, after all, tend to tilt toward the Western side in the world balance of power. Otherwise, successor governments of the dictatorial Left usually align with Moscow, whereas those of the dictatorial Right usually create new liabilities for the Western bloc.

PROBLEMS FOR OFFICIAL DIPLOMACY

Every public policy and program has positive and negative features. A democracy promotion program, with a dual-track approach as described, will be no different. There will be contradictions and a need for coordination. When the original legislation to create the National Endowment for Democracy (NED) was before the Congress in 1983, a number of questions were raised in Congress and the press about the seriousness of the contradictions. A common concern was that if a U.S. private sector program were to aid the opposition in a given country, the incumbent regime might take umbrage, with damage to U.S. government-to-government diplomatic relations.[3]

Experience indicates that this problem is not as serious or as frequent as some expected. The West German political foundations have been working all over the world with many opposition movements, with no major negative results for Bonn's official diplomacy. Also reassuring are the achievements abroad of U.S. labor unions, using U.S. government funding. Most of the nations of the world are governed by dictatorships, and trade unions are often the natural political adversaries of authoritarian regimes. U.S. labor, through its regional institutes for Asia, Africa, and Latin America, has conducted training and other programs with opposition unions in El Salvador, the Philippines, South Korea, Paraguay, Chile, and elsewhere. As in the West German experience, there have been few, if any, cases in which the U.S. labor institutes' programs have damaged U.S. government-to-government diplomacy with the related regimes. Even in the few instances in which the host country's government has expelled a U.S. labor program—Peru in 1971 and El Salvador in 1973—there was little consequence for the warmth or frigidity of official diplomatic relations.

The Soviet Union, it should be recalled, has engaged in assistance to communist opposition movements throughout the world since the days of the Comintern, yet Soviet embassies go right on negotiating trade agreements and maintaining normal diplomatic transactions with many regimes they are trying to subvert. Here, too, the contradictions between the two tracks—official state diplomacy and nongovernmental political institution building—are less than might logically be expected. Only occasionally has a government forced Soviet dual-track policy to choose between state diplomacy and political institution building. One case was Egypt under Nasser. In this instance, the Soviet Union was obliged to end support of the Egyptian Communist party in order to achieve close official alignment between Soviet and Egyptian foreign policies during Nasser's later years in power.[4] Most of the experience supports the conclusion that political aid, thoughtfully fashioned, to another regime's opposition does not necessarily upset official government-to-government relations.

Aiding Democracies

To find out why embitterment is rare, we must divide host country governments into democracies and dictatorships. The factors differ between the two types. In democracies the West German programs and the nascent U.S. program offer aid to the entire family of democratic parties and interest groups in these countries. This usually includes the party in power at some given time and so reduces the incumbent's grounds for complaining that aid is also going to the opposition. With the next throw of the electoral dice, the governing party may well become the opposition, even more eager to receive foreign assistance. What is central in these democratic cases is that foreign assistance is provided in order to strengthen the entire democratic system in the host country, not simply to place a particular party into power. This is a principle that is readily understood by most of the foreign governments and parties in this category and explains their willingness to accept such aid.

Difficulties, however, do occur. One worst case scenario has the party in power in the United States aiding the opposition to a regime in another country.[5] Can the two governments then have cordial diplomatic relations? An answer depends on whether or not the United States had been aiding the entire democratic spectrum, that is, the party in power as well as the opposition. Further, the U.S. political aid would presumably support programs of training, research, and organizing to enable all host country parties to become building blocks for a sturdy democratic polity.

It would be inappropriate for U.S. political aid to fund a particular party's election campaign costs.

Even in such worst case instances, government-to-government relations need not be altered to any great extent by the political aid activities. For example, when West German Social Democrats were in power under Chancellor Helmut Schmidt, this party's Friedrich Ebert Foundation had close ties with Venezuela's Accion Democratica party. When the Venezuelan elections were won by the Christian Democratic party, Comite de Organizacion Politica Electoral Independiente (COPEI), Partido Social-Cristiano, official West German diplomatic relations with Venezuela were not seriously frayed. A major reason was that the governing COPEI party had its own connection with the West German Christian Democratic Konrad Adenauer Foundation. COPEI also understood, correctly, that the overall West German aid program was aimed at strengthening Venezuelan democracy in general, not at getting a particular party into power at a particular time.

Providing political aid may cause inconsistencies in the aid-giving country's own foreign policy more often than it damages relations with other governments. In his article on the German party foundations, Reinhard Meier notes that, in 1982, the Konrad Adenauer Foundation was giving aid to El Salvador's Christian Democratic party under President Napoleon Duarte while the Friedrich Ebert Foundation was aiding part of the coalition supporting the leftist insurgency against Duarte's government. "Since both foundations are financed from the government coffers in Bonn, the German taxpayer finds himself in the grotesque position of having his tax money channeled to two rival groups locked in mortal combat."[6] While it makes sense to aid all the competing parties of a democratic polity, so as to strengthen the polity as a whole, it does not seem sensible to aid both sides in a civil war and thereby aggravate the war.[7]

What any political aid program, West German or U.S., undoubtedly needs is a system by which all parties in a donor nation arrive at a jointly accepted roster of democratic movements in each aid-receiving nation, so that political aid may be confined to the groups on the consensus roster. In the cases of Venezuela and El Salvador, for example, all the West German parties would probably have agreed that both major Venezuela parties are democratic and worthy of aid, but there would probably have been no consensus about which forces in the Salvadoran civil war were democratic. In a decentralized polity such as the United States, most government policies depend on some degree of bipartisan consensus, and a U.S. program to promote democracy abroad is especially dependent upon consensus. Therefore, while each U.S. party should be able to aid its associates abroad, all such aid should be limited to indigenous groups and parties that Democrats and Republicans, liberals and conservatives, agree to be democratic in character. The NED can serve as the forum for arriving at such democratic rosters.

Aiding Dictatorships

Giving political aid to oppositions under dictatorial regimes may prove feasible for reasons other than those pertinent to democratic regimes. In the case of dictatorships, too, government-to-government consequences are less stormy than might be expected.

Many authoritarian regimes allow opposition parties to exist and even to contest elections. The elections are, of course, "managed" so that the opposition has little or no chance of winning. This does not diminish the fact that opposition groups are tolerated and held up by the regime—for the benefit of the United States and Europe—as evidence of its "democratic" character. If it is trying to project such an image, a dictatorial regime can hardly complain if the United States or West Germany endeavors to provide political aid to opposition groups. Since tolerating an opposition is a basis for claiming its own legitimacy, the dictatorship's inclination to vent displeasure by disrupting government-to-government relations with the foreign donor is mitigated.

Even more important is the fact that many dictatorships, particularly those along the periphery of the Soviet bloc, need the United States more than the United States needs them. They are more directly in the path of Soviet expansionism, certainly more vulnerable to communist subversion than, say, California or Maryland. These regimes may have little choice but to accept U.S. political aid programs in support of democratic opposition movements, just as they already accept—with more resignation than enthusiasm—the AFL-CIO training programs for their fractious labor movements. The communist threat to these dictatorships affords political leverage that the United States can use to obtain acceptance of responsible and effective U.S. democracy promotion programs. Sound programs need not perturb official U.S. diplomatic relations with such dictatorships.

In sum, for both democracies and dictatorships, the anticipated danger that U.S. political aid to the oppositions to incumbent regimes may cause friction in official government-to-government diplomatic relations turns out to be more theoretical than real. In contrast, a well-designed U.S. political aid program can provide the United States with a degree of access and flexibility in its foreign relations that has hitherto been impossible through strictly government-to-government transactions. The benefits of a dual-track program of democracy promotion far outweigh the real but minor costs to U.S. state-to-state diplomacy. On balance, a strong U.S. program of government-supported private sector political aid to democratic groups and parties abroad can be effectively carried on in the short term and become overwhelmingly significant for U.S. foreign policy in the long term.

NOTES

1. On the West German *Stiftungen*, see chapt. 5.

2. Reinhard Meier, "Political Party Foundations in Bonn," *Swiss Review of World Affairs*, February 1982, p. 27.

3. For an example of this concern, see Henry Geyelin, "Some Crusade?" *Washington Post*, June 24, 1983.

4. John H. Kautsky, *Communism and the Politics of Development* (New York: John Wiley & Sons, 1968), p. 151.

5. Representative James Leach presented this scenario in the House debate on the original authorizing legislation for the NED. See *Congressional Record*, June 9, 1983, p. H-3816.

6. Meier, op. cit., p. 27.

7. This view was also expressed by Representative Leach, op, cit., p. H-3816.

13 ASSESSING POLITICAL AID FOR THE ENDLESS CAMPAIGN
Ralph M. Goldman

Political aid is a U.S. foreign policy concept whose time has come, particularly as it bears upon the promotion of democratic development. Arriving with political aid are all the issues attendant upon new concepts: definition of its meaning; operationalization of its component features; tactics of implementation in the field; evaluation of program effectiveness; assessment of overall contribution to democratic development. In the case of political aid for democracy, the concept is further burdened by the usual resistance to new policies, modest practical experience, shortages of committed resources, trial-and-error projects and programs, intuitive rather than systematic evaluations of results, and large debates about "best" models of democracy. Nevertheless, the U.S. policy of political aid, particularly in support of democratic development worldwide, is in its incipient stage and, in time, may well replace in importance military and economic aid as the principal foreign assistance program of this nation.

This expectation is currently difficult to support with evidence. Many will greet it with incredulity. Yet, we need only believe that major wars are obsolescent and that the world economy is rapidly becoming an integral whole in order to arrive at the realization that international affairs may well be on their way toward more familiar political forms of ideological and programmatic competition, that is, through party systems, organized interest groups, propaganda campaigns, elections, public debates, and other activities for which an effective program of political aid would be necessary, appropriate, and expensive.

As chapter 1 of this volume recalls, the spread of democracy is a mission as old as the Republic. The Founding Fathers viewed the United States as an experimental model derived from "best principles" of institutional architecture. Many Americans, with understandable patriotism and some chauvinism, continue to refer to the United States as *the* foremost democratic model. Some, with more modesty and greater awareness of the 50 or so other democracies in the world, consider the United States political system as *a* model. Either way, the concern for models of democracy and democratic institutions is likely to remain an important aspect of U.S. political aid well into the future. Inevitably, and perhaps until an association of democracies is created, as described in chapter 11, U.S. aid programs will probably continue to offer as models what has been learned from the U.S. experience.

This look-at-us-as-a-model approach to the promotion of democracy has had the appearance of arrogance and presumption, implying a master-apprentice relationship between the United States and other nations. Furthermore, models as exemplars to be emulated are usually quite different from models as theoretical systems of related empirical variables; compare the democratic nation of Jefferson's and Madison's texts with the variety of nations that conform to their model in name only (e.g., the so-called peoples' democracies of the communist world) or have adapted to the exigencies of national development (e.g., France, Italy, and Japan).

Many Americans have been uneasy about the historical chauvinism of the democratic missionary, the arrogance of the implied master-apprentice relationship, and the scientific weaknesses of available empirical models of democracy. Their discomfort has been increased by policies of nonintervention in the politics of other nations and by U.S. military support for "devils" and dictators in the interest of national security. As a consequence, U.S. political aid policies, often called something else, have been few in number, covert, indirect, ambiguous, apologetic, and largely ineffective or confusing. Chapters 3, 4, 8, 9, and 10 describe innumerable U.S. economic assistance programs that sought indirectly to promote democracy only to fall far short of their economic as well as political objectives.

If the United States and other democracies are beginning to expend significant public and private resources for political aid programs to promote democratic development across the world, how may the objectives, methods, and results of these programs be monitored and evaluated for their effectiveness? The scope and complexity of this question may be compared to an earlier large and complex question: How may the United States land a man on the moon?

The objectives—one political, the other physical—seem quite different. The required "hard" knowledge and technology for each is at different degrees of readiness. The outcomes of the political program may be too "slippery" to measure. Therefore, many would deny the comparability of the questions. Yet, a world of democratic nations and a moon landing were equally visionary goals when first proposed. Their achievement requires the construction of complex systems on the basis of available reliable knowledge. The hard knowledge and technology for a moon landing happened to be, in large measure, available in the 1960s. The knowledge and technology for building democratic nations is still "soft" but, coincidentally, was advanced appreciably also during the 1960s by the researches of political scientists, psychologists, and others in their comparative studies of totalitarian and democratic systems.

At the present time, however, what few political aid projects and programs there are tend to be evaluated more by donor intentions, as ambiguous as these may be, than by attitudinal, behavioral, or institutional changes on the part of the aid recipients. What will be needed, with increasing urgency as political aid programs grow in number, complexity, and cost, are empirically precise formulations of program objectives and valid instruments for the evaluation of program outcomes and effectiveness. These requirements are not readily available, nor will they be fulfilled before much more well-confirmed hard knowledge about democratic institutions has been gathered.

MODELS AND INDICATORS: ADVERSARIES OR PARTNERS?

In the arcane debates of epistemologists, one matter of contention has a chicken-and-egg quality. Which comes first, the creation of a comprehensive theoretical model or the accumulation of observed data about very specific variables? Which comes first, a Platonic portrait of an ideal *polis* or a count of the number of free newspapers distributed under a particular regime? In studying and assessing the evolutionary progress of democratic institutions, must we first design a comprehensive model of democracy or may we begin by gathering facts about selected attributes associated with democracy such as regular elections of public officials, civil rights guarantees, and free speech? Do we use the model to seek out data about its component attributes, or do we build a model from the available data about attributes?

Anyone familiar with the zigzag routes that researchers take and how new knowledge is produced will dismiss these questions as frivolous and usually irrelevant. No matter from which direction systematic inquiry begins—general models or data observations—the investigator must eventually do both: imagine a theoretical model and collect specific data about component attributes.

Despite the fruitlessness of this epistemological argument, it almost invariably intrudes itself into discussions of foreign aid programs generally and will surely accompany the development of evaluation procedures for programs to promote democracy. The argument will emerge—already has emerged—out of the kinds of questions of which the following are examples.

In order to evaluate the effectiveness of a program for the development of democratic institutions, the evaluator must in effect conduct a before-and-after experiment. What were the institutional conditions before the program was introduced? What were the objectives of the aid program; that is, which specific institutional conditions was it supposed to change? What degree of institutional change, if any, was observed at the end of the aid program? Did the introduction of the aid program make much difference?

Methodologically, such questions open up a hornet's nest of definitional and observational problems. At the microsystem level, which of several democratic institutions—election system, interest group formation, press freedom, and the like—does the aid program purport to strengthen? Which specific institutional conditions or attributes will comprise the observed variables in the before-and-after measurements? Hypothetically, what elements of the aid program are expected to accomplish the institutional changes? How much change will be required for the program to be considered effective?

The hornets buzz on to macrosystem issues. How does the institution being subjected to an aid program fit in with other indigenous institutions deemed necessary for the development of a democratic nation? Since pluralism applies to models as well as to democratic polities, which of several models of democracy is pertinent for this aid program? How do all or part of these indigenous institutions add up to one of the models of democracy? Does the particular model of democracy provide for institutional subsystems that create or perpetuate democratic attitudes, behaviors, and relationships? What are the operational definitions of these attitudes, behaviors, and relationships? Does the evaluation procedure of an aid program take these operational definitions into account? Do the macrosystem models provide the goal specifications against which to compare aid program results?

By now, those readers who are old hands in the foreign assistance field, several of whom have shared their observations and wisdom in this book, should be experiencing despair, and rightly so. Democracy, they will say, is not a new idea; discussion of its modern forms has been going on for 300 or 400 years. Yet, the definitions and attributes of democracy are still uncertain and controversial. Empirical measures of degrees of democratic development or maturity are rare, notable exceptions being the contributions of Robert A. Dahl, Lucian W. Pye, Seymour Martin Lipset, Raymond D. Gastil, Samuel Huntington, Arend Lijphart, G. Bingham Powell, William A. Douglas, and a small number of others. With evaluation concepts and instruments so scarce and imperfect, how can program assessment for the foreseeable future be anything more than the informed judgment calls of trained experts?

The answer is straightforward. Yes, informed expert judgments must continue to do the job for today's evaluations. However, the pace and quality of knowledge production about democracy must be stepped up, building on the theories and researches of the last 300 years, perhaps even investing one one-thousandth of the resources appropriated for the moon landing. Next, every 10 years, ask again the above question about evaluation concepts and instruments. If the investment of resources were made, this writer would promise that old hands, trained experts, and political aid program administrators would be amazed at the end of each decade by the extent to which the quality, validity, and reliability of empirical knowledge about democratic institutions and the effectiveness of aid programs had advanced.

This expression of unabashed confidence is based upon several assumptions about democracy and the promotion of democratic development:

1. Democracy is a form and process of government consistent with human behavioral tendencies, needs, and desires. Democracy requires a set of civic values that animate and reinforce the attitudes and behavior of those who live according to its precepts.

2. The basic structure of enduring democratic institutions is observable and generally replicable.

3. Democratic structures, methods, and procedures are transferable, and their institutional forms are adaptable to varying historical, cultural, and other indigenous conditions.

4. As a consequence of centuries of theorization and practical democratic development, there exists enough systematic knowledge about democracy and democratic institutions to provide a strong basis for the production of further well-confirmed knowledge about this system of human self-governance.

DESIGNING POLITICAL AID PROGRAM EVALUATIONS

Designing and testing evaluation instruments and procedures for political aid programs are tasks that, for the most part, are yet to be undertaken on a substantial scale. These tasks have yet to confront the problems of stating fundamental and difficult developmental hypotheses, operationalizing elusive variables, counting units that tend to be spongy, and possibly coming up with findings that may upset existing conventional wisdom about foreign assistance of any kind, political aid included. If evaluation methodology is taken seriously, it will impose rigorous—some would say excessively rigorous—requirements on test instruments and procedures. This short list of requirements suggests what must be developed for a political aid program assessment process.[1]

1. *Program objectives.* The evaluation procedure must ask, What specifically does the political aid program seek to accomplish? The objectives must be defined in observable behavioral terms, including attitudinal changes. The program objectives would have to be logically related to one or more of the attributes of a model or profile of a democratic institution or governmental system.

To illustrate: Let one of the objectives of a political aid program for the imaginary country of Authoria be officially stated as "the enhancement of democratic cultural values." There are many democratic values, one being, in a word, individualism, that is, respect for persons as individuals. Individualism would be one component of most models of democracy. An evaluation instrument would have to include a conversion of this feature of the program's more general objective (enhancement of democratic cultural values) into a variable that represents an observable behavior. In the technical language of behavioral science, the conversion would probably read as follows: Individualism would be one of the democratic values to be enhanced and would be manifest by an increase in positive popular attitudes (which are observable and measurable) toward the priority of individual persons vis-á-vis the regime, the state, or other political persons or entities. This formulation of a program objective would then be testable on a comparative scale.

This example demonstrates what is involved in operationalizing program objectives, that is, translating a broad generality into a specific set of observable behaviors. Educators and behavioral scientists regularly do this kind of operationalization. Their definitions and measurements may be debatable, but they are hardly mysterious, nor do they require rigid models of program goals or political systems.

2. *Behavioral changes.* The promotion of a democratic system presumes a need for change in the existing system. In the illustration above, the aid program sought to change popular attitudes toward persons as human individuals. Evaluation instruments must be able to identify and measure changes.

In its simplest formulation, this follows the before-and-after type of experimental design mentioned earlier. What were the conditions before the aid program was inaugurated? What were the conditions after the program was started or completed? What part (in changed popular attitudes, leadership expectations, governing procedures, distribution of units of power, etc.) did the experimental procedure (that is, the aid program) play in bringing about the changes observed?

The experienced behavioral scientist will immediately recognize the difficulties inherent in isolating cause and effect in the complex setting within which a political aid program must be conducted. For behavioral scientists trained in multivariate data collection and analysis, the challenge is substantial but not overwhelming. Consider the scientific developments in the field of voting behavior over the last 40 years. The multivariate character of mass electorates has been observed, measured, and explained in such detail as to enable practitioners, that is, election campaigners, to fine-tune their campaign efforts in a systematic and verifiable manner. With similar scientific attention and research resources, a comparable degree of knowledge could undoubtedly become available for the planning and evaluation of aid programs campaigning for democracy.

3. *Standardized variables.* Every political aid program or project is a multivariate experiment. Unfortunately, each program moves in a stream of complexity under poorly controlled experimental conditions. The challenge of program evaluation is currently frustrating enough to lead most program administrators to throw in the towel or take refuge behind simplistic generalizations that avoid comment about the complex system of variables with which they must deal.

However, there *is* a body of behavioral knowledge, in the field of educational psychology, for example, that could be relevant for the identification of behavioral variables involved in the development of democratic systems. An incomplete list might be suggestive.

- *Cognitive variables,* that is, specific information that a nation's leaders, citizens, or particular groups may have about democracy and democratic institutions. For example, has a civic education project changed the level of information that union or other group members have about the duties of their governmental agencies?

- *Affective variables,* for example, favorable or unfavorable attitudes toward particular components of their existing system and of a prospective democratic system. For example, has a series of films about the functioning of political parties in various democracies led to a more favorable attitude among peasant groups toward the relevance of this particular political institution for their own needs?

- *Event variables,* that is, the functional characteristics of major political events and rituals, such as coups and elections, in reinforcing or modifying citizen and leadership attitudes and behavior. For example, did participation in a particular local or national election give voters a greater sense of political efficacy?

- *Process variables,* that is, the functions of time and procedure in the governance of the nation, such as frequency of elections, length of terms of office, and the expeditiousness of legal processes. For example, did a seminar for lawyers lead to efforts to change legal rules and practices regarding the right to early trial?

• *Organizational-institutional variables,* that is, descriptions and comparative analyses of the structures and functions of major political organizations, such as armies, bureaucracies, political parties, and court systems, as the basis for comparisons with organizational development in other nations. For example, how does the executive bureaucracy, as described and analyzed by local experts with the assistance of political aid project experts, compare in its structure and functions to similar bureaucracies in other democratic nations? As scores of U.S. management consulting firms will testify, organizational self-analyses are potent tools of leadership and change.

This is an illustrative list, intended to show that multivariate analysis of a democratic system or institution is a finite undertaking for which contemporary behavioral scientists have appropriate knowledge and skills.

4. *Expert opinion.* Precise data and well-confirmed theories are inevitably subject to the intepretations of the experts. This is as it should be. Science is a collective enterprise, and it places high value on skepticism. As political aid program evaluation progresses, new evaluation instruments and procedures will sharpen but hardly displace the informed judgment of trained experts. The kind and quality of relevant expertise may change, but the need for expert opinion will persist. Experts will be needed to intepet evaluation findings, to extrapolate behavioral and political tendencies revealed by the evaluations, and to recommend program improvements that may take advantage of the systematic feedback.[2]

We could go on with this exercise in design specification for aid program evaluation. By now, the more skeptical readers may have dismissed the entire discussion as unrealistic and visionary. Others will recognize it for what it is: an agenda of difficult work to be accomplished.

COMPONENTS FOR DEMOCRACY MODELS

Identifying the component attributes of a democratic system of government is no small or uncontroversial task. A political system presumably falls within the meaning of *democracy* if all or several of the attributes in the following incomplete list are present. The list is intended to demonstrate that democracy model building is a finite undertaking if appropriately demystified.

Each attribute listed happens to be the subject of definitional debates of its own. It is also arguable which attributes should comprise a minimum set to qualify the political system as democratic. Several contributors to this volume have suggested such combinations. The intent here is to be illustrative, not definitive. The listing is made to convey a sense that the creation of democratic models is manageable and practical.

1. *Individualism*. Constitution, laws, leaders, and institutional arrangements specify that the purpose of the system of government is to foster the well-being of the human individual, permitting each person to realize his or her full capabilities. Governments are obliged to respect each persons's rights and to protect each individual from deprivation caused by other individuals or groups.

2. *Popular sovereignty*. The people of a political community, that is, all adult individuals regularly subject to its laws, are the ultimate source of all legitimate political authority. The people must explicitly endorse the establishment of the particular government, delegate powers to its public officials, and have legal means (usually elections, impeachment, recall, etc.) by which to hold government officials accountable.

3. *Civil liberties*. Governments may not arbitrarily curtail the individual's freedom to communicate through speech or publication, assemble, associate, engage in religious worship, own property, or be judged by a fair trial and due process. Freedom House has accomplished much toward operationalizing this component.

4. *Majority rule*. Every political community must devise a system for making collective decisions, particularly for the selection of governmental leadership and the delegation of responsibility for declaring public policies. All adult citizens should have an opportunity to participate in the community's basic collective decisions, either directly or through representatives of their own choosing. The preferences of the greater number of citizens should prevail.

Equally important is the right of the minority to dissent and criticize the decisions of the majority, with protected opportunities to seek majority status for itself through established procedures.

5. *Rule of law*. The prerogatives of officials of government are limited by rules that prohibit arbitrary actions against individuals. The supremacy of the law is assured by the existence of an impartial judiciary. All individuals, including government officials, are equal before the law. No one can be convicted of a crime except through standard procedures that provide due process, fair and open trial, and specific punishment only as provided by law.

6. *Natural law*. The laws of nature are presumed to be universally applicable to all human relationships. This docrine supports the assumption of the equality of all mankind. It applies the same moral constraints upon the conduct of all governments and individuals. It agrees with the behavioral scientist's postulate that all human beings act alike under similar conditions.

7. *Constitutionalism*. Whether written or unwritten, a democratic community's constitution is essentially a set of "rules of the game"

allocating units of prerogative (votes, vetoes, etc.) to government officials, the people, and other participants in the system. A constitution also assigns political functions to the organizational components of the nation. Constitutions, when breached, provide early warning of challenges to democratic institutional arrangements.

8. *Accountability*. Accountability of public officials is achieved usually through systems of election, constitutional constraints, the exercise of civil liberties, a competitive political party system, a free press, open political processes, and other institutionalized arrangements. Accountability is rarely precise in its application or fairness. What is critical is its availability.

9. *Civil-military relations*. Any system of self-governance requires civic order and safety as essential antecedents of self-governance and, in democracies, freedom. The military leadership of the nation must be subordinate to civilian public officials, who, in turn, are regularly elected by the citizenry. To separate army from state, office may not be held in both at the same time. The military may intercede to maintain public order when civilian elites resort to violence and breach the rules of the game, but the military leadership may not assume governmental office during this process.[3]

The nine components above, although they may be variously interpreted, add up to an elaborate, albeit incomplete, set of components for any model of a democratic political system. Whatever components are included, an assessment of the extent to which a nation is or may become democratic must employ operational measures of the degree to which those components are present and operative.

Designing operational tests of the components of democracy and their attributes has only been begun, in the work of the scholars mentioned earlier. There is much yet to be accomplished. For example, different democracies may define and implement each component in somewhat different ways, as Lijphart's research shows.[4] Each component may be at different stages of development in older and new democracies. Other differences can be identified. The existence of these issues of definition, observation, and measurement simply tells us that more systematic theorization and research need to be accomplished in order to construct one or more useful models or profiles of a generic democratic system of government. It has been done in other fields of knowledge and can undoubtedly also be done for democratic systems and political aid program evaluations.

MEANWHILE, IN THE REAL WORLD, THE ENDLESS CAMPAIGN . . .

The activities, events, and trends of world politics will not pause while sound evaluation instruments and procedures are being successfully constructed. Dictators will not postpone their programs of oppression and exploitation while democrats improve their programs of democratization and liberalization. World politics is a dynamic process in which an endless campaign is being conducted. At this historical moment in the campaign, two-thirds of the world's nations are governed by autocrats of one kind or another. Only one-third are, by generous definition, democratic. Even acknowledging how much democracy has spread over the past 300 years, the campaign for democracy seems only just begun.

The call for improved tools for evaluating political aid programs signals an important feature of the present juncture in world politics. The call reflects a growing awareness that a campaign is in progress, that the promotion of democracy requires sound knowledge as well as ringing symbols, and that an essential cost of promoting democracy is the development of methods for assessing campaign effectiveness.

Awareness of the campaign has been painfully stirred by this century's struggles against the most heinous totalitarian systems in human history. With the defeat of the Axis in World War II, the leaders of democratic nations responded to their new awareness by helping West Germany, Japan, and Italy build new democratic institutions. Conquest alone did not create postwar democracy in these countries. Conquest simply brought the opportunity for providing comprehensive political aid, and the aid programs have been effective. In the special case of West Germany, where Axis totalitarianism had its most extreme manifestation, postwar leaders went an extra distance by creating the political *Stiftungen* to provide their citizenry with programs of civic education for democracy. Three decades later, in the United States, the establishment of the National Endowment for Democracy (NED) in some measure confirms a new U.S. awareness that a campaign is going on.

Campaigns evoke symbols and emotions, which are also the essential equipment of ideological contests. While the promotion of democracy may have many of the qualities of an ideological campaign, it should be evident from many of the chapters in this book and much of the scholarly literature in this field that democratic institution building also requires sound knowledge. Wishing to have a democracy, as important as the wish may be, is simply not enough. Information about how it works, what to do, and how to do it is at least equally important. The researches of the West German *Stiftungen*, the proposal for an international institute for democracy, the publications of Freedom House, the work of many scholars, and even the preparation of this book are evidence that knowledge and social technology are critical elements for the democracy campaign. Consequently, the search for more and better knowledge about democratic institutions is likely to burgeon over the next decade or two.

As that knowledge increases, so will the interest in its application and effectiveness. Campaigns seek real results. Can today's 50 democracies improve their institutions? Can 50 other nations be successfully added to the roster of democracies? Can the totalitarians be convinced of the desirability of being less so? The energetic application of improved knowledge about democratic development, particularly through political aid programs, will create an insistent demand for valid and reliable program evaluation. As in any purposive cybernetic system, sound feedback will become increasingly essential if the campaign is to reach its goals.

Meanwhile, the campaign for democracy gathers partisans and resources. Coalition formation and mutual aid among devotees of pluralism are becoming more frequent, more explicit, and more legitimate. For example, the presidents of three transnational political parties—Christian Democrats, Social Democrats, and Liberals—recently jointly declared their commitment to protect and promote political pluralism throughout the world. The Reagan administration has embarked upon the Democracy Initiative, which includes the establishment of the NED. The International Committee for a Community of Democracies have been working to establish an intergovernmental association of democracies and a caucus of democracies at the United Nations.

In other examples, a return to dictatorship is prevented in Spain and Portugal because local democrats in those nations received political aid from colleagues elsewhere in Europe. Several Latin American nations managed to set aside military dictatorships in favor of democratic institutional forms. However, suspecting an imminent military coup, a Peruvian civilian president, Alan Garcia Perez, has taken the unusual step of openly soliciting possible military support from the United States and other democratic nations in his region.

Thus, there is substantial evidence of a mounting international campaign for democratic development. There is prodemocracy energy, organization, and momentum in the practical realm of world politics. Practice is bound to carry theory along with it. As a consequence, program evaluation will increasingly provide the vital link between theory and practice in political aid for democratic development.

NOTES

1. There is a substantial literature in many fields on the methodologies of program evaluation. A particularly relevant compendium is Scarvia B. Anderson et al., *Encyclopedia of Educational Evaluation* (San Francisco: Jossey-Bass, 1975). The administrators of AID projects have found a matrix known as the logical framework, or logframe, to be a useful guide in organizing project evaluation reports. Logframe was prepared by Leon J. Rosenberg and Lawrence D. Posner of Practical Concepts, Inc., Washington, D.C.

2. In recent years, the Delphi Method for summarizing expert opinions has become popular. The method usually presents a selected sample of experts with a questionnaire calling for forecasts, interpretations, and extrapolations about a specific problem or trend. Most responses are quantifiable, allowing for statistical treatment of the degree of agreement among the experts. Delphis could well become part of the armory of evaluation instruments used by aid programs.

3. The developmental process by which civilian control of the military occurs is a central but neglected area of inquiry in democratization research. See Ralph M. Goldman, *From Warriors to Politicians: The Critical Transition to Civilian Supremacy and Representative Democracy* (forthcoming). The building of political party and representative institutions as agencies for countering and circumscribing military techniques of elite conflict is a long and difficult process. One aspect of this process is often a matter of assuring continued employment for officers and enlisted men in the competing armed camps, that is, a kind of full employment guarantee for the military.

4. Arend Lijphart, *Democracies: Patterns of Majoritarian and Consensus Government in Twenty-one countries* (New Haven: Yale University Press, 1984).

FURTHER READING

Berger, Peter L. "Democracy for Everyone?" *Commentary*, September 1983.

Douglas, William A. *Developing Democracy*. Washington, D.C.: Heldref, 1972.

Fraser, Donald M. "The Dynamics of Growth in Developing Nations." *Foreign Service Journal*, March 1970.

Gastil, Raymond D. "The Importance of Ideas: How Democratic Institutions Become Established." In *Freedom in the World, 1978*, edited by Raymond D. Gastil. New York: Freedom House, 1978.

_____. *Freedom in the World: Political Rights and Civil Liberties, 1984-1985*. Westport, Conn.: Greenwood Press, 1985.

Goldman, Ralph M. *Transnational Parties; Organizing the World's Precincts*. Lanham, Md.: University Press of America, 1983.

_____. *From Warriors to Politicians: The Critical Transition to Civilian Supremacy and Representative Democracy* (unpublished).

Goodell, Grace, and John P. Powelson. "The Democratic Prerequisites of Development." In *Freedom in the World, 1982*, edited by Raymond D. Gastil. Westport, Conn.: Greenwood Press, 1982.

Hapgood, David, ed. *The Role of Popular Participation in Development*. Cambridge: Center for International Studies, Massachusetts Institute of Technology, 1968.

Holbrooke, Richard. "East Asia: The Next Challenge." *Foreign Affairs*, Spring 1986.

Huntington, Samuel P. "Will More Countries Become Democratic?" In *Freedom in the World, 1985-1986*, edited by Raymond D. Gastil. Westport, Conn.: Greenwood Press, 1986.

Huntley, James. *Uniting the Democracies: Institutions of the Emerging Atlantic-Pacific System*. New York: New York University Press, 1980.

Kohli, Atul. "Democracy and Development." In *Development Strategies Recon-*

sidered, edited by John P. Lewis and Valeriana Kallab. (New Brunswick, N.J.: Transaction Books, 1986).

Manglapus, Raul. "Human Rights Are Not a Western Discovery." *Worldview*, October 1978.

O'Donnell, Guillermo, Phillipe C. Schmitter, and Laurence Whitehead, eds. *Transitions from Authoritarian Rule*. Baltimore: Johns Hopkins University Press, 1986.

Packenham, Robert A. *Liberal America and the Third World*. Princeton: Princeton University Press, 1973.

Powell, G. Bingham, Jr. *Contemporary Democracies: Participation, Stability and Violence*. Cambridge: Harvard University Press, 1982.

Rostow, Dankwart A., and W. Howard Wriggins. *Political Development*. Reprint no. 65. Washington, D.C.: Brookings Institution, 1962.

Samuels, Michael A., and William A. Douglas. "Promoting Democracy." *Washington Quarterly*, Summer 1981.

Somjee, A. H. *Political Capacity in Developing Societies*. New York: St. Martin's Press, 1982.

Wright, Theodore Paul, Jr. *American Support of Free Elections Abroad*. Westport, Conn.: Greenwood Press, 1964.

INDEX

ABOUT THE CONTRIBUTORS

WILLIAM A. DOUGLAS. Consultant and instructor on democratic development, American Institute for Free Labor Development. Senior consultant, the Democracy Program study, which led to the creation of the National Endowment for Democracy. Formerly education director and country program director for Peru, American Institute for Free Labor Development. Associate director, International Labor Program, Georgetown University, and professorial lecturer in the Liberal Studies Program of the same university. While a fellow of the Center for International Studies, New York University, wrote *Developing Democracy*. Doctorate in politics from Princeton University and graduate of the School of Advanced International Studies, Johns Hopkins University.

RAYMOND D. GASTIL. Since 1977 director of the Comparative Survey of Freedom, Freedom House, and since 1978 has authored its annual yearbook, *Freedom in the World: Political Rights and Civil Liberties* and has conducted conferences on supporting liberalization in the Soviet Union, Muslim Central Asia, and Eastern Europe. Doctorate in social science and Middle Eastern studies from Harvard University. Taught anthropology at the University of Oregon. Analyzed national security issues at the Hudson Institute. At Battelle Seattle Research Center, wrote *Cultural Regions of the United States*; also, *Social Humanities: Toward an Integrative Discipline of Science and Values*, as well as numerous scholarly articles.

ROY GODSON. Associate professor of government and director of the International Labor Program, Georgetown University, specializing in international relations and foreign policy. Also currently a consultant to the National Security Council and director of the Washington office of the National Strategy Information Center. Author and editor of numerous books and articles on labor and world politics, including *Labor in Soviet Global Strategy*; and *American Labor and European Politics: The AFL as a Transnational Force.*

RALPH M. GOLDMAN. Professor of political science, San Francisco State University. Formerly dean for faculty research; chairman, Political Science Department; director, Institute for Research on International Behavior, all at San Francisco State University. Research associate, Brookings Institution. Taught at Michigan State University. Visiting professor, University of Chicago, University of California, and Stanford University. Author of *Dilemma and Destiny: The Democratic Party in America; Arms Control and Peacekeeping; Contemporary Perspectives on Politics; Behavioral Perspectives on American Politics.* Editor of *Transnational Parties: Organizing the World's Precincts.* Co-author of *The Politics of National Party Conventions; Presidential Nominating Politics in 1952.*

RICHARD L. HOUGH. Consultant on rural political and economic development, specializing in agrarian reform and popular peasant organizations in Asia, Latin America, and Africa. Retired U.S. Foreign Service officer. Adjunct professor, Georgetown University; formerly visiting professor, Fletcher School of Law and Diplomacy; and senior research fellow, National Defense University.

JOHN R. SCHOTT. Has taught at Harvard University, Wellesley College, and, as visiting professor of political development, at the Fletcher School of Law and Diplomacy. Served as head of the Agency for International Development's Title IX Division in the mid-1960s and helped define AID's policy concerning the promotion of democratic political institutions. Since 1971 a consultant to multinational agencies, private voluntary organizations, the U.S. government, and the governments of developing countries.

IRA STRAUS. Executive director, Association to Unite the Democracies. Former editor, *CCD Courier*, newsletter of the Committees for a Community of Democracies. B.A. in Russian history from Princeton University; M.A. in Russian history from the University of Virginia; graduate studies in international relations at the University of Virginia.

JOHN D. SULLIVAN. Director of public and congressional affairs, Center for International Private Enterprise; also responsible for liaison with the National Endowment for Democracy and its affiliated grantees, as well as for research, clearinghouse, and business and economic education program development. Formerly associate director of business affairs, Democracy Program, which led to creation of National Endowment for Democracy. Has served on the staff of the U.S. Chamber of Commerce, on the staff of the Gerald Ford presidential campaign, and as research associate with the Institute for Economic Research. Doctorate in political science from the University of Pittsburgh.

TED WEIHE. Executive director, U.S. Overseas Cooperative Development Committee. Formerly coordinator for cooperative programs and congressional liaison, U.S. Agency for International Development. Author. Lobbyist for trade and civic organizations.